NFANTRY

Mark Blackwell

THE
BEDFORD BOYS

THE
BEDFORD BOYS

One American Town's Ultimate
D-Day Sacrifice

ALEX KERSHAW

DA CAPO PRESS
A Member of the Perseus Books Group

Designed by Brent Wilcox
Set in 11-point Fairfield Light by The Perseus Books Group

Cataloging-in-Publication data for this book is available from the Library of Congress.
First Da Capo Press edition 2003
ISBN 0-306-81167-7

Published by Da Capo Press
A Member of the Perseus Books Group
http://www.dacapopress.com

Da Capo Press books are available at special discounts for bulk purchases in the U.S.
by corporations, institutions, and other organizations. For more information, please
contact the Special Markets Department at the Perseus Books Group, 11 Cambridge
Center, Cambridge, MA 02142, or call (800) 255-1514 or (617) 252-5298,
or e-mail j.mccrary@perseusbooks.com.

1 2 3 4 5 6 7 8 9—07 06 05 04 03

For Bedford,
veterans of D-Day,
and those who died that others might be free.

CONTENTS

ACKNOWLEDGMENTS

This book could not have been written without the help and cooperation of many extraordinary people in Bedford. On several visits to this enchanting town below the Peaks of Otter, I was treated with the utmost kindness. It was a great honor to spend so much time trying to commemorate such a wonderful group of men and the families and community that reared them. Bedford represents all that is great and gracious about America.

I would like to thank the following relatives, veterans, and various experts for providing me with information and photographs, and in some cases enduring several hours of interviews and many, many phone calls over the last three years: Eloise Rogers, Johnny Powers, Earl Boyd Wilson, Dorothy Goode, Hazel Clifton Pierce, Linda Gilley, Carol Tuckwiller of the National D-Day Foundation, John Barnes, Harold Baumgarten, Marcia Apperson, Mitch Yockelson of the National Archives, Elizabeth Teass, Major Jimmy Kilborne of the Staunton Armory, Russell Pickett, Bob Slaughter, Lucille Hoback Boggess, Ellen A. Wandrei and her wonderful staff at the Bedford County Museum, the astonishingly helpful Michael Edwards of the Eisenhower Center, Bettie Wilkes Hooper, the outstandingly patient Roy and Helen Stevens, Ray Nance, Eleanor Yowell, Elaine Cockes, Allen Huddleston, the marvelously hospitable Pride and Rebecca Wingfield, Bertie Woodford, Billy Parker, Gamiel Draper, Bob Sales, Jimmy Green, Ivylyn Hardy, Mabel Phelps, Jack Mitchell, Earl and Elva Newcomb, Verona Lipford, Anna Mae Stewart, Billy Parker, Mary Daniel Heilig, staff of the *Bedford Bulletin*, Beulah Witt, Ellen Quarles, David Draper, Michael Zimmerman, Sibyle Kieth Coleman, Gary Bedingfield, Laura Burnette, Octavia White

Sumpter, Kevan Elsby, Judy Monroe, George Gillam, Peter Viemeister, and Linda Gilley.

The staff of the following institutions provided invaluable help with my research: The New York Public Library, the Sawyer Library at Williams College, Loyola Marymount Library in California, the Imperial War Museum, Bedford County Museum, the National D-Day Museum, the McCullogh Free Library in Bennington, and the Eisenhower Center.

I have been exceptionally lucky to have had such an astute, skilled, and enthusiastic editor as Robert L. Pigeon of Da Capo Press. I cannot thank him and his team enough for their support for this project. My agent, Derek Johns, once again helped in every way he possibly could. I am enormously grateful to him for his long-standing patience, support, and generosity. My wife, Robin, and son, Felix, once again tolerated my absence and obsession and brought untold joy. I would also like to thank the Loerch family, and of course my own, for their long-standing support.

THE BEDFORD BOYS

Company A:

Abbott, Leslie C., Sergeant
Broughman, Cedric C., Technician
Carter, Wallace R., Private First Class
Clifton, John D., Private First Class
Coleman, Andrew J., Private First Class
Crouch, George E. Technician
Draper, Jr., Frank P., Sergeant
Edwards, Jr., Robert D., Sergeant
Fellers, Taylor N., Captain
Fizer, Charles W. Private First Class
Gillaspie, Nicholas N., Private First Class
Goode, Robert L., Sergeant
Hoback, Bedford T., Private
Hoback, Raymond S., Sergeant
Huddleston, Allen, Sergeant
Lancaster, James, Private First Class
Lee, Clifton G., Private
Marsico, Robert (Tony) E., Sergeant
Mitchell, Jack, Sergeant
Nance, Elisha R. (Ray), First Lieutenant
Newcomb, Earl R., Sergeant
Overstreet, Glenwood (Dickie) E., Private First Class
Parker, Earl L., Sergeant
Powers, Henry Clyde, Sergeant
Powers, Jack G., Private First Class
Reynolds, John F., Private First Class
Rosazza, Weldon A., Private First Class
Schenk, John B., Sergeant

Stevens, Ray O., Sergeant
Stevens, Roy O., Sergeant
Thurman, Anthony M., Sergeant
Watson, James W., Private First Class
White, Jr., Gordon H., Sergeant
Wilkes, Harold E., Sergeant
Wilkes, John L., Master Sergeant
Wingfield, Pride, Sergeant
Wright, Elmere P., Sergeant
Yopp, Grant C., Sergeant

Company C:
Dean, John W., Master Sergeant

Company F:
Parker, Joseph E. (Earl's brother), Sergeant

Companies A, C, and F were part of the 116th Infantry Regiment commanded by Colonel Charles D.W. Canham. The 116th was part of the 29th Division commanded by Major General Charles H. Gerhardt. Brigadier General Norman D. Cota was Assistant Division Commander of the 29th.

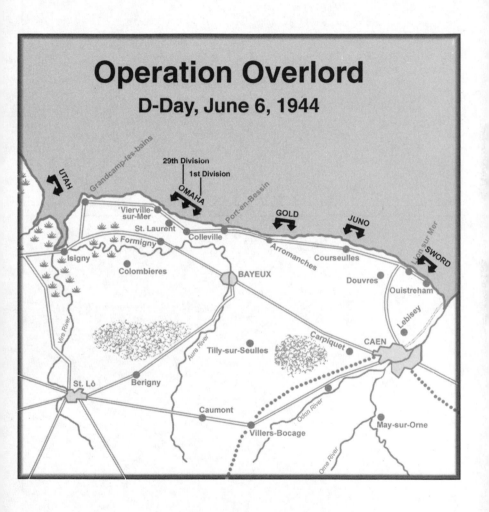

Operation Overlord
D-Day, June 6, 1944

UTAH

Grandcamp-les-bains

29th Division

1st Division

OMAHA

Port-en-Bessin

GOLD

JUNO

LCT-sur-Mer

SWORD

Vierville-sur-Mer

St. Laurent

Colleville

Arromanches

Courseulles

Formigny

Isigny

Colombieres

BAYEUX

Douvres

Ouistreham

Lebisey

Vire River

Aure River

Carpiquet

CAEN

Tilly-sur-Seulles

Odon River

St. Lô

Berigny

Caumont

Villers-Bocage

May-sur-Orne

Orne River

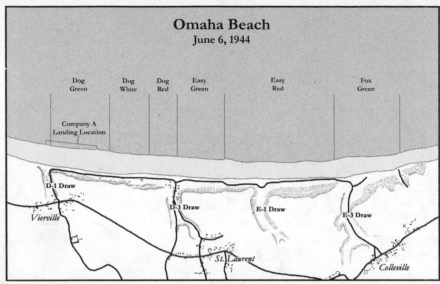

Omaha Beach
June 6, 1944

Dog Green · Dog White · Dog Red · Easy Green · Easy Red · Fox Green

Company A Landing Location

D-1 Draw

Vierville

D-3 Draw

E-1 Draw

E-3 Draw

St. Laurent

Colleville

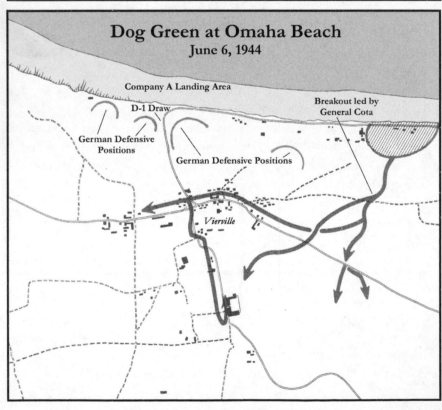

Dog Green at Omaha Beach
June 6, 1944

Company A Landing Area

D-1 Draw

Breakout led by General Cota

German Defensive Positions

German Defensive Positions

Vierville

1

D-Day, H–360

JUNE 6, 1944, 12:30 A.M.: The British troopship, the *Empire Javelin*, steamed steadily across the English Channel. Among her passengers were thirty-four young men from the small Virginia town of Bedford. They belonged to the 116th Infantry's Company A, a select two-hundred man unit. After twenty months of arduous training, Company A had been chosen from among the 15,000 GIs in the Army of the United States' 29th Division to spearhead the most dangerous and critical American assault of the entire war.

Below decks, twenty-five-year-old Sergeant Frank Draper Jr. scribbled notes in his diary. The army had been the making of him. Draper, naturally ebullient, with finely chiseled features and a superb physique, had grown up on the wrong side of the tracks in Bedford, poor even by the woeful standards of the Depression. Since leaving home, he had become a first-rate soldier, and he was determined to bring honor to his unit as well as to his hardscrabble neighborhood back in Bedford, where he'd scavenged for coal as a boy to keep his family warm. As ever, he wanted to be sure he was prepared for the next day, so he wrote himself a note: "Sleep in your trousers, shirt and gas mask. Breakfast—2.30 A.M. Departure—4 A.M. Hit water—4.30 A.M."[1]

Twenty-four-year-old Sergeant Roy Stevens, a handsome farm boy, tried to get some sleep but was too afraid, so he went on deck. Fellow Bedford boys and other GIs were crouched in small groups in the darkness, trying to keep cards and dice from flying or tumbling away across the heaving deck, betting fortunes in poker and craps games: "It

1

didn't matter whether you won or lost. You knew you probably weren't going to get a chance to win your money back anyway."

Roy scoured the blacked-out deck for his twin brother, Ray. Back in England at a training camp, Roy had "hit a streak at blackjack and won a whole lot of money and given Ray half of it, maybe a couple of hundred dollars."[2] Perhaps Ray was using the last of it to play a final few hands of rook, the Bedford boys' favorite card game.

The Stevens brothers had shared everything except women since they could remember: poker winnings, uniform, Red Cross parcels, news from home, and their most intimate fears and hopes. But in a few hours' time, after years of being inseparable, they would not share the same landing craft bound for the beaches of northern France. For the first time since they had joined the National Guard, a week apart in 1938, they would not be side by side. They would not face their greatest test together. They would arrive on Omaha Beach in different boats.

Roy looked around. He wanted to talk to Ray before the ship's alarm sounded and they went to their action stations. He wanted to remind him of the farm they had bought together, and of their dreams of making it successful after the war, and he wanted to arrange to meet at the crossroads of a small village above Omaha Beach called Vierville sur Mer.

A fellow Bedford boy, Lieutenant Ray Nance, twenty-eight, managed to get a few hours of sleep. Nance could trace his heritage to British aristocracy, George Washington, and Huguenot exiles. Like other Bedford boys, he had joined the National Guard as far back as 1933 out of necessity as much as patriotism. Nance was highly intelligent and soft-spoken. He was also fastidious in everything he did and awoke around 2 A.M., dressed in full combat gear.[3] He had not even removed his boots. Nearby were five fellow officers from Company A. By lunchtime, three of them would be dead.

In the noncommissioned men's berths, a few men dozed fitfully. Most men sat in silence, alone with their thoughts. Other Bedford boys lay in bunks writing last-minute letters home. Nance knew that some would not live to write another. He felt responsible for them all. He had grown up with these men, trained them to be superb soldiers, censored their love letters to girls he knew back in Bedford. The men under his command were family. Their parents and lovers had entrusted Nance and Company A's Captain Taylor Fellers with their lives.

At the same time that Nance got up, twenty-one-year-old British Sub-Lieutenant Jimmy Green was woken by an orderly and told that his flotilla commander wanted to see him urgently. Green was second in command of the flotilla but in full command of the first wave of boats that would land Company A in France. The flotilla had twenty craft all told: eighteen LCAs [Landing Craft Army] and two LCPs [Landing Craft Personnel].

Green's commander told him the boats would have to leave earlier than planned because weather conditions in the English Channel were so bad. Green grabbed a cup of tea and a "bite to eat" and then drew his weapons from the *Empire Javelin*'s store. He had no illusions about what lay ahead. There would be heavy casualties. In his last shore briefing, he'd been told to expect to lose a third of his men and his boats.[4]

As Green told his men about the weather conditions and consequent changes in course and timetable, Ray Nance went to the officers' mess to eat breakfast: pancakes, sausages, eggs, and coffee. Few actually ate the hearty meal, served by upbeat orderlies in starched white uniforms.

"Over breakfast, we sat around and shot the breeze," recalled Roy Stevens. "We were laughing, joking, carrying on but you could tell it was phony—everybody was scared. They were putting on a good front."[5]

After breakfast, Nance gathered his kit and climbed up a gangway. A heavy canvas curtain stopped light seeping onto the deck from below. Nance stepped through and into pitch blackness.[6] He went to the rail and looked out at the dark waters, swelling ominously. Suddenly, he noticed Captain Fellers at his side. Fellers had, like Nance, grown up on a farm outside Bedford. The two were cousins.

Twenty-nine-year-old Fellers was tall and thin, with a prominent chin and rolling gait. He was suffering badly from a sinus infection and looked tired and concerned. Before embarking for France, Fellers had confided in Nance, telling him that very few of the officers and men in Company A would come back alive. Fellers had studied the Allied intelligence and countless aerial shots and concluded that Company A was being sent to face certain slaughter.

Fellers and Nance both looked out to sea.

"We stood there awhile," recalled Nance. "We didn't say a word, not a single word to each other. I guess we'd said it all."[7]

An anti-aircraft gun broke the silence, tracer bullets spitting through the sky, and then a searchlight caught the blaze of an exploding plane.

"That brought it home to me," recalled Nance. "This thing is real. It's not an exercise."[8]

Fellers still didn't say a word and then turned away and went below.

A loudspeaker called the British naval crew to its stations. The troops knew they would be next. Ray Nance made his way quickly to where Company A would assemble on deck.

Bosuns' whistles sounded.

"Now, hear this! All assault troops report to your debarkation areas."[9]

As thirty-four Bedford boys emerged from below into the cold darkness, Nance touched every one of them lightly on the arm.[10] "It was a gesture, a goodbye," he recalled sixty years later. "They were the best men I have ever seen in my life. It was a privilege to be their officer. I loved those men."[11]

The men included husbands, three sets of brothers, pool-hall hustlers, a couple of highly successful Lotharios, a minor league baseball player destined for great things, and several Bible-reading, quiet young men who desperately missed their mothers and dreamed of home cooking.

Although they were supremely fit, many of the Bedford boys moved slowly to their debarkation stations, weighed down by their kit. "We had been issued an assault jacket, a sort of vest-like garment with many pockets and pull-strap fasteners to yank off in a hurry," recalled one of the few privates who would still be alive by nightfall. "In the various pockets we stored K-rations, a quarter pound of TNT with fuses, hand grenades, a smoke grenade and medical kit with syringe and morphine.

Besides our regular M-1 clips [for the M-1 Garand rifle], we had two slings of ammo belts across our shoulders. On our backs, we carried an entrenching tool, a bayonet, and a poncho and whatever else we could stuff in."[12] The men's kit weighed well over sixty pounds.

The men's M-1 Garand rifles, among the few Allied weapons that were superior to the German equivalents, were wrapped in cellophane wrappers to protect their working from sand and water. Some men had finally found a use for their Army-issued condoms and tied them around keepsakes, lucky charms, and even small Bibles that they wanted to keep dry. Around each man's waist was buckled a "Mae West" lifebelt which would inflate by squeezing a CO_2 tube.

The Bedford boys checked weapons and kit, exchanged scribbled home addresses "just in case," wished each other good luck, and tried to bolster others who suddenly looked terrified.

"This is it, men," a loudspeaker blared to the men of the 29th Division. "Pick it up and put it on, you've got a one-way ticket and this is the end of the line. 29, let's go!"[13]

2

Going to War

NONE OF THE BEDFORD BOYS had intended to see combat, let alone spearhead arguably the most critical American assault in history. The boys had not volunteered for military service. Back in the thirties, they had joined their local National Guard outfit, more akin to a social club than a military unit, for a "dollar a day" and to play soldier with their brothers, cousins, and buddies. "We were one big family," recalled Roy Stevens. "We'd dated each other's sisters, gone to the same schools, played baseball together. . . . And we were so young!"[1]

Roy and his twin brother, Ray, had joined the National Guard a week apart in 1938 at the age of eighteen. "There had been one opening [in Company A] and we'd matched for it and he'd won," recalled Roy. "I joined a week later. We thought we were something else. We wore these [World War I] brown uniforms and leggings that we never did manage to get wrapped up just right."[2]

Bedford's prettiest girls, sipping sweet lemonade on the porches of whitewashed antebellum homes, watched the Stevens brothers and their fellow National Guardsmen march through Bedford every Fourth of July and could not help but be impressed. The Depression was still felt acutely in Bedford and other rural communities throughout the South in the late thirties: Smart uniforms were a bright contrast to the cast-offs and hand-me-downs that were all most young men in Bedford could afford.

The Stevens brothers and their buddies enjoyed the attention their uniforms brought and the sense of civic pride the National Guard engendered. Then there were the two weeks of paid training each summer, at Manassas or in New York and sometimes on Virginia Beach, close to the swank hotels where city girls wore revealing woolen bathing costumes and the Bedford boys would sweet talk them as they jitterbugged the night away. But above all the Bedford boys were looking to pocket a dollar every Monday night after marching practice at the Bedford armory.[3]

Like most of the men in Company A, the Stevens brothers had grown up on a farm just outside Bedford, a tight-knit community of three thousand whose English ancestors had settled the area in the 1700s. By 1754, the town lay at the heart of arguably the most bucolic county in all Virginia: 764 square miles of rolling hills and lush valleys with mountains reaching 4,200 feet above sea level. The county was named after John Russell, the fourth duke of Bedford, who served as Britain's secretary of state before the Revolutionary War.

Even in the 1930s, Bedford was still a quintessentially English town. The names carved into headstones in its Greenwood cemetery were almost all British; several of the town's merchants could trace their trades back to English craftsmen and artisans; and in many homes furniture and heirlooms dated to the early colonists. The town was first named Liberty after the Colonial victory over Cornwallis at Yorktown. It was renamed Bedford in 1890 and to this day has signposts boasting that it is "the best little town in America."

The Stevens family had farmed in Bedford since anyone could remember. Roy and Ray were two of fourteen children (including triplets) and had attended a one-room schoolhouse before finding jobs to help their family through the Depression. Fiercely competitive, they learned to box at an early age and by the mid-thirties were regularly fighting each other to earn a few cents: "There was a filling station near our home and we would go out there some nights with an older brother who had boxing gloves," recalled Roy. "He'd put up a kind of ring, call folks over, and then take a collection. We never did see much of that money. Soon as we were done he'd take the money, ask somebody for a lift, and go see a girlfriend in Roanoke."[4]

The Stevens brothers were no strangers to tragedy. The triplets all died shortly after birth. In 1934, Roy had watched helplessly as an older brother died from a seizure. "I was putting his socks on and he just tightened up so much, the doctor later said, that his veins burst. I was standing right beside him. First person I ever seen die. He was a real good boy."[5] The loss had left Roy heartbroken but also determined to do all he could to protect his remaining siblings.

After leaving high school, Roy worked on the production line at one of the town's largest employers, a mill called Belding Hemingway, and Ray in a grocery store. Once they knocked off for the day, they were inseparable. "A twin is a little bit different than an ordinary brother or sister," recalled Roy. "They depend on each other a lot more. We were close."[6] For a few months, they even dated two sisters, Emma and Jane Thaxton, sometimes taking them to one of Bedford's two movie theaters which showed such classics as Bette Davis in *Jezebel* and Spencer Tracey's *Boys Town*. The Liberty Theater, at the heart of Bedford, was the more conservative of the two cinemas. In 1937, under pressure from Bedford's powerful Ministerial Association, the theater's manager had stopped showing movies on Sunday.

In 1938, the Stevens twins acquired a 136-acre farm as a home for their parents and as a place they hoped to work on full-time when the Depression ended.[7] They got the property, complete with several pastures ideal for dairy farming, at a bargain price—$3,700—and payments were deferred for several years, but they knew they would have to wait until the economy rebounded before they could hope to make a living working it.

After the Wall Street crash in 1929, prices of crops had collapsed in America, and hundreds of thousands of farmers had been forced to sell. In 1930, the Brookings Institution discovered that 54 percent of the nation's farm families—17 million people—earned under $1,000 per year.[8] By the late thirties, little had changed in rural areas. Small-holders who could actually afford to support families were a rare breed. Although farming had been in their blood for generations, however much they yearned to farm, all the Stevens brothers could do was hope and wait until prices of crops rose again. In the meantime, their day jobs and the extra dollars they earned in the National Guard helped feed their siblings.

In August 1939, the Stevens brothers joined other Bedford boys for their yearly exercises, sharing a tent for thirteen days in northern Virginia near the town of Manassas. They camped beside a hundred other young men from Bedford in Company A, who spent each day attacking imaginary lines, wearing gray armbands and shouting the battle cries of some of their great-grandfathers who had won undying glory in previous wars.

Company A belonged to the 1st Battalion of 116th Infantry Regiment of the 29th Division, which had not seen combat since the trench battles of World War I. The 1st Battalion's Company B was drawn from the city of Lynchburg, Virginia, twenty-five miles to the northeast of Bedford. Company C hailed from Harrisonburg in northern Virginia. Company D comprised men from Roanoke, thirty miles to Bedford's southwest.

Many Bedford boys would still be in Company A on D-Day. By then, Corporal Elisha Ray Nance, from a respected tobacco-farming family, would be a lieutenant. Second Lieutenant Taylor N. Fellers, the son of the chairman of the Bedford County board of supervisors, would command the company after a series of rapid promotions.

Company A's privates first class that summer of 1939 included road-digger Earl Newcomb, ex-miner John Wilkes, and twenty-six-year-old Earl Parker, a lighthearted young man madly in love with one of the prettiest and most popular girls in Bedford, Viola Shrader, who worked at Belding Hemingway.

Then there were the buck privates: Weldon Rosazza, nineteen, whose family was named after an Italian town; twenty-three-year-old John Schenk, slightly built with penetrating blue eyes and a passion for gardening, who worked in a hardware store; and Grant Yopp, eighteen, who had lived with the Stevens family since the age of thirteen after his father had deserted his family. By D-Day, all three would have earned three stripes on their arms, becoming sergeants.

Many of these Bedford boys were aware of their town's distinguished history in arms, including Elmere Wright, a twenty-four-year-old minor league baseball player. He had joined the National Guard as far back as 1934, listing on his application an uncle who had fought with the 29th Division in World War I and two other relatives, William Henry Newman and William Wright, who had enlisted in General Thomas J. Jackson's 1st Brigade, Army of the Shenandoah, during the Civil War.

During the First Battle of Manassas on July 21, 1861, Wright's ancestors and other Virginians had fought so valiantly that they inspired their fellow Southerners to victory. General Barnard Bee of South Carolina was reputed to have shouted to his men: "Look! There stands Jackson like a stone wall. Rally on the Virginians!" Ever after, the Virginians would be known as "Stonewallers."

The Bedford boys reenacted the First Battle of Manassas during their annual exercises that August of 1939. They won the reenactment against a group of 29ers, recruited from above the Mason-Dixon line, who wore blue arm-bands. To have lost would have brought permanent shame on their hometown. Then they returned to Bedford sweltering in the lee of the hazy Peaks of Otter in the Blue Ridge Mountains. The peaks—Sharp Top and Flat Top—had inspired generations of Virginians to rapture and poetry and accounted for Company A's nickname in Bedford, "The Peaks of Otter Rifles."[9]

The boys had barely unpacked their kit, and stowed it in their spotless lockers in the Bedford armory, when they learned that Nazi Germany had attacked Poland. Although the Poles put up a fierce resistance, their antiquated army was no match for the ruthlessly trained and superbly equipped Wehrmacht, which stormed towards Warsaw at stunning speed. On September 4, 1939, Britain and France declared war on Germany. World War II had begun.

On Labor Day, Bedford gathered around radios—there were more than thirty million in U.S. homes by then—to hear President Roosevelt pledge neutrality: "I have said not once but many times that I have seen war and that I hate war. I say that again and again. I hope the United

States will keep out of this war . . . and I give you my assurance and re-assurance that every effort of your government will be directed to that end."[10]

When Company A next met at the Bedford armory in the basement of the courthouse at the center of town, some men predicted that they would be called to active duty for a year. Politicians were openly calling for America to come to the aid of imperiled democracies in Europe.

Other Bedford boys disagreed. Hitler wasn't America's problem, Roosevelt would keep his word. Isolation was the sanest option and fitted with many Americans' reluctance to go to Europe's aid barely a generation after the Great War of 1914–1918—the war to end all wars, they had been told. As long ago as 1796, America's first president George Washington had warned in his Farewell Address against "interweaving our destiny with that of any part of Europe."[11]

Besides, the last thing most boys in Company A wanted was to leave families and jobs for twelve months of serious military training. Fighting the Battle of Manassas was one thing; a year in Uncle Sam's army was quite another. But as 1939 drew to a close, mobilization looked more and more likely. Events across the Atlantic indicated that democracy would soon be under threat across the globe.

The Poles had surrendered on October 5 to the Germans and to the Russians, who had also invaded from the east. There followed what the American press called a "phony" war lasting until spring 1940 as the French and British argued and prevaricated about what course of action would be in both countries' interest. Meanwhile, Hitler laid plans to impose National Socialism on all of Europe. Denmark fell to the Nazis in early April. Later that month, German stormtroopers frog-marched through Oslo, capital of Norway.

On May 10, Britain's Prime Minister Neville Chamberlain, an architect of appeasement in the thirties, was replaced by Winston Churchill. But even the "Bulldog," as he soon became known, could not halt Hitler's lightning advance across Western Europe. Late that spring, Hitler's most brilliant generals, notably Erich von Manstein and panzer commander Heinz Guderian, orchestrated stunningly successful Blitzkrieg attacks on Holland, Belgium, Luxembourg, and then France.

By July 1940, the British had barely evaded capture of their expeditionary force at Dunkirk and stood alone. Only twenty-three miles of the English Channel and brave young RAF pilots prevented the Nazis from gaining complete hegemony over Europe: France had fallen to the German onslaught of Stuka dive-bombers and massed tank formations in less than six weeks.

That August, as the Battle of Britain raged above England's summer skies, Company A again gathered for its annual training camp, this time at Virginia Beach. Once more the Bedford boys spent two weeks playing soldier by day, drinking beer around campfires at night, and speculating about the availability of girls in the nearest town. But now there were debates as well as drunken sing-songs of old Confederate war tunes. Should America remain isolated or should she save the world from fascism?

There were new faces around the fireside, many of them fresh out of Bedford High School. Eighteen-year-old John Clifton, who had five older siblings, was nicknamed "J. D." and was known all around town because he had delivered the *Bedford Bulletin* to local homes as a boy. "He was a real nice kid," recalled Gamiel Draper, a schoolmate. "He wasn't mean or ferocious. He was quiet, and nice."[12] He was also strikingly handsome, thanks to a Cherokee ancestry: high cheek bones, warm eyes, and lips that always seemed set to smile.

Another recent high school graduate was Gordon "Henry" White, who had joined the National Guard in October 1939, a few weeks after Hitler invaded Poland. Of all the Bedford boys, White was most passionate about farming. As a young boy, he had raced home from school every afternoon, changed into work clothes and stuffed apples into his pockets to snack on as he labored until nightfall on his family's farm. "He liked to plow, he just liked to be out on the farm," recalled his sister Octavia White Sumpter. "He just liked the dirt."[13]

Eighteen-year-old Raymond Hoback had joined the National Guard that spring, wanting to be with his older brother, Bedford. Like the

Stevens twins, the Hoback brothers had been raised on a small farm just outside town.

Bedford, twenty-four, had served in the Regular Army with Company E of the 35th Infantry before joining Company A in February 1937. Nicknamed "Motor-Mouth," he told tall stories and pretended to be a carefree Don Juan but everyone knew he was devoted to his fiancée, Elaine Coffey.

"Everybody thought [Bedford] was married to her," recalled Roy Stevens. "If you asked him, he'd say, 'I'll bet you a dollar I am, and I'll bet you a dollar I'm not.' You never knew what he'd say next."[14]

Elaine Coffey and Bedford Hoback had a tempestuous relationship, often arguing about Bedford's wild ways. But they had been in love with each other for most of their young lives. Elaine, twenty-one, a petite brunette with a snub nose and slim hips, had ditched her previous boyfriend for Bedford as soon as he had returned, tanned and lean, from a posting to Hawaii in 1936. Since they could remember, they had always wanted to be together. They had in fact been childhood sweethearts, passing notes to each other at age nine in a two-room grade school.[15]

In contrast to his brother, Raymond was modest, hard-working, and self-disciplined—ideally suited to army life in the eyes of Company A's officers and men such as Ray Nance, who had been with the guard for several years. Raymond had left school in the eighth grade and worked as a laborer building New Deal roads, saving enough to buy a $750 two-door Chevrolet. He was often to be found with his head in a Bible.

"Raymond was more sincere [than Bedford]," recalled Roy Stevens, who would eventually become his platoon sergeant. "And he was a great soldier but he could never keep in step. Finally, we just gave up on him—he just couldn't get the rhythm."[16]

In September 1940, Congress passed a selective service bill, ushering in the first peacetime draft in American history. Eight hundred thousand men were called to arms, dwarfing the numbers in the Regular Army, which had been limited to seventy-five thousand men. Senior officers in the National Guard talked ominously of mobilization. Subtly, things began to change in Company A. Officers grew more serious. Older men and those with "essential" civilian jobs left the unit. On September 8, President Roosevelt declared a state of emergency and called for the creation of an Office of Production Management, which would produce armament and other materials to defend America and help Britain in every way "short of war."

In October it was announced that Company A would be mobilized into the federal army for a year, beginning in early 1941. None of the Bedford boys had seriously considered that joining the National Guard would actually lead to twelve months in the Regular Army. Most had never been outside Virginia. All but the married men still lived with their parents, and not one had ever fired a shot in anger. For all of them, mobilization would be the first great test of their lives.

The Bedford boys spent the next few months arranging to leave their jobs, finding relatives or friends to fill their places on the farms, making out wills, and in many cases arranging life insurance. On Monday, February 3, 1941, they reported to the Bedford armory, were issued new woolen uniforms, and then sworn in. The new shoulder patches on their uniforms, inspired by the Korean monad symbol that represents life, were one part blue, one part gray, explaining the 29th Division's popular name, "The Blue and Gray." The colors represented the deliberate mix of Northerners and Southerners in the division, which had been formed after Reconstruction.

"Six officers and ninety-two enlisted men of Company A, 116th Infantry . . . were duly inducted," reported the *Bedford Bulletin*. "The ceremonies were brief but impressive as the khaki-clad line took the oath of transfer and allegiance. . . . In and around the armory, young stalwart men wearing their country's uniform casts an atmosphere reminiscent of the war-torn days of 1917–18. Crisp, sharp commands; quick, snappy responses. . . . Induction into the United States Army adds credit to that great organization of fighting men who know no defeat; and upon whom . . . hangs the future of this nation."[17]

Just twenty-four hours before, Wallace R. Carter, barely eighteen, had enlisted in Company A.[18] A popular player for the Mud Alley Wildcat baseball team, which drew its players from the poorest streets in Bedford, Wallace had worked at a Bedford pool hall after high school. The job paid a pittance but Carter usually had a thick wallet thanks to his winnings "playing eight ball."[19]

"[Wallace] was a fun-loving guy," recalled Morris Scott, a childhood friend. "His family was poor. We were all poor, but we didn't know it; we had so much fun together. He attended lots of movies. He always had an extra dime for a movie."[20] Beneath his fun-loving exterior, however, was a young man of fierce emotions. He once, according to Roy Stevens, jumped off a bridge after falling out with a girlfriend. Fortunately, his fall was broken by a bank and he was only slightly injured.

Before Wallace Carter and his fellow Bedford boys left the armory on the day of their induction, National Guard officers read out the fifty-eighth and sixty-first Articles of War concerning the crimes of desertion and going absent without leave. It was a disturbing introduction to the rigors of military discipline. They now faced far greater penalties than they'd received for any misdemeanor at school. "The officers would read out those articles a few more times in the coming months," recalled Roy Stevens. "They wanted to make sure we hadn't forgotten them."[21]

Stringent medical examinations the following Saturday reduced the enlisted in Company A to eighty-six men. Roy Stevens was deemed fit but ordered to get dental repair work, as were other Bedford boys whose teeth, like those of so many inductees in 1941, were so bad that the U.S. Army embarked on a massive dental program to prevent hundreds of thousands of its soldiers from becoming casualties of severe gum disease. In 1939, the U.S. Army had just 250 dentists. By 1945, 25,000 dentists had pulled more than fifteen million teeth from American men allowed to wear general-issue uniforms so long as they had "sufficient teeth (natural or artificial) to subsist on the Army ration."[22]

Because new barracks to house the 29th Division at Fort Meade in Maryland were not completed, the Bedford boys stayed on in Bedford for a fortnight, attending training sessions at the armory and going home in time for supper. It was a strange interlude, more akin to being at college than in the army. Boys sat around the kitchen table in their new uniforms, listening to the Grand Old Opry on the radio, doing their chores before bedtime, milking the cows before dawn.

On February 17—the day before their departure—the Bedford boys marched behind the town's widely acclaimed Fireman's Band to Bedford High School, a stately brick building fronted by forty-foot white columns, where a farewell party and dance were held until the early hours. Over two hundred people danced the night away, alternating between formal square dances and wild and often drunken jigs.

Cans of "Old Virginia" beer, brewed in nearby Roanoke, were all of ten cents. A thick haze of cigarette smoke—a pack of Camels or Lucky Strike also cost just a dime—hung in the air above the khaki-clad boys and their girlfriends as they "shook a leg" to twanging banjos playing hillbilly classics by Old Grandpa Jones. When the home-stilled whiskey ran out, the band packed up and the Bedford boys took off home or into the night with their dates.

The next morning was "right cool"23 as the Bedford boys gathered at the rail station at the heart of town near the hardscrabble neighborhood called "Mud Alley." It was a clear day with wonderful visibility—the Peaks of Otter, snowcapped, pierced the bright blue skies. Roy Stevens remembered that perhaps as many as three-quarters of the boys nursed heavy hangovers from the night before. Most of the town seemed to turn out for the send-off before the boys boarded trains headed for the 29th Division's main camp at Fort Meade.

As the Bedford boys embraced families and loved ones, many looked sad and close to tears. None cried, however, afraid that they would shame themselves and their friends. But plenty felt like it, according to Roy Stevens, who was leaving home for the first time. Spirits rose when several more bottles of whiskey were produced and the men mixed it with the Cokes they were drinking to ease their hangovers. The Fireman's Band broke into an upbeat marching song and then Company A finally formed up on the platform, ready to board the train.

Twenty-one-year-old Jack Powers, over six feet tall and weighing two hundred pounds—all of it muscle—stood proudly in line, a few yards from his brother, Clyde, five years his senior, "a clean-cut guy, more conservative and a little shorter than Jack, who was more outgoing."[24] The Powers brothers had grown up in Bedford not far from the Hampton Looms mill, where their father worked.

Jack could see his little sister, sixteen-year-old Eloise, beaming at him as she played clarinet in the forty-strong Fireman's Band. "We'd been let out of school to see them off," she recalled. "They looked like they were all going on a big adventure."[25]

Sixty years later, Eloise would remember Jack being a handsome, big-hearted man who loved to dance and play the guitar. "He was always practicing. Some of the neighborhood children got together and recorded some songs. Those wax records didn't survive long."[26]

Jack could jitterbug to Tommy Dorsey tunes as well as any man in Company A, and many a Bedford girl enjoyed a spin around the dance floor with him.[27] "One of my best memories of [Jack] was [when] I had a kitten, and I had taken him out of the box and was playing with [him] on the front porch," recalled Eloise. "[Jack] stepped on one of the kittens, and he was so heartbroken, he gave me his skates to make up for the kitten."[28]

Also standing in formation was Harold Wilkes. The same age as Clyde, curly-haired, five-foot-eleven-inch Harold was nonetheless the Powers's uncle. "My mother's father was married three times," explained Eloise over sixty years later. "With his third wife, he had two children— one of them was Harold. He lived just over the road, so we were always over at each other's houses. Harold was very close to us all, and he considered my mom as his mom."[29]

A front-page report in the *Bedford Bulletin* raved about how splendid the boys looked in their new uniforms. "Not only the physical appearances but the splendid attitude which they have shown has been the subject of discussion and commendation," the hometown paper added. "There has been an entire lack of grousing or complaining. . . . The town feels strangely empty."[30]

At first, most of the Bedford boys found life at Fort Meade an exciting challenge. They learned how to salute and address officers properly and how to strip a weapon and put it back together so mechanically that some could do it blindfolded, and they were given physical tests and immunization shots. After painting their hastily built barracks, they were issued M-1 Garand rifles, allowed to fire them, and sent on exercises with new radios and motorized vehicles. The nightlife in local towns was even better than at Virginia Beach, and unlike many of the Bedford men's homes, Fort Meade had central heat and running water.

According to the 29th Division's official history, "cold, freezing weather blew across [Fort Meade]. . . . Barracks orderlies stoked fires clumsily in their inexperience, as they cursed the complicated furnace units. But the weather was no complaint of the men, for it meant frozen roads, and less time spent in cleaning of overshoes, or in pushing the old two-wheel-drive trucks out of the mud, an assignment which became theirs when the temperature moderated."[31]

By summer 1941, boredom had become a problem. The constant, mind-numbing routine and close-order drilling began to grate on men not used to taking orders week in, week out. Above all, the Bedford boys were homesick. Leave was rarely granted and passes issued for no longer than two days. Yet the drive to Bedford alone was seven hours, weather permitting. Despite the distance, Bedford Hoback got home most weekends, often taking several other Bedford men with him in his wood-sided station wagon. "He charged two dollars a piece," recalled his sister Lucille, "and would pack in as many as he could fit."[32]

At Fort Meade and other bases in the United States discipline became a widespread problem that summer as morale fell to distressing lows, mostly because of resentment that the men were being kept from their families and jobs for no clear reason. Very few were convinced by warnings in Congress and the press that America would be next on Hitler's list for conquest.

Life magazine printed a story on August 18 about "the growing restlessness and boredom of the great civilian army," and the *New York Times* ran an article that caused an uproar among the army's general staff when the paper reported that most men did not believe they were needed in the Army: "They compare it to a football team in training without a schedule of games."[33]

That November, Company A again played war, this time in North Carolina. The entire 29th Division split into "Red" and "Blue" armies which chased each other through woods and frosted river valleys. The Bedford boys again joked and argued around campfires each evening about who had been killed or taken prisoner that day. To the fury of many a 29er, the outspoken broadcaster Walter Winchell claimed that the men of the "29th are hiding in the hills of North Carolina."[34]

The military games stretched into early December. The Bedford boys were soon shivering in sleeping bags and cursing army life as never before. When December 7 arrived, they were slogging through North Carolina mud and ice. A bitter wind blew. Their destination was a tented camp at A. P. Hill in Virginia. They would then take trucks back to Fort Meade, where they expected to be discharged and sent home early in the New Year.

As the men trudged along with upturned collars, rubbing their hands together to keep warm and talking about finally getting out of the goddamned army and back to their families and jobs, orders suddenly came along the line that they were to stand down. There was astonishing news. Men quickly gathered around radio sets. That morning, the Japanese had bombed Pearl Harbor in Hawaii.

Waves of torpedo-bombers and fighters had killed more than 2,500 American citizens and wounded another thousand. Six of the U.S.'s greatest battleships had been irreparably damaged or sunk: *West Virginia, Tennessee, Arizona, Nevada, Oklahoma,* and *California.* In a matter of minutes, an estimated half of the United States' naval power had been lost. Nearby Hickam Field airbase had been peppered with bombs. The

Air Corps lost all but sixteen of its bombers. America had never before been attacked so viciously and effectively.

In Bedford, people also learned of the attack on their radios. Lucille Hoback, twelve-year-old sister of the Hoback brothers, returned from church that Sunday morning and listened to reports with her parents, a sister, and another brother. "Everybody was very worried because we thought it meant the boys would be sent off to war," she recalled. "That day, my father never left the radio. In the coming days, there was a rush of local men eager to sign up."[35]

At Camp A. P. Hill, the Bedford boys reacted with a mixture of shock, outrage, and anger. Roy Stevens, his brother Ray, and Lucille's brother Bedford Hoback went to see a Gene Autry western that night at a cinema in nearby South Hill, Virginia. Another news flash on the bombing interrupted the movie. The men went to a local bar and started drinking. Bedford described the Schofield Barracks that had been bombed in Hawaii—he had been stationed there in 1936. They ordered more beers, growing angrier with every sip. "I didn't even know where Pearl Harbor was," recalled Roy Stevens, "but we had those beers and we got right mad. Man, we were so confident—we were going to wup them and still be home for Christmas."[36]

The day after Pearl Harbor, Company A boarded trucks bound for Fort Meade. During the trip, the caravan stopped so that the men could stretch their legs and have a smoke. Second Lieutenant Ray Nance and several other officers gathered in a ditch below pine trees, out of the biting wind.

A few yards from Nance, the 116th's regimental chaplain set up a portable radio and tuned it to a news station. On a carpet of pine-needles, Nance and his fellow officers soon sat transfixed as they listened to President Roosevelt make what would become perhaps the most famous speech of his Presidency. Dressed in a formal morning suit, Roosevelt stood alone at the rostrum in the House of Representatives and opened a black notebook. The entire Congress then stood in unison and gave him the first joint ovation since 1932.

Roosevelt gripped the rostrum.

"Yesterday, December 7, 1941—a date which will live in infamy—the United States of America was suddenly and deliberately attacked. . . . Hostilities exist. There is no blinking at the fact that our people, our territory and our interests are in grave danger. With confidence in our armed forces—with the unbounding determination of our people—we will gain the inevitable triumph—so help us God."[37]

The chaplain turned off the radio. Company A clambered back onto trucks. They were "in for the duration." The buck a day had saved them from poverty. Now it had bought a ticket to the frontlines. As the trucks neared their camp for the night, the Bedford boys did not sing or joke as usual. "We kept our feelings to ourselves," recalled Nance. "There wasn't much to say. The president had laid it on the line. We were going to war."[38]

3

Moving Out

IT WAS AFTER DARK ON December 8 when the trucks unloaded at Fort Meade. Company A formed up and then marched into the garrison. Extra sentries had been posted around supply dumps and outside the gates: America was now on high alert. In their barracks that night, the Bedford boys wondered what would happen to them next. Would they be shipped out West, bound for the Pacific? Would they be allowed home for Christmas before going to war?

A few days later, Captain Taylor N. Fellers returned from a two-week officer training course in Georgia. The only career military man among the Bedford contingent, Fellers announced that Christmas furloughs would be granted, though they would be short.

A tough disciplinarian and fiercely ambitious, Fellers had worked hard to command his fellow Virginians' respect. The oldest child of a well-to-do family, "a real tall and lanky country boy through and through,"[1] he knew the men he commanded more intimately than did any other officer in the 116th Infantry. He had grown up with them. He also knew that Bedford would be looking to him to bring its boys home.

"A lot was expected of Taylor," recalled his younger sister, Bertie Woodford. "He was always very serious even as a boy and had a very competitive spirit. He was all soldier—everybody thought he would go a long, long way."[2]

Nicknamed "Tail Feathers" by fellow sprinters on his high school track team, Taylor was one of six children and had joined the local highway department straight out of high school, eventually becoming a fore-

23

man. Bertie, ten years his junior, remembered Taylor doting on her and a sister, Janie, who had polio and was forced to wear braces. He paid for piano lessons for Bertie, ferried her to Sunday school at the local Nazareth Methodist Church, wrote to her regularly, and showered her with gifts at Christmas and birthdays. "He was the oldest in the family and we all looked up to him," remembered Bertie. "He just felt like he had to take care of us."[3]

In 1932, Fellers joined the National Guard. He was promoted to sergeant in 1935 and then took military correspondence courses to qualify for officer training. His job on the highways paid better than most in Bedford County in the Depression and he was able to buy a Buick coupe, a notable status symbol in rural Virginia at that time. In the late-thirties, he joined Mason Lodge No. 245 in nearby Forest, Virginia.

In early 1940, Taylor converted a schoolhouse in his birthplace, Cifax, ten miles from Bedford, into a home, and soon after moved in with his bride, a striking blonde named Naomi Newman. He jokingly told his family, after returning from officer's training school in Georgia, that one day he would live like a true Southern gentleman, buy a farm, "and get a black woman from Georgia to cook all his meals."[4] His father, Peter Anson Fellers, and mother, Annie Elizabeth Leftwich-Fellers, were immensely proud when they read in the *Bedford Bulletin* that their eldest son would command Company A.

Back in Bedford County, in the weeks after Pearl Harbor, Fellers's young wife waited nervously to hear from her husband. Several other wives of Bedford men, who shared coffee and gossip in Green's drugstore on Main Street, were also set on squeezing whatever joy they could from what might be their last Christmas together. Eighteen-year-old Bettie Wilkes had, on August 10, 1941, married Master Sergeant John Wilkes of Company A. When she heard about Pearl Harbor, she vowed to see John whenever and however she could before he was posted overseas. If he couldn't come to her, she would go to him.

John Wilkes had grown up on a 149-acre farm nine miles south of Bedford, one of eight children. His father, Leo D. Wilkes, a plainspoken man with a strict moral code, worked as a coal miner in North Fork, West Virginia. He would send money and return to the farm whenever he could, but he was much missed by John and his siblings. "Daddy said he didn't want any of his boys going down a mine," recalled Dorothy Wilkes Goode, one of John's sisters. "That's why he brought us up on a farm. . . . John was all boy. He played ball, protected me, helped my mother with the cows and the two mules we owned."[5]

Money was scarce but the Wilkeses never "went hungry or cold." Their farmhouse was a joyous place, often filled with music. "My Daddy used to say he married my mother because she loved music. We had a record player, and then, when electricity came, a radio, and always there would be something playing. Momma had a banjo, a guitar and a piano. She'd play them all, and John loved dancing to tunes like "Beer Barrel Polka." He was just a natural."[6]

After leaving high school at sixteen, John worked part-time mining feldspar on a local farm. He joined the National Guard to make a few extra dollars and quickly proved himself as tough a soldier as Company A had ever seen. Because of his trustworthiness and immense self-discipline, both inherited from his father, he was quickly promoted to master sergeant. He wanted things done by the book, the army way, or not at all. As with Taylor Fellers, he detested any kind of slacking or insubordination; the men he inspected each morning were careful not to cross him.

"I knew John long before the war," recalled Roy Stevens. "He used to play a lot of pool in town. . . . We also played poker, and he used to joke about how he was on furlough back in Bedford one time and got into a fight with a fellow called Sam Ruff. Sam was seventy pounds lighter than John, but he just happened to hit him right. 'That little fella—he broke my nose!' John would say and then laugh."[7]

Bettie Wilkes saw a different man in John: deeply sensitive, romantic, and as passionate as she was about movies and bowling.[8] They had met at a football game at her high school, the New London Academy, just outside Bedford. "John and I were probably typical of most young people growing up in the prewar America of the late 1930s," she recalled. "[We] had not traveled far beyond the confines of the farm or village, but there were things like the jitterbug to be learned at local dances, songs like "Deep Purple" to be sung, money to be saved to see *Gone with the Wind*, a movie which was an unheard-of four hours long! A time to be envied in most respects, safe and carefree."[9]

Christmas 1941 in Bedford was not carefree. The community crowded the town's Methodist and Southern Baptist churches. A *Bedford Bulletin* editorial advised: "This Christmas season is not a time to give way to forebodings and despair, but rather we should use the anniversary of the Prince of Peace as the most appropriate time in which to dedicate ourselves to the task of striving, with spirit, mind and body, toward bringing to the world the peace and justice he proclaimed two thousand years ago."[10] Special services were held in recognition of the county's men in arms. After singing "O Little Town of Bethlehem," congregations prayed, above all, for the safe return of their loved ones. Some parents were confident that the following Christmas the seventy-odd men in Company A from Bedford would be back home and the war over. Others now regretted the day their sons had joined the National Guard.

That Christmas was especially poignant for the parents of twenty-year-old Dickie Abbott, who lived above a beautiful old inn, "The Dutch," in Bedford. In 1938, aged seventeen, Dickie had begged his father to sign papers allowing him to join the National Guard. Reluctantly, his father had done so. Three years later, with America at war, he now regretted the decision. The papers that had made his son so happy were now a possible death warrant.

Dickie Abbott typified his fellow citizen-soldiers from Bedford. He rode around town on horseback, rolled his own cigarettes from tobacco he grew himself, kept an elaborate scrapbook, and was utterly devoted to his large God-fearing family. There was nothing he enjoyed more than sitting down with them after a long day in the fields and feasting on fresh buttermilk, cornbread, and fried chicken.

Dickie had been raised mostly by his grandmother, Mrs. W. B. Abbott, and shared her infectious sense of humor. A joke was never far from his lips. "He was just a fun guy," recalled his cousin Morris Scott. "He loved to laugh. You could tell him anything and he'd just laugh."[11] Before he returned to Fort Meade, he promised to write to his family and wanted them to send all their news as often as possible, especially about his grandmother.

For the married men in Company A that Christmas, time was suddenly painfully precious. Every moment with their young wives was to be savored. They made love knowing they might not see them again.

In 1940, twenty-six-year-old Sergeant Earl Parker had married nineteen-year-old Viola Shrader. The couple were eager to start a family as soon as possible. One of three brothers, all of whom would experience combat, Earl had worked at the Piedmont Label Company, which printed labels for canned goods, after graduating from Bedford High School. He had grown up on a 300-acre beef farm just outside Bedford.

Earl's youngest brother, Billy, who would later become a German POW, recalled Earl's great passions as a boy being baseball and hunting. Able to hit a dime at thirty-five yards with a .22 rifle, he was forced to take turns with his brothers when they hunted quail and rabbit together with a .410 gauge shotgun. "Every shot counted because bullets were expensive back then," recalled Billy, who was hunting at age eighty-six. "Earl didn't have any clear idea what he wanted to do other than get a job that paid money. Like everyone else he joined the guard for the dollar."[12]

All too quickly the day came for Earl Parker to leave his young wife and share a ride back to Fort Meade.

"I don't know how you'd go shoot anybody," Viola told Earl just before he left.

"If it's me or them," he shrugged, "I guess I'll have to.'"

In bitterly cold weather, in the second week in January, Company A practiced anti-invasion procedures on Cape Henry in Virginia. Their goal was to ward off groups of 1st Division marauders pretending to be the enemy. "Digging gun emplacements in the frozen ground wasn't easy," recalled one of the defenders, "but wading ashore from landing crafts through icy surf was worse. Many 'Leather Necks' were paralyzed after hitting the icy water and had to be rescued. War is hell, real or otherwise."[13] Ironically, three years later it would be the 1st and 29th Divisions who would join forces to invade Omaha Beach on D-Day.

In April 1942, while the Bedford boys tested new weapons and defended the Eastern seaboard, Britain and the United States set up joint planning staffs to coordinate operations against Nazi Germany. Their ultimate goal was a successful cross-channel invasion intended to defeat Hitler in the west. But such an operation, eventually codenamed Overlord, would be the greatest logistical challenge in military history and would not be feasible until, at the very earliest, summer 1943.

Whenever possible, the Bedford boys tried to get home, clubbing together to pay for gas if they were lucky enough to get a weekend pass and the loan of a car. Earl Parker often drove back with Company A's clerk, Pride Wingfield, who owned a shiny 1938 Plymouth. Others paid "motormouth" Bedford Hoback a buck each way for a seat in his station wagon.

Nineteen-year-old mess sergeant Earl Newcomb usually came home with a friend from Roanoke. But when his friend couldn't get a pass, he paid Bedford Hoback the buck without a word of complaint. That spring, he had gotten engaged to a feisty nineteen-year-old mother of three, Elva Miller.

Elva was a remarkably resilient and mature young woman, as were many of her working-class peers in Bedford. She had been brought up to work hard and make the best of even the most meager opportunities. Her father had set the example of how to muddle through come what may—he had turned his hand to anything to make a buck, selling cars and running a filling station to make ends meet in 1932 when the Depression was at its worst.

In 1935, Elva had joined the production line at Hampton Looms, the Bedford woolen mill, and she was married not long after. Then tragedy had struck. She was widowed in 1938 when her husband died in a car crash. Before meeting Earl, she struggled to bring up her three small children, Bill, Nancy, and Garland, on little more than her mill wages of $10 a week. While she was bent over a loom from 7 A.M. to 3 P.M. each day, her aunt cared for her children in Elva's home, a five-room log cabin on the outskirts of town.

Earl Newcomb had joined the National Guard in 1934. The son of a farmer, he dreamed of working the land but was forced, like Elva's father, to take any job he could find. After a period of unemployment, he was lucky to be accepted into the Civilian Conservation Corps, which ran a CCC camp for unemployed men, mostly from New York, at Fancy Farm in Kelso at the foot of the Peaks of Otter.

The Civilian Conservation Corps was one of the great achievements of President Roosevelt's New Deal. Nicknamed "Roosevelt's Tree Army," the 500,000 young unemployed Americans who benefited from the program planted an estimated three billion trees by 1942 as well as preventing soil erosion on more than twenty million acres. The CCC also brought much needed revenue to Depression-era communities like Bedford where enrollees spent their money.

Earl Newcomb enrolled for two years, pocketing $30 a month and helping to build a road up into the mountains. He also learned to cook in the camp's mess. On summer maneuvers with the National Guard, he also prepared meals, and this led to his eventually becoming Company A's mess sergeant.

Elva's and Earl's wedding date was set for June 27, 1942. Unfortunately, Earl could not get a pass in time. But Bedford Hoback was due a pass that weekend and agreed to swap his for a later date. "Bedford was due to come home," explained Elva. "But his brother Raymond didn't have a pass. So Bedford told Earl to take his pass because he would wait until he could ride home in his car with Raymond. It would be cheaper that way."[14] Sadly, neither Bedford nor Raymond made it home that summer: When Earl returned to Fort Meade from his honeymoon, he learned that Company A was moving out.

On August 17, 1942, Company A marched with full kit onto an old train. No one knew where they were headed. Soon, the stale air in their compartments got sticky. After an endless day shuttling between drab depots, the men realized they were headed to Florida. When the train finally stopped, they formed up and marched into the vast military base at Camp Blanding near Jacksonville, until recently home to the 1st Division, which had just departed for England.

The 1st Division would, by November, be part of Operation Torch, an Allied invasion of North Africa. Torch was partly aimed at relieving pressure on the Soviet Union, which had fought a ferocious battle against the Wehrmacht since June 1941 when Hitler hurled more than a hundred divisions of his best soldiers at Stalin's Red Army. But Operation Barbarossa, as the German invasion was codenamed, had failed. When the bitter winter set in, Hitler's finest armies became bogged down in desperate sieges.

In the Pacific, the Americans had just begun to turn the tide against Japanese forces, which had since Pearl Harbor swept across a vast expanse of ocean, conquering Burma, the Philippines, Singapore, Malaya, and the Dutch East Indies in rapid succession. In June 1942, U.S. aircraft had surprised a Japanese fleet cruising towards Midway (a few hundred miles northwest of the Hawaiian Islands) and inflicted so much damage that the Japanese lost naval air superiority in the Pacific. After Midway, the Japanese would fight a largely defensive war against the "third-rate power" they had so viciously attacked at Pearl Harbor.

On the homefront, America was gearing up to produce the vast quantities of material and other arms needed to defeat the enemies of democracy in Europe and the Pacific. Factories throughout the nation were quickly being converted to wartime production.

In Bedford, a plant called Rubatex began to produce rubber gas masks. Hampton Looms was also converted to military production, turning out woolen uniforms. Like many workers across America, Elva Newcomb and her fellow loom-operators had to work harder but started to earn more. Hampton Looms increased wages by six cents an hour after management made a deal with the local Textile Workers Union. Earnings would continue to rise throughout the war: For most Americans, world war had brought an end to the Depression.

Other developments were not quite so welcome. Rationing began in May 1942, with most citizens limited to a pound of sugar every two weeks and twenty-five gallons of gas each month. In Bedford, the restrictions on sugar use caused widespread complaint because so many homes relied on it to produce fruit preserves to sell at markets and for their own sustenance. The limit on consumption of gas was even less popular because Bedford had no public transportation to speak of and cars and trucks were essential to movement around the far-flung community.

While America girded to become the free world's arsenal, and as total war raged around the globe, the Bedford boys got accustomed to their new barracks in Florida. They were further from Bedford than ever—now at least a long day's drive. For the married men, the distance was frustrating. But for the unattached, Camp Blanding's proximity to bustling Jacksonville, forty miles away, was a distinct improvement on every other camp or base they'd stayed in. Jacksonville's nightlife was famous throughout the U.S. Army. The city had dozens of nightclubs, brothels, back-room gaming tables, and cinemas. If a GI had a particular craving, somewhere or some woman in Jacksonville would cater to it.

Despite its vast drabness, with its hastily erected buildings and maze of roads and block-houses that all looked the same, Camp Blanding had another thing going for it. The Bedford boys would not be sleeping under canvas. To their delight, they had bunks beneath roofs that neither sagged dangerously nor leaked. Pristine white sands and palm trees were a short walk away. Finally, the living looked like it was going to be easy; many of the boys quickly developed deep suntans.

At least one of the Bedford boys wasn't the slightest bit interested in what Jacksonville had to offer. All Sergeant John Schenk wanted was to get back to Bedford so he could marry his fiancée, a bewitching and smart elementary school teacher, Ivylyn Jordan.

John and Ivylyn, both twenty-five, had met on a blind date the day Company A was inducted into the federal army. The date was arranged by a mutual friend who had heard Schenk say how pretty Ivylyn was as he strolled past her and a friend one afternoon in downtown Bedford. The two had dined at a small restaurant just outside town and were instantly infatuated. That first night they sat up and talked in Schenk's car in the pitch darkness of Route 122 just outside town. "I talked and talked and talked until three in the morning," recalled Ivylyn. "We fell lock, stock and barrel."[15]

They were rarely apart in the following days. At night, they jitterbugged. By day, they planted rows of vegetables and tended John's garden. "He was a very good gardener. We gardened every day we could. He loved being outdoors," Ivylyn remembered.[16] They were married on August 24, 1942. Then it was off for a two-week honeymoon in a small cottage in Natural Bridge, not far from Bedford. A creek babbled nearby as husband and wife talked of starting a family after the war. John had been a clerk in a Bedford hardware store; the manager had promised to make John a partner when he got out of the army. They would be able to give their children a decent start in life. "We wanted a boy and a girl, at least," Ivylyn said.[17]

The honeymoon ended all too soon. They returned to Ivylyn's apartment in Moneta, a few miles from Bedford, and spent a last night together, wrapped in each other's arms, vowing they would find some time to be alone and think about each other every day. "We had an appointed time—his would be 10 P.M. each night, and mine was to be 5 P.M.," she said.[18]

On her stoop the following morning, Schenk took his slim wife in his arms, kissed her and made her swear not to move an inch until he returned. "He asked me to stand on that porch and wait for him," she said. "I did. . . . I waited a long time."[19]

When Schenk arrived back at Camp Blanding in early September he found Company A again preparing to move out. This time, the 29th Division was headed overseas. But thousands of men were still on furlough, some as far away as Baltimore. Telegrams were dispatched across the States. In nearby towns and Jacksonville, trucks fixed with loud-speakers drove through the streets crowded with soldiers, blaring orders for the division's return to camp. Those watching that summer's hit movies, *Yankee Doodle Dandy* and *Casablanca*, were amazed when the order—"RETURN TO BASE"—flashed on screens, replacing James Cagney and the luminous Ingrid Bergman.

Two rail lines left Camp Blanding. One went north, the other west. Which would they take? No one wanted west. That meant the Pacific, the death islands of Guadalcanal and an enemy who would show no mercy. If it was to be north, they would follow the 1st Division and possibly end up in North Africa. To a man, the Bedford boys preferred sand to jungle.

There was little time to do more than make a quick telephone call or send a hastily prepared telegram. New weapons had to be issued, treated with Cosmoline grease, and stored in massive crates for transport. All other equipment had to be waterproofed, and all insignia had to be removed from uniforms—a precaution against German spies detecting the identity and destination of the 29th Division.

Back in Bedford, Bettie Wilkes heard that Company A was about to move out. She called other wives and fiancées. Did they want to join her and take the train to Florida? It would be their last chance to see the boys. Elaine Coffey worked in the same mill as Bettie. She was up for it. Their manager said they could both take a day off. Viola Parker eagerly joined the group.

The girls pulled out their best summer frocks, crammed a change of clothes and make-up into valises, and headed south. Viola was especially anxious to see Earl: She had just discovered she was pregnant.

The train was packed with soldiers and with other families from Bedford hoping to see the boys one last time. Among them was sixteen-year-old Verona Lipford, sister of Company A's Frank Draper Jr. Verona had never missed a day of school or been tardy. "My mother took me out of school for a whole week so we could go down to Florida together,"

Verona recalled. "It was so full of soldiers that Viola, bless her heart, had to sit on her suitcase in the aisle. That train was just shaking us all to death. But we made it."[20]

Bettie Wilkes got her girlfriends together and slipped with them into Camp Blanding: "We had a great time. I asked one of the men to take a picture with my Kodak Brownie. It was the last of the boys together before they left American soil." To this day, Bettie cherishes the photograph, shown on the cover of this book.[21]

The afternoon of September 22, 1942, Elaine Coffey was able to be alone with her fiancé, Bedford Hoback. He handed her a ring and tried to comfort her. "Now don't you cry,"[22] he told her as tears streamed down her face and they hugged one last time.

It was a sultry and still evening. Company A milled about. Other wives, relatives, and girlfriends mingled with the men, handing over keepsakes, fighting back tears. The light started to fade.

"I'm coming back, you can believe that," John Wilkes told Bettie.

There was time for one last kiss. Then Master Sergeant Wilkes stepped away.

"Well, looks like time we got to shove off," he said.

Wilkes turned towards Company A.

"All right, men!" he shouted. "Fall in!"

The men snapped into perfect formation. Not a head turned towards the women.

"Forward, march!" Wilkes ordered. "Hut, two, three, four! Hut . . . "

Bettie and the other Bedford girls waved goodbye. "Oh my, they looked very fine," recalled Bettie. "They made us feel proud."[23]

Company A marched up an incline towards the train station. The girls jogged alongside until they could follow no more, choking back sobs, watching until the silhouette of Company A disappeared into the darkness over the brow of a hill. Then they traipsed to Bedford Hoback's station wagon and set off in silence for the day-long drive home.

Meanwhile, the Bedford boys sat in their train, chain-smoking, gambling, and joking. "For all we knew, we could be fighting in a few weeks," recalled Earl Newcomb who sat in a nonsmoking compartment with three other men and played poker. "But no one seemed too bothered. We were in a pretty good mood. We'd got used to sitting in trains all day, being moved around all the time."[24]

They were going north, thank God. The Japanese would have to wait until they'd licked Uncle Adolf. Armed guards were posted at the train's doors whenever it stopped. The men were not to say a word to any civilian: The polite stranger asking about life in the army might be an undercover German. When they passed through their old base, Fort Meade, someone said they must be going to Camp Kilmer in New Jersey, the main staging area for troops headed to Britain.

Almost twenty-four hours after leaving Florida, the Bedford boys wearily filed off their train in a downpour at a station in New Jersey. They formed up on the platform before Master Sergeant Wilkes and awaited orders, sodden uniforms soon clinging to their skin.

Overseeing the transfer of the 116th Infantry to Camp Kilmer was a tall and lean officer, Colonel Charles "Stoneface"[25] Canham, forty-six, one of the most gifted soldiers of his generation. In 1921, as a lowly sergeant, he had been accepted into the elite military academy, West Point. A notorious "ball-buster" with a Hitler-like moustache and iron-rod posture, he had been brought into the 29th Division to toughen up the National Guardsmen and turn them into effective killers. Before the year was out, the Bedford boys would fear and detest him.

Around 1 A.M., a major with an artillery battalion noticed Canham.

"Well, we got them off the trains pretty fast, didn't we Colonel?"

"It could've been a lot faster if you'd poked them in the ass," snapped Canham.[26]

In Camp Kilmer, the Bedford boys were surprised to discover that some men's wives were waiting in motels and campgrounds in nearby New Brunswick, thirty miles from Manhattan. Most were from Maryland and Baltimore, home to approximately half the 29th Division.

When the Bedford boys arrived in their new barracks, built to process doughboys headed for Flanders in the last war, they were greeted by a barrage of orders and new regulations. The boys were headed overseas and the army, it seemed, was determined they would take everything they could possibly need with them.

"New coal-scuttle helmets replaced the flat First World War dishpan version and blue denim fatigues were exchanged for new-issue green herringbones," recalled Bob Slaughter of Company D, then seventeen years old. "Photographs were taken and identification cards given that would be carried until our separation from the army. Immunization shots for every disease known to man were given in both arms and where the sun doesn't shine."[27] Slaughter had grown up in Roanoke, the nearest city to Bedford, and at age fifteen, with his parents' consent, had joined the National Guard to be with his buddies. "I was tall for my age—six foot two," he recalled. "We got a dollar every drill and went to Virginia Beach in the summer."[28] Slaughter would grow another three inches by D-Day.

Meanwhile, Bettie and her girlfriends had arrived back in Bedford late on Sunday, September 23. When she got home, Bettie discovered John's new whereabouts and immediately decided to follow him. Viola Parker again eagerly agreed to accompany her. "We thought they might be in New Jersey for a while," explained Bettie. "So, tired and worn out, we boarded a train to New York, where we were due to arrive on Monday night."[29]

Their train was again crammed with troops. The track needed repairs. The journey seemed to last forever. And Viola now had morning sickness. Every few minutes, Bettie asked if she was all right.

"Don't ask me that anymore," Viola finally replied. "If I'm not all right, I'll let you know."[30]

The train shuddered to a halt in New York's Pennsylvania Station. An early autumn chill was in the air. Bettie and Viola crossed a sea of uniforms and suddenly found themselves on a sidewalk, overawed by Manhattan. It was their first time in New York. They couldn't help but look up and marvel at the skyscrapers jostling for attention, lit up so high they seemed to touch the stars.

They walked several blocks until they found a decent hotel. As they were checking in, they heard the familiar sounds of a big band. They followed the notes and peeked into a ballroom. The legendary Tommy Dorsey had just played. His road crew was packing up trombones and double basses and moving on for another gig.

Late into the night, Bettie and Viola tried to get a call through to their men at Camp Kilmer. They were told the camp was sealed. They kept calling, but no messages could be given to the men. They put their heads down for a few hours. The next morning they decided to return to Bedford. "Earl wrote later [that] the camp was surrounded by wire and looking through wire wouldn't have been great," Viola recalled.[31] "It was a foolish trip, but I was trying."[32]

At least two Bedford boys were, however, allowed out of the camp. Ray Stevens and pencil-mustached nineteen-year-old Sergeant Grant Collins Yopp were lucky enough to be issued twenty-four-hour passes. Stevens and Yopp headed for Washington, D.C., and finally got off a streetcar at Third Street Northwest. It was a short walk from there to an apartment shared by Yopp's sister, Anna Mae Stewart, and his young wife, Elsie Foutz, who both worked in the Washington central post office.

After a few drinks, the men got to talking about going overseas.

"I'm gonna go kick the shit out of the Germans," said Yopp, "and then I'm coming home."

Ray wasn't so gung-ho. "Well," he said, "if I go over, I won't be coming back."

"Ray, you know better than to say things like that," said Anna Mae.[33]

Ray was deadly serious. He had already told his brother Roy that he could take his share in their farm—he wasn't going to come home.

The 29th was among the first divisions to pass through Camp Kilmer on the way to Europe. The extensive preparations were infuriating and frustrating as everything, down to packing replacement buttons, was done strictly by the book. Every man was issued two kit bags—A and B—one for a ship's hold, and one to carry on board. The list of contents for each took minutes to read, and there were frequent changes to the lists. The men spent days packing and repacking their bags.

Finally, early on September 26, 1942, Company A formed up outside its barracks and then marched to the nearest train station in New Brunswick. As their train moved slowly towards Hoboken, the men waved to crowds lining the route, flying flags and honking horns. Locals had not yet become jaded at the sight of boys leaving for war.

In Hoboken, the men learned that many of them were to cross the Atlantic on the most impressive ocean liner in history—the magnificent, 81,000-ton *Queen Mary*, launched to great fanfare and praise in 1936, the year Hitler had occupied the Rhineland. Two-thirds of the 29th Division—15,000 troops—would cross the Atlantic aboard the *Mary*. The rest would take her sister ship, the equally imperious *Queen Elizabeth*. The liners had been requisitioned in March 1940 by the British Admiralty.

Ferries took the Bedford boys across the choppy Hudson River after dark. Because of blackout conditions, the ships at the west side Manhattan docks were indistinct silhouettes until the men walked down gangways onto the piers owned by the Cunard–White Star line. Once again, Colonel Canham was on patrol, barking orders. There were no more bands, no cheering crowds.

Nervously, the men formed long lines and then inched forward. Before them loomed the *Mary* but she looked nothing like the dashing Blue Ribbon record holder they'd seen in the pages of *Life* magazine and newsreels. Her bright red, black, and white coloring had been masked with what the British admiralty called "light sea gray."[34] As they got close, the Bedford men had to crane their necks to take in her full size; the sun deck was seventy-five feet above the water line.

Boarding was done strictly "by the numbers": As each man stepped forward with his number chalked on his helmet, his last name was called out. He answered with his first name and middle initial, and was then checked off by Transportation Corps men wearing red and gold armbands. The Bedford boys, carrying heavy duffel bags, wearing full combat uniform—including cartridge belt, canteen, and rifle—then walked aboard and were given directions to their berths. As they headed below, they were handed a letter from President Roosevelt. "You are a soldier of the United States Army," it stated simply. "You have embarked for distant places where the war is being fought."[35]

4

Cruel Seas

THE BEDFORD BOYS DID NOT expect to find the art deco opulence they had read about and seen in newsreels. But they were surprised by how spartan the conditions on the *Mary* actually were. Her six miles of carpet had disappeared, as had 450 deck chairs, 220 cases of china, silver, and crystal from the famous dining rooms, and every wooden door. Now walls of sandbags, endless hinged metal shutters, and a drab décor greeted the new passengers.

In the A section of the ship, deep down in her bowels, a long way from the lifeboats on the upper decks, the Bedford boys dumped their packs and realized this was going to be no pleasure trip. There were just eighteen inches between their bunks stacked in tiers of six. And they would have to lie on them and wait for several hours until the ship's captain, Gordon Illingworth, gave orders allowing them to move about.[1]

Bedford Hoback had crossed to Hawaii aboard a troopship in the mid-thirties. But that was before the war, when there were less than a hundred thousand soldiers in the entire U.S. army. Now there were over ten thousand men on the *Mary* alone. Thoughts of garlanded hula girls serving rum cocktails in coconut shells had no doubt buoyed Bedford's last journey. Now his exact destination was unknown. One thing was certain—there wouldn't be any lounging around on surf-pounded beaches wherever they were going.

Hoback walked over to choose a "rack," as the bunks were called. From experience, he knew he'd be better off in a top bunk. If the ocean was calm, it was better to sleep below and be able to get out of the berthing quarters without having to clamber down over five men. But if the crossing got rough, the top bunk was the only place to sleep. There would be no one puking his guts out just a few inches above.

The Bedford boys felt the *Mary* pull away from the pier and then steam slowly down the Hudson River and through New York harbor. Finally Captain Illingworth sounded the all-clear, and the Bedford boys were able to move around A deck. But they could not yet go up on top, so many opted to stay in their racks. The *Mary*, designed to accommodate three thousand at a push, was bursting at her seams with a vast human cargo. Men crammed every passageway, lugging heavy kit bags, wearing lifebelts, and shouldering guns.[2]

The *Mary* moved down the river leading towards Ellis Island. Finally, Company A was permitted to go up on top. They found a deck already crowded with other companies, all smoking, it appeared, and all watching Manhattan's skyscrapers glide by. From the sun deck, Roy Stevens and his brother Ray watched New York's skyline disappear into the distance to be replaced by endless gray waves.

For many of the men, their last sight of land was an emotional moment. Almost all of Company A's two hundred men were leaving American shores for the first time. They knew many of them would never return. "I feel scared," Ray told Roy, voicing many of the men's feelings. "I never felt scared like this before."[3]

Roy was confident they'd be back soon enough. Ray wasn't so sure: They'd be lucky if they even got to Britain—three thousand miles across an ocean infested with dozens of "wolf-packs" of German U-boats. The enemy was hellbent on sinking the *Mary*, thereby knocking out an entire U.S. division and landing a crippling blow to American morale.

Dubbed the Gray Ghost because of her color and speed, the *Mary* had so far outrun every attacker, her elusiveness so infuriating Hitler that he was now offering a $250,000 reward to the first Nazi submariner who sank her. But how much longer would the *Mary*'s luck last? The Bedford boys were crossing at the height of the Battle of the Atlantic; U-boats were sinking more than 187,000 tons of Allied shipping every month. In fact, the Allies were very close to defeat, barely managing to build more ships than were being sunk. And if the Germans did launch a successful attack, there wouldn't be a chance in hell of the Bedford boys being fished from the Atlantic by a merciful enemy.

The first day aboard the *Mary* was particularly bad for John Schenk, who suffered acute seasickness. Like most men aboard, he had never been to sea. Yet he managed to write to his wife and to think of her each day at the promised time. "He was so sick he could not stand up," recalled Ivylyn. "Whenever he was on water, he got very nauseated."[4]

Perhaps the *Mary*'s only design fault was her tendency to roll heavily when the wind got up. This motion was exaggerated by her zigzag course, which changed at least every eight minutes, and by her speed. The fastest an attacking U-boat could go was twelve knots on the surface and just seven submerged—far less than the *Mary*'s top speed of thirty-two knots. Before long, many men nursed their first injuries of the war—bruises from falling to the floor in corridors and cramped quarters.

But the rolling was nothing compared to the *Mary*'s most serious drawback as a troopship—lack of ventilation. Officers were allowed to take showers. Noncoms could not, and the stench of unwashed thousands quickly filled every deck. To make matters worse, most officers went without showers: None wanted to be caught naked in front of their men when an alarm sounded.

While the weather was brisk and cold, the stench was almost bearable. But when the *Mary* headed south, so she could be out of range of U-boats for as much of the crossing as possible, higher humidity and temperatures forced some men to sleep with handkerchiefs across their noses. There was soon fierce competition to go on deck and fill one's lungs with clean ocean breezes. Many wished they were on a summer crossing when men were allowed to sleep on the top decks under the stars.

Idleness is the enemy of discipline and morale in all armies: As much as possible was done to keep the men occupied. The most popular distraction was the daily testing of the *Mary*'s anti-aircraft batteries, which were commanded from a platform set up on the Veranda Grill on the boat deck. There were sometimes contests between artillery companies to see who could be quickest to fire the guns.[5]

The men were expected to attend several lectures during the crossing. The most popular was about their destination, England. Every man aboard was also given the U.S. Army Special Services Division's pamphlet, *A Short Guide to Britain*, full of advice about how to stay on friendly terms with the Brits.[6]

> You are higher paid than the British "Tommy." Don't rub it in. Play fair with him. He can be a pal in need. It isn't a good idea to say "bloody" in mixed company in Britain—it is one of their worst swear words. To say "I look like a bum" is offensive to their ears, for to the British this means that you look like your own backside. The British are beer drinkers—and they can hold it.[7]

The men's first taste of British food did not bode well. Company A's mess sergeant, Earl Newcomb, was suddenly viewed with a new respect. His meals may not have been much to write home about but compared to British "grub" they were gastronomic marvels. Bob Slaughter of Company D would always cringe at the memory of the *Mary*'s bland, mutton-based meals. Actually, the food was remarkably good given the number eating it, and vastly superior to the average Briton's diet at that time.

It took the Bedford boys most of the voyage to get used to other things British. Only after several rounds of rook, a popular card game, did some understand the British currency, with its mysterious half-bobs, "tuppeny bits," half-crowns, shillings, and bobs. Private Nicholas Gillaspie, an avid baseball player and fisherman before the war, was particularly skilled at rook. "Nick loved rook," recalled his niece Melba Basham. "They all loved that game. They played it all the time."[8] He had grown up with four brothers and gone to a one-room school like the Stevens twins. Tall, light-haired, quiet, and utterly dependable, Gillaspie was known in Bedford for his impeccable manners and constant smile.

The most serious gamblers congregated in bathrooms along with the heaviest smokers—smoking was banned in most other areas. In a fog of Lucky Strike fumes, men kissed the dice and small fortunes goodbye. Spotters were posted to give advance warning of MPs who would break up games. Junior officers, especially "ninety-day wonders" with the rank of second lieutenant, usually turned a blind eye, thankful that the men were preoccupied. In any case, many played stud poker in their own quarters in the former state rooms.

Company A had more than its fair share of heavy gamblers. For twenty-year-old Bedford boy Wallace Carter, nicknamed "Snake Eyes" because of his passion for dice, the crossing passed quickly. Whether he won or lost, "Snake Eyes" always had a spare dime to watch a movie, especially a Western or the thirties film noirs starring Humphrey Bogart.

Then there was Earl Newcomb, the best poker player in Company A, who could sit for hours with an inscrutable face, and sometimes bluffed his way to pots of several hundred dollars.[9] "We used to have some pretty good games around pay day," Newcomb recalled. "Mostly, we'd just bet with quarters because some of the boys didn't like to lose everything in one go. They wanted to take their time about it."[10]

It was not unusual, with so many men on board, to bump into old friends and even relatives in other regiments. On September 28, less than forty-eight hours after leaving America, Grant Yopp ran into one of his four brothers, Herbert, in a corridor. They had not seen each other since January 1942 when Herbert had been drafted and sent to a training camp in North Carolina with an observation squadron of the army air corps. Neither knew that the other was aboard.[11]

The second day out was notable for another incident, one that put many of the Bedford boys on edge for the rest of the journey. Roy Stevens and several buddies were shooting dice in a hallway when suddenly the *Mary* pitched to one side so violently they thought she was going to capsize. Their dice flew against a wall and then the *Mary* quickly righted herself. There was a nervous silence while several men picked themselves up and then loud sighs of relief and even a few brave

jokes. "Some of us thought: 'What if? What if we'd gone over?'" recalled
Roy Stevens. "It could have been the end of 10,000 people. It would
have been a terrible disaster."[12] For the first time, many of the boys realized that from now on life and death would be separated purely by
luck.

When he wasn't gambling, Roy bunked beside his brother Ray on A
deck. Ray could sit for hours and read passages from a Bible or cheap
army-issue paperback edition. Roy couldn't sit still that long but he
would listen for a few minutes as Ray quickly summarized each chapter.

At least once an hour, Roy would go check on the men in his platoon.
"We were berthed close to the privates so we could keep an eye on them.
You knew where they were and they knew where you were. For most of
those boys it must have been almost like being on a trip with Mom and
Dad."[13]

On the third day out, tempers began to fray. There were rumors of
fights between men sick of waiting in line at water fountains, tired of
being woken by the snores of men inches from each other's faces, unable to get air on deck after dark, and resentful of the officers' privileges.

For those with appropriate rank, it seemed, the *Mary* was still a pleasure boat. In addition to showers, the officers had stewards to clean
their kit and serve food; it was rumored that they even had the run of the
sun deck at night. Most noncommissioned men soon shared the senti-
ments of a Private Sam Shapiro who had written to *Yank* magazine that
June: "We'll win this damn war but I can't face the trip back."[14]

Eventually, the temperature dropped and the weather closed in as
the *Mary* began her approach to Britain. They were now in waters latent
with menace, close to the U-boat pens in the Brittany port of Brest. On
October 1, the *Mary* entered the Irish Sea and was met by a convoy of
British cruisers that would escort her to the Scottish port of
Greenock.[15]

When October 2, 1942, dawned, the sun shone and there were no
clouds in the sky. Several Bedford boys walking around up top enjoyed
exceptionally clear views. They were in high spirits; soon, they would be

rid of the pitching *Mary* and be able to get a bath or shower, decent food, and a good night's sleep.

Five destroyers and a British cruiser, HMS *Curacoa*, were sent out to escort the *Mary*, who continued her zigzag course that morning. The *Curacoa* was an anti-aircraft cruiser and provided essential protection since the *Mary* did not yet have enough guns to ward off a serious air attack by the Luftwaffe.

Just about 10 A.M., the *Curacoa* reached her designated rendezvous position five miles ahead of the *Mary*.[16] The two boats were then to accompany each other to the Forth of Clyde, weaving back and forth in a zigzag pattern. For its armament to be effective, the *Curacoa* had to stay close.

The *Curacoa*'s captain, John Boutwood, a veteran of World War I, had serious reservations about the close-in escort system because communications were not good between the ships. On a previous escort run, it had taken two hours for a message to be passed to the *Mary* by signal lamp. What bothered Boutwood more were the standing orders forbidding the *Mary* from slowing down under escort. It was extremely difficult for the *Curacoa*, built before the last war, to stay ahead of the *Mary*. Even on her zigzag course, the *Mary* clipped along at 26.5 knots—1.5 knots faster than the *Curacoa*'s top speed.[17]

At 12.30 P.M., the *Curacoa* signaled, "I AM DOING MY BEST SPEED 25 KNOTS ON COURSE 108. WHEN YOU ARE AHEAD I WILL EDGE ASTERN OF YOU." Captain Boutwood went below to have lunch just after the signal was sent. When he got back to the bridge around 1 P.M., he saw that the *Mary* was catching up with the *Curacoa*, so he ordered a change of course for the *Curacoa*.[18]

Aboard the *Mary*, Senior First Officer Noel Robinson had been on watch since noon. At 2:04, the wheelhouse clock chimed. A few minutes later, Robinson noted that the *Mary* was now quickly gaining on the *Curacoa*. He ordered the quartermaster to "port a little" and then went into the wheelhouse to check his course. When Robinson got back to the bridge, he was shocked by how close the ships now were to each other. When the *Curacoa* rolled, Robinson could see "down her funnels."

Robinson turned to the wheelhouse.

"Hard-a-port!"[19]

The *Mary*'s quartermaster spun the wheel as fast as he could. But turning such a mammoth vessel was a slow process. . . .

Telegraphist Allin Martin was a radio operator on the *Curacoa*'s lower bridge:

> The upper bridge speaking tube clanged and my "oppo" [opposite number] indicated that if any camera was to hand a particularly good view of the *Queen Mary* was available. Unclipping the bulkhead door, I stepped outside, where, to my horror, I saw the enormous bulk of the *Queen Mary* bearing down on our port quarter at about fifty yards range. Her huge white bow wave seemed as tall as a house and it seemed inevitable that we were within seconds of being torn apart. I dived for my lifebelt.[20]

It was 2:12 P.M. Suddenly, the 81,000-ton *Mary*, now moving at 28.5 knots, hit the *Curacoa* 150 feet from her stern, breaking through three-inch-thick armor and bulkheads as if they were cardboard.

On deck, the Bedford boys could not believe their eyes. "There were several of us there," recalled Earl Newcomb. "We knew we were getting close to land and we'd gone up to get a first look. The *Mary* just cut her clean in two."[21]

Corporal Bob Slaughter was sunbathing when he felt the collision. Men shouted and ran to the ship's rail. "My first thought was that we had been torpedoed. . . . I saw the *Curacoa*'s stern going down one side of the *Mary*, and the bow down the other—cut right in two. The *Curacoa*'s crow's nest was parallel to the water, and there was a sailor in there still doing semaphore signals. His eyes looked enormous—he was so frightened. All we could do was throw life-jackets. I remember thinking: "'God, here we are, haven't even got overseas, and we've killed all these British sailors.'"[22]

Deep below on the *Mary*, the collision felt as if a rowing boat had gone over a log—a jarring and a screech but nothing spectacular. Twenty-one-year-old Sergeant Allen Huddleston, who had worked as a soda jerk in Lyle's drugstore in downtown Bedford before the war and was married to Private Nicholas Gillaspie's cousin, Geraldine, was lying on his bunk when he suddenly felt a "small" jolt. "I looked out the porthole and saw half a ship going down," Huddleston said. "There were people still in her."[23]

Roy Stevens was getting ready to disembark when the collision happened. "The boat jarred. It was very quick. Soon, everybody was running upstairs to see what happened." When Stevens got to the top deck, he saw the *Curacoa* sinking in the *Mary*'s wake.

The *Mary*'s Captain Illingworth was also below when the ships collided. He immediately rushed to the wheelhouse.

"Was that a bomb?" he asked.

"No, Captain," the *Mary*'s quartermaster replied, "we hit the cruiser."[24]

Aboard the forward section of the *Curacoa*, Captain Boutwood was still alive.

"Abandon ship!" he shouted.[25]

There was suddenly a deafening screech as steam pipes ruptured. Men jumped off the ship wherever they stood. Clouds of dense black smoke shrouded the area, and oil from the cruiser's fuel tanks soon covered the surface, making it harder for men to hold onto wreckage. The burnt and badly wounded started to slip into oblivion. Among the ship's officers, only Captain Boutwood and a Lieutenant Holmes were still alive.

Survivors swam from the ship, knowing they could be sucked under with it. Suddenly, the bow lurched into the sky and what remained of the *Curacoa* sank. Escaping air created a final anguished groan. The *Curacoa* disappeared beneath the waves at 2:24 P.M., ten minutes after being struck.

Aboard the *Mary*, Captain Illingworth struggled to contain his emotions. Although he could see many survivors in the water, he ordered his men to continue their course. There were more than 11,000 troops on board: To stop would be to risk all their lives.

Seventeen-year-old Private Bob Sales of Company B had gone on deck to get some air. He couldn't understand why the *Mary* did not stop to pick up survivors.

"You're crazy as hell, man," a soldier told him."The *Mary*, sitting still in the water—a German submarine could blow [us] off the face of the earth."[26]

They were only hours from Scotland, but would they make it? Indeed, how badly damaged was the *Mary*? Captain Illingworth ordered Staff Captain Harry Grattidge to find out. Grattidge had been awakened by the impact and had arrived on deck just as the remnants of the *Curacoa* disappeared beneath the ocean.[27] Now he rushed to the *Mary*'s forepeak to assess the damage:

> The speed was still on the ship when I reached the forepeak. By the light of a torch I could see the water racing in and out of the forepeak, a great column of it forming a kind of cushion from the collision bulkhead, the watertight reinforced steel wall that rises from the very bottom of the ship to the main deck. If that bulkhead were weakened I did not like to think of the *Mary*'s chances. I sweated through my silent inspection. But finally, not a crack. Not a break. I turned to the bosun and the carpenter: "Get every length of wood you can find, bosun. Get it down here and strengthen that collision bulkhead as much as you possibly can. I'll report to the Captain." . . . I was sick at what we had done, yet I marveled, too, at the strange and terrible impregnability of the *Queen Mary*. It came home to me that she had no equal anywhere in the Atlantic, perhaps not anywhere in the world.[28]

Relieved that the *Mary* had suffered no life-threatening damage, Illingworth set a course, at thirteen knots, for Greenock. He also ordered the destroyers in the escort to go to the *Curacoa* survivors' rescue. It was well over two hours after the collision when the rescue ships reached the scene of the disaster. Survivors clung to rafts and floatnets. Some held on with their last strength to debris. Captain Boutwood was pulled near death from the water by the crew of a whaleboat from the Bramham destroyer.

Only 101 men from the *Curacoa*'s crew of 439 were saved. Twenty-one bodies would later wash ashore along the coast of Scotland. No one from the stern of the boat survived. All but a few of the men who had marveled at the *Mary* from the boat's quarterdeck had been killed. The Gray Ghost was the last thing they saw.

Later that afternoon, Lieutenant Ray Nance and ten other officers in his quarters were called down to the *Mary*'s main lounge. The chandeliers had been taken down and the floors planked over. Hundreds of 29th Division officers sat waiting nervously. Captain Illingworth informed them that the tragedy could not be mentioned under any circumstance. Information about the sinking would not be public until the war ended.

The tragedy's impact on the Bedford boys was enormous. "It was a great shock to see that happen," recalled Roy Stevens. "We'd not been in combat before. We'd never seen people die like those who drowned there. The men were very disturbed."[29]

Was the collision yet another bad omen? The near capsizing had set the superstitious on edge. Now many others worried that such a gut-wrenching catastrophe, before they had even encountered the enemy, meant the 29th Division was cursed with bad luck. One thing was certain—with their own eyes they had now seen how expendable men were in war.

On October 3, a bitterly cold and overcast day, they finally arrived in the Forth of Clyde and boarded "lighters" (old channel ferries) that took them to Greenock harbor. As the Bedford boys formed up on the dockside, the war suddenly felt very close. Barrage balloons filled the dirty skies as they marched through terraced streets to Greenock's station, where they boarded an old train of the London, Midland, and Scottish Railway. "It was gray, cold, raining," recalled Roy Stevens. "We were not too happy that day."[30]

The men had no idea where they were headed. Some hoped for a training camp in the south of England. But others predicted they were going directly to another port to board another troopship, this time bound for Africa. Considering their luck, they could be digging foxholes in the desert just in time for Christmas.

5

England's Own

COMPANY A SAT CRAMPED together in old British railway carriages. Drab terraced homes gave way to country. Men were soon crowding the greasy windows to catch glimpses of the fall landscape in the Scottish border country, some parts uncannily similar to Virginia's—rolling hills dotted with patches of bluish heather, crumbling stone walls, crooked lanes, and sheep farms. In northern England, at some junctions, gaggles of grubby schoolchildren, evacuated from London because of the Blitz, called for candy and gum. At several stations, pale-faced Red Cross girls offered refreshment—crumpets and tarts, served with piping hot tea.[1]

As darkness fell, blackout blinds came down in the train. Suddenly, an air raid siren wailed. The Bedford boys had never heard a real warning before. The war was above them and all around them—they were traveling through a county that had been under attack for over three years. "I tried to get some sleep," recalled Bob Slaughter. "Other boys gambled and shot dice. We were all ready to go to war. But of course back then we didn't know what war was."[2]

Early on October 4, 1942, the Bedford boys shouldered their hundred-pound barrack bags and marched into an old British army base on Salisbury Plain, southwest of London. Their new home, said an officer, was called Tidworth Barracks. It dated back to Elizabethan times and had been used at the turn of the century as a cavalry post. To most of the men it looked like a Dark Ages prison, all "steel, brick, rock—not a plank of wood anywhere, very cold, austere."[3] The nearest towns were Andover and Salisbury with its magnificent cathedral, and just ten miles away stood the ancient wonder of Stonehenge.

The Bedford boys' first task was to "go get sacks." The men discovered a mass of straw and were told to fill cloth bags to form a mattress. They then placed them on "double-decker beds" knocked up by a bad carpenter. Any man over six feet slept with his knees to his chin. It was freezing, yet their only source of warmth—two ancient pot-bellied stoves—was extinguished at lights out. The next morning, each of Company A's four barracks discovered there were just two bathtubs with claw feet for fifty men.[4]

By the second morning at Tidworth, the 116th's 1st Battalion was laid low with a scabies epidemic caused by infested straw in the mattresses. "Everybody was just scratching and clawing all over," recalled Company D's Bob Slaughter. "To make matters worse, the British food rations were pretty meager. Breakfast was maybe a smoked herring—what the Brits called a kipper. It stank. Then there was bread and marmalade. The bread was hard. The marmalade was bitter—just orange peelings and no sugar. And they gave us cups of tea. Not coffee. We felt like we were being starved. Each night, we'd go to the PX [the company store] and spend all our money on candy bars. But the Coca-Cola had no sugar and was served warm. Everything was just horrible."[5]

Far worse was to come. As soon as the men had recovered from scabies, they began the longest training program any American infantrymen endured in World War II. It would last over twenty months, from October 1942 to May 1944. The U.S. chiefs of staff had not yet decided when to invade Europe and they were concerned about the American forces' lack of combat experience and rigorous training. So they opted to turn the 29th into as strong an invasion force as possible. For seven days a week, broken once a month by a forty-eight-hour pass, Company A was pushed to its physical limits. Fifty men from Bedford had arrived at Tidworth. Each week, that number fell as one man after another was weeded out or assigned to a different unit.

The 29th Division's commander, Major General Leonard Gerow, wanted to prove that his troops, largely made up of National Guard outfits, could be made just as tough and battle-ready as any others in the army of the United States. A plainspoken and popular graduate of the Virginia Military Institute, Gerow was keenly aware of how some of his fellow generals, namely Lt. Gen. Lesley McNair, Chief of Staff of U.S. Army Headquarters in Washington, D.C., belittled the National Guard troops under his command. If Gerow had to work his men twice as hard as other division commanders to prove West Pointers like McNair wrong, then so be it.

"Endurance and strength tests called 'burp-up' exercises were given to monitor physical fitness," recalled Corporal Bob Slaughter. "Those who passed earned the Expert Infantryman's Badge and an extra five dollars in the monthly paycheck. Failing to qualify meant transfer to a noncombat outfit."[6]

To qualify, first the men had to run a hundred yards in twelve seconds in army boots and uniform, do thirty-five push-ups and ten chin-ups, get across an obstacle course at a sprint, and then show themselves to be deadly accurate with a Colt .45, the Garand M-1 rifle, and a BAR [Browning Automatic Rifle], the standard issue submachine gun.

All of this was done beneath sullen skies on the damp and wind-exposed Salisbury Plain. "It seemed to me the first few months in England the sun seemed to be rationed," recalled Slaughter. "Thick fog, a biting wind and cold drizzle were typical weather during November and December. We accepted bland, scanty food; little sleep and rest; and not enough warm clothing."[7]

To mark its first Christmas away from home, the 29th Division held parties for evacuated British kids. Men took items from care packages and gave them as presents. For propaganda purposes, there were actually two Christmas dinners: one in early December, staged for newspapers back home, and one on Christmas day.

At 10 P.M. on Christmas, John Schenk took time to be alone and think about Ivylyn. It had recently snowed and John had sent her a photograph of him and two other Bedford boys clowning about in their shorts, wearing British helmets. It cheered Ivylyn—he seemed to be enjoying himself.

The highlight of any day for Schenk and the Bedford boys was mail call. Company A's mail clerk, a Pennsylvanian named Ned Bowman, would deliver mail first to Fellers, Nance, and other officers, next to Master Sergeant John Wilkes, and then walk into the barracks and call out men's names. Some boys would fall into deep depression if they failed to get a letter from home or a Red Cross parcel. Packages from home were shared around, and delicacies and ethnic foods were often tasted for the first time. By 1943, the average GI received fourteen letters each week and wrote one letter a day unless in combat.[8]

Like many Bedford boys replying to letters from home that Christmas, Schenk masked his homesickness with humor. He'd been forced to give up his habit of smoking a cigar after dinner. "A cigar over here is quite a treat," he explained. "The English think that Churchill is the only one who can smoke one."[9] Ivylyn promptly went out and bought a humidor. "I drew a picture and sent it," she remembered. "I told him it would be waiting when he got back."[10]

Sometimes relatives sent clippings from the *Bedford Bulletin* which fascinated many of the boys who had grown nostalgic since leaving America. By New Year's Day, 1943, over 1,500 Bedford County men were in service and death notices were starting to appear in the *Bedford Bulletin*. Among the first to die was John Canaday, twenty-one, a classmate of several of the Bedford boys. He had been killed fighting the Japanese in the South Pacific. More men from Bedford were being drafted every week and those who had been deferred so that they could work farms were "not happy over having to explain constantly why they are not in service. One man, whose son was deferred for this reason, went out one morning and found his fence posts leading to the highway painted yellow."[11]

The big news from home that winter was the crash of a B-25 bomber into the side of Sharp Top, one of the twin Peaks of Otter. Five men lost their lives when the plane hit head-on at 10 P.M. on February 2, 1943. Many townspeople saw the bomber fly over Bedford so low that they feared it would crash in the town itself. "Those who reached the scene of the disaster were sickened by the sheer horror of what they saw," reported the *Bulletin*. "All the bodies were cruelly crushed and mangled, some were dismembered, and one of the searchers said that the head of one of the men had not been found when he left."[12] For the first time, the war had truly hit home.

Back in England, the Bedford boys grew ever more miserable: The winter of 1942–43 was one of the coldest on record in England, yet the boys' training program, much of it spent outside, got far tougher as the weather got worse. By February, shortcuts were no longer tolerated on marches; MPs were posted to make sure every man completed the weekly twenty-five-mile "yomps." One New Yorker in Company A recalled that it was "not unusual to march out with heavy overcoats, covered with our ponchos and be fighting frozen icicles on one side and sweating on the other."[13]

The damp chill in England seemed to penetrate everything. "Us yanks can't figure the weather here like we could at home," Captain Fellers wrote his parents. "I remember back there when Dad used to go out in the yard and take a look at the mountains, and if he saw any snow flurries on the Peaks [of Otter] he would come in and pull his chair closer to the fire. Here the people don't seem to mind the weather at all."[14]

Eventually, the conditions on Salisbury Plain began to improve as spring approached. The colors brightened. Crocuses appeared and then the first daffodils. And Company A began to earn the praise of battalion commanders: Captain Fellers was shaping a first-class fighting force. On average, the men were seven pounds heavier—most of it muscle—than when they had left America. Their chest sizes had increased by an inch at least and their self-confidence had soared. Several sergeants were selected for officer training and Jack Powers earned the rare honor of being chosen to join the 29th Division's elite combat unit, known as the Rangers, the American counterpart of the British commandos.

On March 27, 1943, Captain Fellers wrote his parents "from somewhere in England" about Company A's swift progress:

I am beginning to think it is hard to beat a Bedford boy for a soldier. Out of less than a hundred we left there with I would say about a dozen have made officers and several more will be soon. They are good practical officers too with a year or more of regular non-commission service behind them. I am truly proud to be commanding my old hometown outfit and just hope I can carry them right on through and bring all of them home.[15]

In early May, the 29th Division was ordered to vacate Tidworth and move to warmer climes. On May 23, 1943, the Bedford boys formed up and began a six-day journey that would take them 160 miles to the southwest. Four days were spent marching and two in the back of trucks. Exhausted, the Bedford boys finally dropped their packs in a new barracks near Ivybridge in Devon, twelve miles from the channel port of Plymouth. The move was part of "Operation Bolero," a long-range plan for transferring and then accommodating almost two million American servicemen in Britain in the run-up to an invasion of Europe, which Allied commanders had now set for the summer of 1944.

When the Bedford boys explored nearby towns and especially coastal villages, they were astonished to find palm trees growing in some parks because of the more temperate weather brought by the Gulf Stream's effect along the entire southwest coast of England. But when they ventured north, they discovered far less hospitable terrain—a deserted, godforsaken stretch of moorland called Dartmoor.

Some of the men recognized Dartmoor from the successful Hollywood horror movie, *Hound of the Baskervilles,* starring Basil Rathbone. Even in mid-summer, the area could be just as bleak as the ghoulish wasteland portrayed in the film. To a GI without a compass, Dartmoor was also potentially lethal, mired with boot-sucking bogs and peaty quicksand. But on the odd day when the sun broke through dirty clouds, it was also starkly beautiful. There were wild ponies and delicate wildflowers, and the moss and heather changed color with the weather.[16]

Company A began to camp out on the moors, even in the most deplorable conditions. "You couldn't stay dry," said Allen Huddleston. "Water would always seep into everything. You'd lie down on your bed sheet and before long the water would come through. It was horrible."[17] Roy Stevens remembered one awful evening when the men set up their pup tents on the moors in a hurry because of a downpour: "Captain

Fellers came along and knocked down several tents that weren't in proper line. There were still guys in them."[18]

Men did their best to fend off the blues. Wallace "Snake Eyes" Carter filled his water can with whiskey he'd bought on the black market and took a good swig every few miles.[19] Others chanted caustic songs to take their minds off their sore feet and blisters.

One verse was particularly popular:

> I want to go again to the moors,
> To follow their winding trails,
> To stand again on their lonely slopes,
> In the cold and the rain and the gales.
> Oh, I'll go out to the moors again,
> But mind you and mark me well:
> I'll carry enough explosives,
> To blow the place to hell.[20]

When the boys passed through villages, locals often lined the route, shouting encouragement, sometimes providing snacks and cups of tea. If the Bedford boys came across English children, they would toss chocolate bars and shower the prettiest girls with strips of Wrigley's Spearmint gum from their C rations.

More often than not, Roy Stevens walked ahead of the company beside Captain Fellers. "Fellers and I would get up on the line in a hike, just the two of us up front together." For hours on end, out of earshot, they would joke, needle each other, and reminisce. "I'd ask Fellers about the old days back home, and kid him about what a tough kid he was, and get him going. We would talk all the way, sometimes for twenty-five miles. At night, he'd sometimes say it was as 'black as midnight's asshole.' He just loved saying that. He didn't waste his words. When he told you something, he meant it."[21]

It was not all "yomp" and hard slog. Many evenings, the Bedford boys strolled down winding lanes to nearby pubs where they shared news from home and drank "bitter." "We called it beer," recalled Earl New-comb, "but we didn't know exactly what it was—it didn't taste like beer I'd been used to. But we consumed it all the same."[22]

The few hours sat supping warm pints beside roaring fires would be among the men's fondest memories of Britain. Weldon Rosazza, Glen-wood "Dickie" Overstreet, and other sociable Bedford boys were soon copying the Brits, treating the lounge of their "locals," Ivybridge's "The Sportsman's Arms" and "The King's Arms," as a home away from home where they would tuck into good "pub grub," play darts, gossip, read the "funnies" in *Stars and Stripes*, and listen to American jazz on the radio.[23] Liquor, or "spirits" as the Brits called it, was strictly rationed. What little could be found was drunk within an hour of opening. Around seven, the landlady would cry out: "No more spirits tonight, gentlemen."[24]

Corporal Weldon Rosazza, twenty-two, was the neatest and perhaps the most cosmopolitan of the Bedford boys, having lived for a while in Washington, D.C., as a boy. "He was very charming, outgoing, and he had the prettiest dimples," recalled his cousin, Ellen Quarles. "He hated them and hated to be teased about them."[25] Rosazza had joined the Na-tional Guard upon graduating from Bedford High School. His father, Calisto, had worked as a mechanic at Bedford's People's Garage. His grandfather had emigrated from the small Piedmont town of Rosazza in Italy in the 1890s.

Twenty-two-year-old Dickie Overstreet, one of eleven children, had labored since he was a small boy for his father who owned a farm just outside Bedford. He and his family had somehow got by in the worst years of the Depression through supplying vegetables and meat to Dickie's aunt, who owned the Dutch Inn, a boardinghouse in Bedford. "We were very, very poor," recalled sister Beulah Witt. "My parents were very upset when Dickie went away. He was essential to running the farm. When he left, my father, Wilton, who was a carpenter, went to work in the shipyards in Newport News to keep us all."[26]

Just before nine o'clock every evening, silence descended in Ivy-bridge's pubs as everyone sat and waited for the BBC news on the wire-less. The reports were mostly uplifting. On the Russian front, the Germans were in retreat after suffering a devastating defeat at Stalingrad. In Africa, the Axis had been routed, losing 349,206 in dead and prisoners. Now the Allies were working their way up the jagged spine of Italy. Throughout England, General Bernard Montgomery was worshipped with almost the same fervor as Churchill.

The 1st Division, after a shaky start, had proved their mettle, decisively answering the snide British accusation that the GI was an inferior soldier to the Tommy. After the capture of Oran in Algeria, "The Big Red One" had fought its way across Tunisia, defeating Erwin Rommel's Afrika Korps, and then spearheaded the invasion of Sicily. They would shortly return to England to prepare for an invasion of France. As for the 29th Division, it was now dubbed by other GIs, somewhat derisively, as "England's Own." All but a few dozen of its 15,000 troops had yet to see combat and the division was still the only army based in Britain.[27]

After closing time at 10 P.M., the Bedford boys would trudge back to their barracks where some would write and read letters—there was precious little time in the day to one's self. Through letters from relatives, they learned that wartime Bedford was now very different from the small town they'd left in early 1942.

Shortages were starting to be felt and by Saturday nights most shelves in grocery stores were bare. Lines were common outside many stores because there were too few employees waiting on customers. Butter was rationed at four ounces a week; Tuesdays and Fridays were designated national "meatless days." Kitchen fat was saved to be processed into explosives. To men's delight, women's hems rose, in some cases as far as the knee, in a patriotic fashion craze aimed at saving material for uniforms.

Mrs. George P. Parker noted in a bimonthly report to Virginia authorities on morale in Bedford that "labor shortage is acute in rural areas. . . . Women and children are picking berries who have never been in a blackberry patch before. Huckleberries are being brought down from the mountains and are bringing unheard of prices but are in great demand . . . housewives are canning chickens and making sauerkraut."

Driving for pleasure had been banned and in its place many couples, reported Parker, had started to play croquet. The townspeople were "calm but anxious about the conduct of the war on the homefront. Disgusted with John L. Lewis and his strikers; felt the president was too lenient with them, perhaps remembering his obligation to labor and not unminding of that vote in case of a fourth term for himself."[28]

John L. Lewis was leader of the United Mine Workers and had ordered over half a million of his members back to work on May 20 twenty minutes before Roosevelt went on national radio to denounce a two-day strike that had threatened to bring war production to a standstill. Although Lewis called off the strike, he and other labor leaders were granted wage increases.

The underlying cause for Lewis's militancy was a widespread resentment among blue-collar workers that they were not sharing in the soaring profits of corporations, for whom the war represented no less than a rejuvenation of American capitalism. Approximately seventy big companies controlled three-quarters of wartime production and in the textile industry, for example, profits had risen 100 percent each year. For the bosses at Hampton Looms and other Bedford factories, times had never been so good.

The Bedford boys also learned, through reports in *Life* magazine and *Stars and Stripes,* that while Bedford was adapting well to wartime conditions elsewhere in America there was precious little harmony. As the Bedford boys prepared to fight Adolf Hitler, in several cities racial tensions had boiled over. In June 1943 in Los Angeles, white GIs had attacked blacks wearing "zoot" suits, sparking riots that led to the military declaring the city a no-go area for all American servicemen until it had regained control of the streets. In Detroit that June, where 300,000 whites and blacks had migrated to work in war factories, thirty-five people were killed, 600 wounded, and thousands jailed in two days of rioting.

The most popular attraction for the Bedford boys other than the local pub was the American Red Cross's Tidworth House, a magnificent mansion that actually adjoined the 29th Division's barracks and had once belonged to the great British general, Wellington. The stately country home was now given over to entertaining the troops, and the Bedford boys attended weekly dances where, for the first time, many met English girls.

Many of these women belonged to the Land Army, responsible for Britain's wartime agricultural production. "There were some robust women in that army," recalled Lieutenant Ray Nance. "They'd pitch you over a fence if you stepped over the line."[29] Delicate or robust, they had all endured three years of strict rationing and bombing, and a well-paid Brylcreamed Yank was the ideal wartime boyfriend. "We had chewing gum, smart uniforms, American cigarettes, and money," confirmed Roy Stevens. "We really were 'over-paid, over-sexed and over here' as the Tommies said."[30]

Radio operator John Clifton was particularly successful with English women due to an unbeatable combination of Southern charm, penetrating brown eyes, courtesy of his Cherokee Indian ancestry, and a slim but muscular build. "He was a real Cassanova—he and Rosazza ran together," recalled Stevens. "They knew how to get the girls. Some of the guys would go with them just to get their rejects. That little Rosazza, I bet he wasn't more than five foot six. Clifton was a great guy, too, but he'd snatch your girlfriend from under your eyes all right."[31]

At Bedford High School, "J. D." had been a quiet, trustworthy pupil with a gentle spirit. His mother, Minnie Lee, was proud that he had ignored the taunts of anti-Semitic local boys when he had started to date Edith Bornstein, the Jewish daughter of a manager at the Hampton Looms. Edith's delicate features and wonderful singing voice had captivated Clifton. But in England, according to letters home, he quickly found solace in the arms of an English girl he met at a dance and was soon engaged to her.

Raymond Hoback also fell in love with an English girl. His brother Bedford wrote to their sister, Mabel: "Ray is not married yet but is courting heavy. I saw him the other night with a little Jewish girl, right good looking."[32] Raymond later wrote to his parents about his new girlfriend.

"My mother got terribly worried that he would stay on in Britain after the war and marry her," recalled Lucille, his younger sister.

John Reynolds, Company A's runner, fell for an American, Kathleen Bradshaw, a nurse from Quinby in Virginia, who was working in a nearby hospital. According to relatives they were soon so in love that it seemed certain they would be married when they returned to Virginia after the war.

One of seven children, Reynolds, twenty-one, was remarkably close to his mother, Willie, whom he had begged to let him join the National Guard so he could be with his friends. "It was like they had a special bond with each other," recalled sister Marguerite Cottrell. "She would spend a lot of Sunday afternoons just reading his letters over and over."[33] When war had broken out, Willie had bitterly regretted she had agreed to John's joining the National Guard. As a runner, Reynolds was responsible for ferrying messages between Captain Fellers and battalion headquarters.

One night, Company A was invited to a dance organized by English women working in the fire service. "I was talking to a great girl," recalled Roy Stevens, "and then Fellers comes on over, pulled rank on me, and takes her away! I tell you, he got the biggest kick in the world out of that! He laughed about it for a long time."[34]

From their marches together, Stevens knew Fellers's marriage was pretty much on the rocks. "Fellers and his wife had fallen out. Before we went overseas, I'd heard through the grapevine that they were about to separate. He called her the blonde bomber but otherwise never said too much about her—he'd just go out at night and have a ball."[35]

Fellers also enjoyed a platonic relationship with a local widow, a Mrs. Lunscomb, who was soon mothering him and several other officers. "She kind of adopted him," recalled Fellers's younger sister, Bertie Woodford. "She lived on a farm and would fix Taylor hot meals. . . . Taylor said he couldn't believe she had a barn right next to the house."[36] Back in Bedford County, where cleanliness was next to godliness, swine were kept much farther from the kitchen.

Within a year, Sergeant Clyde Powers would be considering marriage to a sweet-natured "rose" named Pam Roberts whom he met in

Plymouth; Sergeant Roy Stevens would be dating a chirpy Liver-pudlian, Mickey Muriel Peake;[37] and company clerk Pride Wingfield would be seeing Doreen, Mickey's cousin. They shared cigarettes, taught their girls to jive and jitterbug, and tried to forget the war. The next dance, the next pub, the next forty-eight-hour pass were all that mattered.

When the Bedford boys ventured into towns and cities, they saw how fleeting life could be. Since 1939, there had been over 295,000 dead and injured in air raids. John Wilkes wrote Bettie: "It is very nice to know our homes and towns aren't being bombed as they have over here."[38] Bombed-out streets and orphaned children, meager meals, and nightly blackouts were continual reminders of the suffering and sacrifice of wartime Britons. They worked, on average, fifty-hour weeks and subsisted on rations that would have been unimaginable back in Bedford. Most had forgotten what fresh eggs, real coffee, a sweetened cup of tea, or an orange tasted like. But three years of total war had not dented their resilience nor diminished their generosity. Many families boarding GIs saved rations to provide birthday cakes and other treats.

Passes in hand, some Bedford boys took their English dates to the grave of Pocahontas, the Indian princess from Virginia, who was buried at Winchester. Some visited another Virginian—Nancy Astor, Britain's first female MP, who invited groups to tea and sandwiches. Astor had been born near Charlottesville, one of the 116th Infantry's hometowns. Rumor had it she had lobbied the American high command so that the Virginia boys would stay in Britain as its principal army of defense, long after other Yanks had been sent into battle.

Others from Company A headed straight for the nearest train station, bound for London, specifically Piccadilly Circus. "That was where the ladies, or rather the women, hung out," Roy Stevens explained.[39] As often as not, the men were overcharged for everything they bought in London, and sometimes fleeced by canny English "gals" who could see a horny Yank coming a long way off, even in the blackout. Roy Stevens lost a month's pay when his libido got the better of him and a buddy one night: "We met these two girls and were going to have a great time with them. They said: 'You give us some money and we'll get all of us a room.' We handed them some money but didn't see them again."[40]

Private Bob Sales of Company B was typical of the young Virginians in the 116th Infantry who saved their wages and then headed for Piccadilly Circus at every opportunity, hell-bent on painting the town red, white, and blue. As soon as they arrived in London, they hopped on a "tube" to Soho, army-issue rubbers and crisp "quid" notes stuffing their wallets. In Gerard Street, Sales and his fellow Virginians then bartered with "cheeky tarts" sitting on stoops, mascara lines drawn on their calves to resemble stockings, calling out their price: "Half a pound, occasionally a pound if she was real good looking. It was just unreal when it came to that. . . . There was also a Red Cross hostel where we'd spend the night for nothing. A bunch of girls from Spain worked as maids there. They'd sing, carry on, and laugh as they made our beds. When you were screwing one of them, the others would sing so the supervisor wouldn't catch on. It was the darndest thing you ever seen. Then you'd slip them two shillings."

The nice girls were to be found in Covent Garden: "Churchill had Covent Garden opera house converted into the biggest dance hall you ever saw in your life. They had two bands there. One would play for a while then the stage would rotate and another would start up. If you were dancing with a girl you didn't like, you waltzed over to the stag line and got another. Wrens, Wacs, always two hundred standing waiting to dance. They loved to dance, those English girls. Man, it was as close to heaven as you could get."[41]

Bedford boy Earl Parker also visited London but did not enjoy it quite so much as Sales. He couldn't stop thinking about his new family. Back in Bedford, Viola had given birth. He had been convinced the baby would be a boy, and had agreed on a name with Viola: Danny. A few weeks later, a letter reached Earl. Viola had named the girl Danny. Earl pulled out a photograph to show his buddies. She was every bit as beautiful as her mother.

6

"29, Let's Go!"

IN JULY 1943, THE 29TH Division received a new commander. General Charles H. Gerhardt, forty-eight, replaced Major General Leonard Gerow, who had been promoted to command V Corps. It was said that Gerhardt was another polo-playing West Point prima donna hell-bent on knocking even more sense into the apparently slovenly National Guard.[1]

Gerhardt immediately confirmed the rumors by appearing before the men dressed like a northern dandy in shiny cavalry boots and wearing "a polished leather holster and belts, and decorative neckerchief."[2] But the division's new chief martinet surprised everyone and ordered an end to the relentless training schedule and gave all the men seventy-two hours off. Suddenly, Gerhardt was affectionately being called "Uncle Charlie" throughout the division.

Gerhardt also devised a new battle cry—"29, Let's Go!"—and insisted it be used in every drill and even had it emblazoned on signposts. And he ordered as much weapons practice as possible: The men enjoyed firing guns; it made them feel like true soldiers. Typically, he led by example, terrifying locals by pulling out his Colt .45 and blazing away at rabbits or any other convenient target from his spotless jeep, the Vixen Tor, as his driver roared along narrow country lanes. Before long, many 29ers had become particularly adept at letting loose salvos at signs and gateposts as British cars approached. But Gerhardt didn't stop at impromptu fusillades. He was especially fond of dropping hand grenades from Piper Cub spotting planes as he watched his men practice maneuvers on the moors.

The honeymoon lasted a few weeks. Then Gerhardt began to crack down on officers and noncoms alike. Whether a colonel or a buck private, every man under Gerhardt was ordered to look immaculate at all times and keep helmets strapped under the chin. Equipment and vehicles were to be polished and as spotless as the men's uniforms. Stubble was forbidden, a cold-water shave mandatory every morning. And officers were to keep their distance when conferring with "Uncle Charlie." If they didn't, he would quickly bark: "That's far enough!"

Although soon detested by many officers, Gerhardt didn't appear to care. He had waited twenty years, rising through the ranks to command an infantry division. Besides, there was good reason for driving his officers and men harder than his predecessor. Gerhardt had been briefed on plans for a massive Allied invasion of France, codenamed "Overlord." If they proved up to the challenge, the 29ers could be selected for the most audacious and risky amphibious operation in U.S. military history. Gerhardt's time had come.

Overlord had been the goal of the U.S. Army and President Roosevelt since the beginning of the war. If successful, it would, as Churchill said, mark the "beginning of the end" of World War II in Europe. In January 1943, President Roosevelt, Prime Minister Churchill, and the Allies' Combined Chiefs of Staff had met at Casablanca and decided to set up an Anglo-American headquarters in London that would investigate possible locations for the invasion. The planning team, soon known as COSSAC, would be responsible for the details of Overlord. The invasion the team planned was set to take place as early as possible in 1944.

Overlord would entail landing three divisions of thirty thousand men on beaches and dropping two airborne divisions nearby. The Allies had succeeded in two previous amphibious invasions—in Sicily and North Africa—but had yet to attack a fortified coastline defended by seasoned troops. Overlord would be the greatest military gamble of the war. Its failure could deal a catastrophic blow to Allied unity, doom the Jewish race in Europe to probable extinction, and leave Europe under Nazi control. Success would depend on absolute surprise, superlative teamwork, the weather, secrecy, a vast armada's effective deployment, air superiority, and then a full frontal assault by tens of thousands of young men who had never experienced combat.

In early September 1943, Lieutenant Ray Nance returned from a special intelligence training program in Derbyshire. Captain Fellers told him that the 116th Infantry could possibly be chosen to spearhead a 29th Division assault on Europe. There were no specifics about where or when. That was far too sensitive information. But from now on they were to train to land on a heavily defended beach and seize it. "We knew we had a very important job to do," recalled Nance. "That's when the real work began."

COSSAC had, in fact, decided in August at a conference in Quebec on the section of French coastline where the invasion would take place. Instead of the obvious stretch of beaches along the Pas de Calais, closest to Britain, COSSAC opted for those of Normandy, southwest of the port of Le Havre, between the mouths of the Orne and Vire rivers.

This stretch of the Atlantic Wall, as Hitler had called beach defenses from southern France all the way to Holland, was not as well defended as the Pas de Calais. If bridges across the Seine could be destroyed, and the Wehrmacht's response to the invasion thereby impeded, the Allies would have a greater chance of landing enough men and armament to enable an attack directly into the heart of Nazi Europe.

The Bedford boys were soon climbing cargo nets hung from thirty-foot beams, scaling cliffs, digging shapes in the peat moors to resemble landing craft, and storming banks of heather that doubled as imaginary shores. Every man, from Gerhardt down to the lowliest private, had to take swimming lessons. And there was no warm indoor pool to hand. Whatever the weather, the men had to swim in nearby ponds and across rivers.

That autumn, the increasingly chilly swimming lessons were forgotten for a few days as the entire division focused on baseball. Three men from Bedford played for the "116 Yankees" in the Allied Armed Forces

Inter-Army championship finals in London in late September: Elmere Wright, Frank Draper, and Robert "Tony" Marsico.

The son of Bedford's deputy sheriff, Wright had pitched for the Bedford High School team and then for a St. Louis Browns farm team in Texas. The summer before Pearl Harbor, several scouts from the St. Louis Cardinals and Chicago Cubs had watched Wright and been impressed. Of all the Bedford men, his future seemed most promising. "Before the war, wine, women and song had got to him," recalled Roy Stevens. "But in England he settled down and did real good. He was very tricky with the ball. I tried to hit [his pitched ball] one time, and man, the catcher got the ball before I even started to swing. Everyone knew he'd be in the majors after the war."[3]

Another outstanding player in the 116 Yankees from Bedford was twenty-three-year-old Sergeant Frank Draper Jr., who had played for his tough neighborhood's "Mud Alley" baseball team and then for the Hampton Looms factory team. He had also been a star in high school basketball, football, and track.

Frank's two younger brothers, Gamiel and David, had also played for Hampton Looms. "We were one, two, three in the batting order," recalled David. "My mother and father hadn't wanted us to play because they didn't want us to get hurt. But we did anyway. I was nicknamed 'Hammerhead' because of playing football. We called Frank 'Piggy' because when we were real young he would jump on the back of pigs and ride them like they were a horse. He was happy-go-lucky, sang in the choir, never drank, or smoked when he was back home."

By 1943, Frank had matured into a superbly consistent outfielder and powerful hitter. "He could do everything," insisted David. "He could hit, run, field. He had a good arm. He could have made it in the big leagues."[4]

Draper was as capable a soldier as he was an athlete: resourceful, calm and decisive under pressure, and highly organized. Alone among the Bedford boys, he kept a diary—a black notebook in which he would mostly jot a few quick reminders of his duties the next day.

Thirty-four-year-old Staff Sergeant Tony Marsico was the oldest Bedford boy by five years and a gifted catcher. One of ten children, Marsico had grown up in Roanoke, Bob Slaughter's hometown, where he had worked for a time at the Blue Hills golf course. His father, John, had come to Virginia from Italy in the 1890s.[5]

The 116 Yankees faced twenty teams drawn from all the services in the European Theatre of Operations, and played four games over four days at the Eighth Air Force Headquarters, Bushy Park, in London. Each team was allowed to field fifteen enlisted men and one officer. "They let those guys play ball because they wanted to keep them busy," explained Verona Lipford, Frank Draper's sister. "It was to get their minds off what was going to happen."[6]

The services newspaper *Stars and Stripes* contained the following report on the final between the 116 Yankees and the Fighter Command Thunderbolts:

> Led by their peppery captain, Corporal Douglas Gillette, of Springfield, Mass., who came from behind the plate in the fourth to hurl his way into the hearts of the spectators, the field force Yankees copped the ETO World Series by defeating the Fighter Command Thunderbolts, 6–3, in the final played here this afternoon. The Thunderbolts' stickmen got to Elmer Wright, of Bedford, Va., for a single in the second and third innings, but without success. . . . The winners took the lead in the sixth when two men were safe on errors and scored when a batted ball got past the second baseman and went into right field. They rallied again in the seventh, Sergeant Frank Draper, of Bedford, Va., getting his second triple of the game, but was out at the plate trying to score when Private First Class Joe Gubernot, of Shamokin, Pa., hit to second. Gubernot came home on an error at first for the final tally of the game. Wright allowed four hits and struck out five, while Gillette, who worked on the batters all the way, was touched for three blows and fanned five.[7]

Within eight months, three of the winning team's players would be dead, and another 116 Yankees player, "Chubby" Proffit, would be awarded the Distinguished Service Cross for gallantry.

Soon after the final game, Wright wrote to the St. Louis Browns. The club's vice president, William O. DeWitt, replied: "We are mighty glad to know your curve ball and your control are better. I think you will be ready for some high class baseball when you get back."[8]

Back in America, on October 11 the New York Yankees had defeated the St. Louis Cardinals four games to one in a classic World Series final. It was sweet revenge for the Yankees, who had been humiliated by the Cardinals in 1942 and had lost three of their best players in the 1943 season—Joe DiMaggio, Phil Rizzuto, and Red Ruffing—to military service.

As winter returned, the Bedford boys' impatience to "get the job done and get home"[9] grew with every bitter frost and gale. "If you want to know any thing about England," wrote a thoroughly dejected Grant Yopp to his sister, Anna Mae, "you will have to wait until the war is over and come and see for yourself. This is one part of my life I am aiming to forget."[10]

Yopp and his buddies had now been in England for fourteen months without home leave. They were the best-trained men in the U.S. Army, but also among the most resentful. They had had enough of waiting and many felt that the 29th Division had become guinea pigs, endlessly being tested and ordered to try out new techniques in training and weapon use and to comply with every new addition to the army's regulation book. "Everybody was always complaining, 'Get it over with. We've been here long enough!'" recalled Bedford boy Allen Huddleston, "but a few didn't mind. I remember Earl Parker saying he'd stay another five years if he didn't have to hit a beach."[11]

When an American evangelist erected a sign in Ivybridge asking "where will you spend eternity?" someone scrawled "in England" across it.[12] If the exact location of the Bedford boys' afterlife was in question, one thing was not: If the 116th Infantry didn't get out of Britain and into action soon, its hard-won unity and resilience might crumble. After three years in the regular army, there was one thing every man agreed with: Gerhardt's intuitive war cry—"29, Let's Go!"

There was, however, one morale booster—Gerhardt's assistant, forty-eight-year-old Brigadier General Norman "Dutch" Cota. Tall and rangy, quiet and unassuming in private, from dawn to dusk Cota could be found up to his knees in mud, clutching an old walking stick as if it were a baton, and chomping on an unlit cigar. His resonant voice could be heard even amid heavy explosions as he yelled encouragement and charged across banks of heather fifty yards from artillery units he had instructed to open fire to simulate the sound of war. A specialist in infantry tactics and particularly amphibious assault, Cota would be the division's highest-ranking officer in actual front-line combat. "He was a plain, sound man," recalled Lieutenant Ray Nance. "You believed in him."[13]

Captain Fellers would often watch Cota and the far shorter Gerhardt confer: "Uncle Charlie," all swagger, barking orders at "Dutch," who stood at the appropriate distance with his chin strap hanging loose. Cota was the only man in the 29th Division allowed to do so.[14]

Yet again, another Christmas away from home approached. On December 3, a friend of Captain Fellers sent news from the homefront: "Things are moving along fairly well, we have our difficulties such as strikes and complaints yet considering everything, these are at a minimum. Nearly all staple items are now rationed, but they are rationed so generously that if a person uses any judgment at all there is no reason for complaining. There is plenty to buy. The streets are full of Christmas shoppers."[15]

The weeks before Christmas were particularly hard on Earl Parker, ever more desperate to see his daughter. "Dear Danny, Maybe Santa Claus will bring you lots of things if you are a good little girl," he wrote in early December. "I sure hope I will be there next Christmas. I don't suppose you will know your Daddy when he comes home. I don't believe it will take us long to get acquainted. Don't tell mother that I said this, but I love her a lot and think she is real sweet. I wish I could be there with you and Mother tonight. With all my love, Daddy."[16]

By New Year's day, 1944, the 29th Division no longer had Britain to itself. Being a Yank armed with pass and a fat wallet was no longer so much fun. In a massive build-up to the invasion of Europe, over 1.6 million other Americans were soon crowding an area not much bigger than Virginia. They would share this "occupied territory" with well over ten million civilians, 1.7 million British troops, over 150,000 Canadians, and 60,000 from other Allied nations, including a Polish armored division and parachute brigade. In total, the Americans in Britain would comprise six armored divisions, thirteen infantry divisions, and two airborne divisions. Ports would soon be jammed with over 4,000 landing craft and 1,300 warships. Added to this colossal force were 165 U.S. Air Force squadrons.

As this "American occupation" gathered pace, many 29ers discovered that some Brits had finally had enough of the braggart Yanks, spreading venereal disease, packing every decent restaurant and pub, and stealing their girls: over 70,000 British women would marry their Yank boyfriends immediately after the war and return to the United States with them.

New faces started to change things in Company A too. By February 1944, it was under strength; less than a third of its remaining men were from Bedford. Many of the original Bedford boys had received commissions and been transferred. Others had failed increasingly stringent physicals and stamina tests. Having formed the nucleus of the unit since Pearl Harbor, however, most of those issuing orders were still Bedford born and bred.

To bring the 116th Infantry up to full strength, replacements arrived in batches of up to fifty men. Most were drafted northerners like nineteen-year-old John Barnes, the son of devout Catholics, who arrived with twenty other New Yorkers in the back of a freezing truck one grim afternoon.[17] A pound over the cut-off weight at his induction medical in 1942, Barnes was "full of foreboding" and still wondered what he'd have done if he had weighed 119 pounds rather than 120. Like so many others, would he have gorged himself and returned to the scales?

Barnes's truck stopped and the New Yorkers filed into a Quonset hut. They included a cocky and streetwise Jew from New York City, Hal Baumgarten. The son of Austrian immigrants and a superb athlete, Baumgarten had made a remarkable fifty-four-yard return punt for his high school team the day that Pearl Harbor was bombed. In June 1943, he'd been offered a college exemption from the draft. His professors had advised him to take it, but he did not. Determined to repay his country for the opportunities it afforded his family, he was sworn into the army on July 10, 1943, and soon proved to be a spectacularly gifted marksman, especially with a 1903 Springfield bolt-action.

"The first officer we met was Colonel Canham," recalled Baumgarten. "He told us: 'Two out of three of you are not going home.'"[18]

Barnes and Baumgarten were ordered to go to one of the First Battalion's four companies: "Able, Baker, Charlie or Dog."[19] They walked down a foggy pathway between more huts and then someone barked: "You, you, you—fall out here!"[20] Barnes and Baumgarten entered a well-lit building. There they found a heavy set, tough-looking Virginian with three stripes on his shoulder.

"My name is Wilkes. Master Sergeant John Wilkes."

The men stood at attention.

"You men have been assigned to A Company. We have been in the ETO [European Theatre of Operations] for eighteen months and we are *ready* for combat. You men *will* be ready too."

Another man stepped forward—tall and lean, with two silver bars on his uniform.

"My name is Captain Taylor Fellers," he said in an almost unintelligible Virginia drawl. "This company will be in the leading wave of infantry in the invasion of Europe. You men will be part of a great force to end the war. Good luck!"[21]

Barnes's heart sank. "What have I gotten into?" he thought.

That first night, the replacements bunked in Company A's Nissen huts. "Why are they sending you kids over here?" several Virginians asked nineteen-year-old Baumgarten.

A couple of days later, the replacements were ordered to sleep in tents nearby. For several weeks, they lived under sodden canvas without heat in an increasingly muddy field. To other recruits such as riflemen George Roach, Gil Murdock, and Thomas Valance, it seemed that the Southerners were deliberately testing the northern replacements, ostracizing them until they were deemed tough and fit enough to eat and sleep beside the stalwarts of Company A. "The Bedford men were like one big family," recalled Baumgarten. "When we came out of our tents to line up in the morning for reveille, they were all calling each other by their first names, kidding with each other. The captain knew every one of them."[22]

After a month, the replacements were finally allowed to join the rest of Company A under a roof. Hal Baumgarten slept on a top bunk opposite Jack Powers. "He was very good to me. He'd trained to be a Ranger and wasn't too happy to be back [his unit was disbanded]. He was a great soldier and taught me a lot of tricks. Bedford Hoback was also friendly."[23]

At first, however, most replacements made uneasy bedfellows. "Those boys from up North, you had to ride them or they'd ride you," recalled Mess Sergeant Earl Newcomb. "You had to holler at them sometimes or they'd forget who you were. They didn't want to be disciplined like you had to have them."[24]

Other men bridled at some of the new city boys' preconceptions of the Southerners in the 29th Division as dumb hicks. Accents got thicker, drawls even slower. Some shared their grandfathers' contempt of the infernal Yankees. The Civil War was not over yet, and there was many a fierce but mostly good-natured debate about slavery, reconstruction, and the key battles of the war.

Each night, Captain Fellers would do a bed check before lights out. "I still find the battle of Bull Run and Gettysburg going on," Fellers wrote his parents. "They sit around and smoke their pipes and fight it all over again. Among them are diplomats, statesmen, politicians, and guard house lawyers. It is really interesting just to listen. And when one of them gets back from pass and starts telling about a girl he met, from his description you would wonder how Heddy Lamar and Lana Turner ever got so popular."[25]

Before turning in, one of A Company's four lieutenants or Captain Fellers would censor the men's mail to be sent to America the following day. The rhyming slang and private codes men used to express their feelings fascinated Fellers. "Those boys really have a technique on some of their phraseology to the girls they left back there," Fellers told his parents. "And from the local mail it seems that the same tactics work with the local lassies too."[26]

As Fellers became more involved with preparations for Overlord, he relied more than ever on Master Sergeant John Wilkes to deal with problems of morale or discipline. Wilkes was particularly tough on replacements who didn't adapt quickly enough to Company A's rigid discipline and strict regulations. A bunch of rowdy, slack city kids were not going to undermine the fighting force he and Fellers had primed since Fort Meade.

Wilkes had put on twenty pounds since leaving Virginia and when angry was so intimidating that one New Yorker thought he looked like a huge "wall" about to fall on him. He often chewed a potent brand of Virginia tobacco and on several occasions reminded new arrivals how to stand to attention by spitting a large wad between their legs. Men quickly learned to salute correctly with their heels firmly locked together.

One morning, John Barnes woke up with a terrible pain in his jaw. He couldn't bear shaving in cold water. Knowing Wilkes would make him shave, Barnes reported sick to another company's medical station. "I was desperate. I knew I couldn't show up to roll call with stubble because I would be really chewed out."[27]

It didn't take long for Wilkes to find out what Barnes had done.

"I've had a skin infection for the last three weeks," he barked, "and I've shaved every day! Go back and shave."

From then on, Barnes toed the line. He soon realized that Wilkes was mild in comparison with the regimental commander of the 116th Infantry, whose camp was known to many in the 29th Division as "Colonel Canham's Concentration Camp."[28]

"The officers in England were scared to death of Canham," recalled Roy Stevens. "I had a sore on my foot one time from all the marching and

I had to go to first aid so I wore a tennis shoe. Canham saw the shoe. 'If you can't wear a proper shoe on that foot, you'll go barefooted. Take that shoe off!' He must have been ashamed of himself sometimes—he was so tough on the men. But it takes men like him to win a war."[29]

Even if men returned from forty-eight-hour passes just a few minutes late, perhaps having missed a last train from London, they were fined thirty dollars and kept in camp for a month. Canham had decided on the punishment, which led even Major General Gerhardt to complain one day that he was "too hard on the men."

"Goddamn it," Canham replied, "this is my regiment and I am the one commanding it."

"You know," said Gerhardt, "the men don't mind that thirty dollars but they hate that thirty days."[30]

The 116th's officers took their cue from Canham, driving their men harder and harder that winter as the planned invasion got closer. When Company A now formed up for drill, Fellers would prowl along the ranks. If he saw a sloppy uniform or stubble, he shouted angrily: "This parade will never march!"[31]

Increasingly, soldiers vented their anxieties and frustrations outside camp. By 1944, there were outraged reports about GIs' heavy drinking and boorishness throughout Britain. Lady Astor now told the Virginians she invited to her home: "Boys, if you're out on the town and have too much to drink and any English people ask you where you are from tell them New York, New Jersey, or anyplace but Virginia. I have told the English people that Virginia boys don't drink and rough it up."[32]

But Virginia boys did drink and many loved to rough it up. "Most of the boys never really drank before," recalled Roy Stevens. "The Tommy knew how to drink. We didn't. They could take a bottle of beer and sit down for an hour and drink it, but if it lasted two minutes with us, that was a record! We drank it down in one."[33]

Snake Eyes Carter and John Reynolds were among Company A's heaviest "boozers." Both narrowly avoided being thrown in the lock-up for drunken behavior. "Poor old Jackie [John Reynolds], he was a real wild guy," recalled a Bedford contemporary. "He drank so much one night he came back to the barracks and peed in John Clifton's bed. He was like a lot of those boys. Most of them didn't have much chance here in Bedford but they were good-looking, and over there they put that uniform on and they were something."[34]

Knowing their "number would soon come up," other "good-time guys" in Company A started to "come a cropper," as local landlords put it. Discovered without a pass by MPs one night, Dickie Overstreet suddenly found himself in charge of a flamethrower, arguably the most dangerous job in the infantry.[35] Sergeant Jack Powers, one of the finest soldiers in Company A, also got busted, apparently for going AWOL. Although pleased to be back with his childhood friends in Company A after his 29th Rangers had been disbanded, Powers was also dismayed that his months of intensive training, some spent with British commandos in Scotland, had been in vain. For going AWOL, Fellers stripped him of his sergeant's stripes, making him a private first class. Fellers had done the same to Bedford Hoback for eating a sandwich without permission during a march.

The demotion didn't seem to bother Bedford too much. In a letter to his sister Mabel he expressed an ever more nonchalant view of life. He was smoking far too much, but what the hell, life was short and he was going to enjoy himself come what may: "Smoking never kills but so many people and they were going to die anyway. So why not let them die happy? I smoke too many, more than a pack each day, and I cough much too but I will die happy with my cigarettes."[36]

In nearby Ivybridge, the town center was now a battleground at weekends as drunken GIs slugged it out. There was nothing like a good fight to relieve bottled-up aggression. New replacements were advised to head to the nearest city and bypass the town when they received their first pass. John Wilkes spent many Monday mornings disciplining men who had fallen afoul of MPs in Ivybridge over the weekend.

Increasingly often, the fights in Ivybridge had to do with race. In America, blacks were still segregated. But in Britain there was no color divide. Black soldiers were treated the same as white GIs, to the fury of many Southerners. "The truck company over there was black," recalled Lieutenant Ray Nance. "They'd meet the outfit in the pubs, and the troublemakers would get to work. There was something going on pretty much all the time with the black men."[37]

What most upset many Southerners was the sight of English women dating black Americans. "The men were not used to seeing that, and couldn't get used to it, though I'm sure they could if they had tried," Nance said.[38]

A black lieutenant, Joseph O. Curtis, was also stationed in the area. That March, he wrote to a friend back in segregated America: "You know, the more I see of the English, the more disgusted I become with Americans. After the war, with the eager and enthusiastic support of every negro who will have served in Europe, I shall start a movement to send white Americans back to England and bring the English to America."[39]

In local pubs, Company A ran into blacks but also weary veterans from the 1st Division. They were brutally honest when asked what combat was like: horrific and very short, especially for officers of Nance's and Fellers's ranks. They could expect to fight for no more than a couple of weeks. If they were lucky, they'd receive a "million dollar" wound and be shipped home as an invalid. The only other way back to Bedford would be in a coffin.

One day, as the 29ers marched along in perfect formation, chanting "29, Let's Go!," a 1st Division soldier shouted back: "Go ahead 29, we'll be right behind you!"[40] "England's Own" were so goddamned eager, so naively gung-ho, and so well-disciplined they even kept their chin straps buckled.

7

Slapton Sands

THE COUNTDOWN TO THE real thing finally began in early March 1944. Company A's four platoons were reorganized into six boat teams and the exercises became serious.[1] From now until D-Day, the thirty men in each boat team would train, eat, and sleep together. The teams included two officers, a four-man 60mm mortar crew, a four-man machine gun crew, five men responsible for demolition of beach obstacles, five riflemen, and four men armed with Bangalore torpedoes for blowing holes in wire. Everything they did was focused on working in harmony to "assault enemy beaches and be able to establish a beach-head by neutralizing all obstacles and pillboxes."[2]

Suddenly, the Bedford boys found themselves with very specific roles that they would perfect on the moors and at a specially built series of assault training centers (ACTs) around Woolacombe and Braunton on the south coast. Buck privates as well as General Gerhardt praised these facilities as superb.

Ray Stevens, Roy's brother, led a mortar squad and was widely thought to be the most accurate man in the company with the 60mm. He was so proficient, in fact, that he was placed in charge of training the company's other squads.

John Schenk, Company A's communications sergeant, was now responsible for making sure that the six boat teams all had operational walkie-talkie radios and that the men operating them could do so under enormous pressure. Far shorter than Captain Fellers, Schenk would scurry after his captain on maneuvers relaying orders to each of the

81

teams. "Tail Feather" Fellers darted around with a sprinter's pace, prompting some Bedford boys to nickname Schenk "Duck Legs" and Fellers "Long Legs." When the Bedford boys did not form up quickly enough or exited mock-up landing craft clumsily, Fellers would bark "too slow, too slow, too goddamned slow!"[3]

"Several times we left our headquarters at Ivybridge to go on a full dry-run operation," recalled John Barnes, a rifleman in Roy Stevens's boat team. "This would involve marching to the railroad station near the village or a truck assembly point. We left camp at night and marched through Ivybridge, its houses dark and people silent, up the hill to the railway tracks. I often thought at the time, why did we go? . . . Were we lining up like sheep off to the slaughter that we knew was ahead? What forced us to obey when our heads, our hearts, and our feet wanted to go no further? Was it the fear of military discipline? Was it patriotism, love of flag and country?"[4]

The trains and trucks took the Bedford boys to a sealed camp near Weymouth. Then the men would walk in their boat teams up gangways onto a British troopship, the *Empire Javelin*, to be ferried to Slapton Sands. An area designated on England's south coast since 1943 for practicing large-scale amphibious assaults, Slapton Sands resembled several beaches in Normandy: gently sloping stretches of sand and shingle flanked by a five-foot-deep salt marsh.

Several miles out at sea, in pitch blackness, the Bedford boys would crawl down cargo nets flung over the ship's side and step into bucking LCVPs (landing craft, vehicle and personnel), which would take them to Slapton Sands. The Allied Supreme Commander, General Dwight D. Eisenhower, would later credit these craft, commonly known as Higgins boats, with winning the war.[5]

Over 20,000 Higgins boats would carry more Americans into combat than all other crafts combined. The boats were thirty-six feet long and ten feet wide, made from plywood with a metal ramp that lowered to allow a fast exit, and could carry up to thirty-six men quickly to shore even in rough seas. Highly moveable and powered by a very reliable

"We were poor but we didn't know it." The Powers family in 1928; oldest brother Clyde stands to the left of Billy and above Jack. To sister Eloise's right is Archie Russell. Clyde, Billy, and Jack would all experience combat. One would be killed on D-Day; one would endure a brutal POW camp; and the other would be severely shell-shocked. *Eloise Rogers.*

"We were so young!" Left to right: Billy Parker, Pride Wingfield, and Earl Parker at Wingfield's childhood home, where he lives to this day. Earl Parker would be killed on D-Day. Wingfield transferred to the Army Air Force in 1943 and was at home in Bedford on D-Day. *Rebecca and Pride Wingfield.*

"Who said eat?" The Schenks run to supper outside their home in Bedford. John Schenk is to the far right beside his young bride Ivylyn. *Ivylyn Hardy.*

The wrong side of the tracks. Frank Draper Jr.'s childhood home was only yards from the Norfolk and Western railway line in Bedford. Draper collected coal from passing trains to keep his family warm during the Depression. *Warren Draper.*

The Bedford Fireman's Band, 1940. Sixteen-year-old clarinet player Eloise Powers—sister of Company A brothers Clyde and Jack Powers—stands to the left of the band leader at center. The band played when the Bedford boys were mobilized and left Bedford in February 1941. *Eloise Rogers.*

"A time to be envied in most respects, safe and carefree." Master Sergeant John Wilkes with his young bride Bettie near a waterfall in Bedford County, summer 1941. *Bettie Wilkes Hooper.*

Top left:
Harold Edward Wilkes, one of the fortunate few to return home. *Eloise Rogers.*

Top right:
Frank Draper Jr., superb athlete and even better soldier. *Warren Draper.*

Above:
Glenwood "Dickie" Overstreet, who would be badly wounded on D-Day, one of the most sociable and popular Bedford boys. *Beulah Witt.*

Right:
Dickie Overstreet, center, with family shortly before shipping out. *Beulah Witt.*

Clyde Powers and Jack Powers on furlough in Bedford, summer 1941. *Eloise Rogers.*

Bedford boys at camp A. P. Hill in Virginia, 1941. Earl Parker combs his hair at center of front row. *Pride Wingfield.*

"He was all soldier." Captain Taylor N. Fellers, the Bedford boys' hometown commander. *Bertie Woodford.*

"We shared everything." Sergeants Roy and Ray Stevens, twin brothers. *Roy Stevens and Virginia Historical Association.*

"Exact opposites." Brothers Raymond and Bedford Hoback. Both would be killed on Omaha Beach. *Lucille Hoback Boggess and Virginia Historical Association.*

Left: Leslie Abbott, the first of the Bedford boys to come home in a casket. (This and the following seven photos are details from a group photograph.) *U.S. Army.*

Right: Wallace "Snake Eyes" Carter, Company A's best dice player. *U.S. Army.*

Left: John Clifton, Company A's "Casanova" who had Cherokee Indian ancestors. *U.S. Army.*

Right: Charles Fizer survived D-Day only to die a few days later in the hedgerows of Normandy. *U.S. Army.*

Left: Nicholas Gillaspie, the mild-mannered Southern gentleman. *U.S. Army.*

Right: "He just liked the dirt." Quiet and deeply religious farmboy Gordon Henry White. *U.S. Army.*

Left:
Andrew Coleman, the first Bedford boy casualty. *U.S. Army.*

Right:
Clifton Lee, fiercely patriotic and thought to have died beside several of his friends within minutes of landing on Omaha Beach. *U.S. Army.*

Earl Parker, the only father among the Bedford boys. *Mary Daniel Heilig.*

Above:
Earl Parker on maneuvers in North Carolina a few months before Pearl Harbor. *Pride Wingfield.*

Below:
Company B from Lynchburg, Virginia. The boys from this company would land just after the Bedford boys in the second wave on Omaha Beach. Picture taken at Fort Meade, February 1941. Seventeen-year-old Bob Sales kneels at front. *Bob Sales.*

Top left: Ace poker player and Company A mess sergeant Earl Newcomb. *Elva Newcomb.*

Top right: Robert "Tony" Marsico, one of the few who landed on Omaha and then came home. *Laura Burnette.*

"He had the prettiest dimples." Weldon Rosazza, one of the Bedford boys who enjoyed great success with English women. *Ellen Quarles.*

"116 Yankees." Bedford boys who played for the undefeated "116 Yankees" in 1943. Photograph taken in London, summer 1943. Left to right: Elmere Wright, Tony Marsico, Pride Wingfield, Frank Draper Jr. *Pride Wingfield.*

E.T.O. World Series Baseball Champions, 1943. Victorious "116 Yankees" players with uniformed Colonel Charles Canham, center. Middle row: right to left— Bedford boys Draper, Wright, Marsico. Three of the team would die on Omaha Beach in a matter of months. *Bettie Wilkes Hooper.*

Lieutenant Ray Nance, the only surviving officer who landed on D-Day with Company A. *Ray Nance.*

Company A's officers a few weeks before D-Day. Left to right: Lieutenant Ray Nance, Lieutenant Edward Gearing, Lieutenant John Clements, and First Sergeant John Wilkes. *Ray Nance.*

Left:
John Wilkes and John Schenk in England before D-Day. *Ivylyn Hardy.*

Below:
"Who says England doesn't get snow?" John Schenk, far right, and friends standing outside their barracks, winter 1942–43. *Ivylyn Hardy.*

Pride Wingfield and John Schenk in Ivybridge, England, summer 1943. *Ivylyn Hardy.*

"We really were overpaid, oversexed and over there." Dickie Overstreet, in uniform on right, with two English "gals," a Company A buddy, and English children outside a swimming pool, summer 1943. *Beulah Witt.*

diesel motor, the Higgins boat's only defect was that it shipped water and bounced around in heavy seas, causing acute seasickness. The British equivalent, the LCA (landing craft assault) was produced in far fewer numbers, but had benches to sit down on and some protection from the elements.

Over several weeks, Company A refined their landing techniques on two-day exercises and tried to keep their nerve: Bullets flew overhead now as they crawled through barbed wire blown by Bangalore torpedoes. "The beauty of the Bangalore was that they blew aprons of barbed wire by exploding sideways and not towards the men in front of the barbed wire," recalled rifleman Hal Baumgarten of boat team number six. "They enabled us to blow a path through many rows of barbed wire rapidly."[6] The men fired at targets. They tested different forms of grenades. At first, smoke was used to provide cover but then it was decided that the smoke caused too much confusion and would not be employed on D-Day itself.

Machine-gun operators practiced jumping down into craters, blown or dug in the beach, and then firing from awkward positions—it was assumed in all beach exercises that craters would pepper the real beach on D-Day, thereby providing crucial protection. Mines had to be scouted and then carefully uncovered with bayonets. Dummy positions stormed and concrete pillboxes blown with TNT. When the beach had been secured, the Bedford boys had to climb bluffs and seize homes emptied of British residents only months before.

Assistant flamethrower George Roach was in Master Sergeant John Wilkes's boat team. Fifty years later, he would vividly recall the procedure for storming a beach:

> As the boat would land at the beach, the ramp was dropped. The lieutenant would be the first one off the boat, usually, followed by four or five riflemen who would be in a position to fan out, followed by Bangalore torpedo people and wire cutters, then the flame thrower and his assistant, then the demolition team which carried pole charges of TNT, then second in command, in [my boat], Sergeant Wilkes. . . . The Bangalore tor-

pedo people would run up to where the barbed wire was, throw a pole charge across the barbed wire, explode it so that the riflemen could then follow on and fire at the pillbox which was usually situated at a distance from us, and then the flame thrower would activate his flame thrower at the embrasure and then the pole charge people would come up and lay their TNT packages against the embrasure and blow a hole in it.[7]

"Man, Slapton Sands was tough," recalled Roy Stevens. "You realized very quick you had to stay down as low as you could to keep your head."[8] The U.S. army allowed for 5 percent casualties in training, far less than the Germans and Russians. In some elite SS combat units, the allowance was 10 to 15 percent: a cathartic masochism attended the ritualistic preparations for killing among Hitler's most fanatical followers.

According to Hal Baumgarten, there was "loss of lives and casualties, which were hushed up," in every fullscale rehearsal on Slapton Sands. In Company A, there were minor injuries—sprained ankles, cuts, and bruised egos—but no serious casualty until one particularly cold day when Bedford boy Andrew Coleman collapsed with pneumonia aggravated by the cold and wet conditions.

Coleman had grown up in a lovely old two-story home on Grove Street in the heart of Bedford, the son of a widely respected carpenter. Perpetual pain had cast a long shadow over his life: For most of his youth, Coleman's mother had been severely crippled with arthritis. "She lay in bed in a room downstairs," recalled Sibyle Kieth Coleman, the wife of one of Andrew's nephews. "She couldn't move her arms, her legs, any of her fingers, hands. She had terrible pain."[9]

In the hospital in England, Coleman developed a kidney complaint, Bright's disease, which made his "whole body and stomach swell up."[10] The infection rapidly developed into chronic nephritis which causes progressive, incurable kidney damage. In the days before dialysis and kidney transplants, patients could expect only a slow and agonizing death. Coleman was soon so ill that he was shipped back to America by the end of April 1944.[11]

Boat teams practiced over and over until the assault procedure went like clockwork. If teams couldn't get it right, they were taken out onto the moors where they trained until Captain Fellers was satisfied. On a drizzly Sunday in late March a boat team was trying to perfect the technique for blowing up a pillbox when the man assigned to lobbing a TNT package into the pillbox's slit was killed; the TNT exploded in his face, perhaps because of a faulty or damp fuse.

The death stunned the Bedford boys. No one had yet seen a man killed by an explosion. "Seeing that [man die] hurt those boys more than anything else the whole time we were in training," recalled Roy Stevens. "They all seen it, you see. And his body was mangled, blown pretty well [to pieces]."[12]

Even on practice invasion runs, John Schenk found time each night at 10 P.M. to stop and think about Ivylyn. Back in Bedford, she was struggling to recover from headaches and partial paralysis provoked by nightmares. On March 17, she had woken up screaming. In the nightmare, God had told her John would not come back.[13]

"I was awakened with this violent headache," explained Ivylyn. "It was the beginning of understanding that I would probably be a widow. I had exchanged sentences with God. I said to him that I didn't think he could take my husband because we had not had our children and our lives together. John and I wrote all the time to each other about having children when he came back."[14]

By April, Company A was also on edge. Tempers flared. Officers seemed on particularly short fuses. Men wondered how they would perform in actual battle. Would they disgrace themselves or would they find the courage to fight and kill? There was no way of knowing, veterans said, how they would behave under fire for the first time. Over and over, they speculated as to where and when they would finally gamble with death.

That April, some of the Bedford boys read *Liberty* magazine's bold prediction: "There will be no needless loss of life in the American Army in World War II if the orders and plans of our High Command are carried out."[15]

But the experience of American troops in Italy that spring was far from reassuring. At Anzio, the Germans had contained the Allies effectively, preventing them from reaching Rome, and causing demoralizing casualties as they bombarded trapped troops for week after week. At Monte Cassino, the Allies had also met fierce resistance and become bogged down in a battle of attrition that threatened to become as bloody as those fought in Normandy in World War I. Italy was no "soft underbelly" as Churchill had predicted—far from it. The slog up the country's mountainous spine did not augur well for the Allies once they had arrived on French soil.

The Germans were formidable soldiers able to impose severe casualties as they fought defensive actions in Italy and on the Eastern Front, where the Russians had yet to launch their massive summer 1944 attack. But they were far inferior to the Allies in matters of military intelligence. In order to maximize this critical advantage, Overlord's planners set up Operation Fortitude, a plan to convince the Germans that the Overlord forces were double their actual size and that the invasion would take place on the Pas de Calais far from the Cotentin peninsula. Fortitude created phantom divisions, a British Fourth Army preparing to invade Norway, and a U.S. First Army Group, commanded by General George S. Patton, that was poised to land on the Pas de Calais any day. Run by an ultra-secret intelligence committee, "The Twenty Committee" (so-named after the Roman numerals XX—double cross), Operation Fortitude was arguably the most successful of all preparations for Overlord. It so convinced the Germans that even after D-Day they still believed that the main Allied attack would be in the region of the Pas de Calais.

On April 13, Sergeant Raymond Hoback wrote to his parents, who had told him that most of Bedford's young men had now been drafted: "Looks like they will get all the boys before we come back. Well, the army won't hurt them much."[16] On April 26, Company A performed its final dry-run invasion on Slapton Sands, Operation Fox, sailing on the troopship *Empire Javelin* from Weymouth and landing at dawn in

British-built LCAs. The boat teams worked in perfect harmony. Gaps in barbed wire were quickly blown, the beach exits secured, and there were no casualties. The men returned to their barracks confident and keyed up for the real thing. Company A had proved it was good enough to be the first 29ers to land in France. "We had worked especially hard and competed to be the first on the beach," recalled Ray Nance. "We had tried to be the best in training. It was a matter or pride and honor. And it worked. We *were* chosen to be the first to land."[17]

Many 29ers believed they deserved, simply by virtue of having spent so long in England, to be first in line to invade Europe. They had trained longer and harder than any other American division. Although they had never seen combat, they were tough, risk-taking, and aggressive troops. General Gerow and General Gerhardt's training regimes had given the Bedford boys great stamina and a proud, almost cocky, confidence.

Time and again, British officers would later concede that while the American buck private was not as good as the Tommy in saluting and other barrack-room discipline, he was often more gung-ho. The Yanks were paid three times as much, had been reared with a "can-do" attitude, and were supplied by a vast industrial capacity. But the crucial difference lay in memory. The Somme, Paschendaele, and other horrific bloodbaths of World War I had left permanent scars on the British psyche. There was no enthusiasm for full frontal assaults among British tacticians—a generation had been culled between 1914 and 1918 due to callous orders to "go over the top," and then walk across No Man's Land in the direct line of fire of German machine guns. The Bedford boys' ancestors had charged towards death during the Civil War but that was three generations ago. Company A had not grown up with a loathing of war or the resentment of senior officers that had resulted from the massacre of Britain's youth.

Their lack of combat experience actually increased their confidence, some historians have argued. It was to the Allies' advantage that so many men had not seen combat; young men who have seen the horror of war are far less likely to rush headlong towards it. Naïveté can perhaps be a powerful weapon. Only one of the eleven American divisions in Britain before D-Day—the 1st Division—had seen combat.

The Bedford boys' senior commanders were also confident—they believed the troops would meet little resistance. The boys didn't need to be combat veterans, they figured, because they did not envision a prolonged firefight on the beaches.

Confidence was vital to success in such a risky operation as Overlord. But in the last weeks before D-Day confidence evaporated among many senior American generals and officers. What caused their self-assurance to slip was witnessing one of the greatest military disasters of World War II. Near Slapton Sands, in one night of miscommunication, panic, and organizational chaos during an invasion dress rehearsal, more Americans died on all but one of the Overlord beaches. Many survivors and witnesses viewed the catastrophe as a terrible omen.

On April 27, 1944, barely twenty-four hours after the Bedford boys had practiced their Omaha-invasion scenario by storming Slapton Sands for the final time, Operation Tiger—an invasion rehearsal for the 4th Division—began after dark. Twenty-five thousand men were due to land on Slapton Sands, which had been prepared to resemble Utah Beach in Normandy. Three hundred thirty-seven ships were involved, with the British Royal Navy providing an escort and protection from attack from any German craft patrolling the channel. The men needed the practice because the 4th's previous exercise on Slapton Sands, "Exercise Beaver," had been "far from successful: co-ordination between units broke down and the men who took part remember it mainly for the confusion."[18]

Shortly after midnight on April 28, nine German torpedo boats moved into Lyme Bay, close to Slapton Sands. Lured by heavier than normal radio traffic, the E-boats suddenly found themselves in the midst of Operation Tiger.

German E-boats, "Schnellboote," were designed to wreak maximum havoc in the channel. A hundred feet long, armed with two torpedoes and powered by 6000-horsepower Daimler Benz engines, painted black for nighttime camouflage, able to attack at a maximum speed of 40 knots, the boats also carried two 20mm cannons, which fired green tracer bullets that lit up far from their source to prevent Allied vessels from quickly identifying their position. The rehearsal's slow moving LSTs (landing ship tanks) were no match.

Because of widespread confusion among the British escorts, that night the E-boats were able to get close enough to the Tiger convoy (codenamed T-4) to launch their torpedoes. Warnings had been issued about the Germans' presence but no preventative action taken. The result was an unmitigated disaster. One LST was seriously crippled. Another burst into flames, trapping many of the victims below deck. A third sank immediately, sending hundreds of U.S. 4th Division soldiers to their deaths.

As bodies washed ashore along England's South Coast in the days after, the official death count rose to 749. Quartermaster soldiers on board LST 531 were among the hardest hit. The 3206th Quartermaster Service Company was virtually destroyed. Of its 251 officers and men, 201 were killed or wounded.

U.S. Navy Medical Corpsman Arthur Victor survived the sinking of LST 507, which had been "packed with about 500 soldiers . . . amphibious [vehicles], jeeps, trucks . . . loaded from one end of the ship to the other, top deck and tank deck. We were a floating arsenal."[19]

Like hundreds of other survivors, Victor would spend the night clinging to a life raft as his countrymen slipped into death by hypothermia. By 3 A.M., the channel waters were "almost unbearably cold. . . . I had also been swallowing oily tasting salt water that made me nauseous, and I started puking. I pissed my pants to feel the warm. I remember how good it felt pouring over my thighs."[20] Victor watched buddy after buddy fall away into the black waters, unable to struggle on. Soon, more than half of those who had clung to the life raft after 507 sank were dead.

After three hours in the water, a man shouted that he could hear a ship's engine. Another LST, Number 515, had come to the rescue. The 515 lowered three LCVPs into the water and one of the boats designed by Andrew Higgins to storm enemy beaches quickly made its way towards Victor. He had held a fellow survivor's hand most of the night but now, only minutes from rescue, the man gave up. "I was so mad that the ludicrous thought came to mind that I could have killed [him]."[21]

Julian Perkin, a British warrant officer candidate, arrived off Slapton Sands aboard HMS *Obedient* near daybreak on April 28: "The sight was appalling. There were hundreds of bodies of American servicemen, in full battle gear, floating in the sea. Many had their limbs and even their heads blown off. . . . Those the doctor pronounced dead were pushed back into the sea [where] small American landing craft with their ramps down were literally scooping up bodies. It was a ghastly sight!"[22]

The dead were buried in military graveyards around England. The wounded were segregated for days from other troops and, according to some survivors, told not to say a word to anyone before the invasion. "We were told to keep our mouths shut and taken to a camp where we were quarantined," recalled 4th Division infantryman Eugene Carney. "When we went through the mess line we weren't even allowed to talk to the cooks. If, for example, we wanted two potatoes, we were told to hold up two fingers. If three, three fingers."[23]

On April 29, corpsman Arthur Victor joined other survivors who were taken to a "dilapidated barracks, under guard, for three days, and ordered, under threat of court martial, not to discuss the incident with anyone outside our immediate group."[24]

On the evening of April 29, General Eisenhower wrote to General George C. Marshall, chairman of the Joint Chiefs of Staff, in Washington. The disaster meant that the Allies had no reserves of LSTs, vital to Overlord's success. "We are stretched to the limit in the LST category," wrote a concerned Eisenhower, "while the implications of the attack and the possibility of both raiders and bombers concentrating on some of our major ports make one scratch his head."[25]

More worrying to Eisenhower than the communications failure that had exacerbated the disaster was the 4th Division's woeful performance once it had actually landed on Slapton Sands. Harry Butcher, Eisenhower's aide, was, like his boss, deeply troubled by "the absence of toughness and alertness of the young American officers whom I saw on this trip. They seem to regard war as one grand maneuver in which they are having a happy time. They are as green as growing corn. . . . We should have a more experienced division for the assault than the 4th which has never been in a fight in this war."[26] But there was only one division that was not green, the 1st Division, and due to concerns about the 29th Division's inexperience, it had been slated to join the 29ers in the joint operation to seize Omaha Beach.

Secrecy about the Slapton Sands disaster was crucial. If it became common knowledge, it would have an irreparable impact on morale and alert the Germans to Overlord. Yet despite the gag order imposed on many survivors, rumors spread fast through many officers' quarters. Some were so shocked by the scale of the botch-up that they began to question their roles in Overlord. The tragedy also affected Company A's commanding officer, Taylor Fellers, who may have heard about the disaster because some survivors were temporarily housed at Blandford, near the holding area for the 116th Infantry. "He was all excited when he told me about the disaster," recalled Lieutenant Nance. "It upset him a whole lot. He said it could have been us guys. We had done exactly what they had done, only two days before them. [Operation Tiger] made us even more aware of our responsibilities. We had these young men's lives in our hands. It deeply affected us."[27]

Officers Nance and Fellers did not say a word to anyone else in Company A about the disaster. According to Roy Stevens, this was just as well: "It would have given us something else to worry about. . . . We already had a lot on our mind."[28]

So did the Allies' senior intelligence officers. What, they wondered, had happened to the officers involved in Operation Tiger who knew the details of Overlord? Staff headquarters for General Montgomery was in a panic. "There was a whole day when it was seriously contemplated trying to alter the [D-Day] operation because of the knowledge which the enemy must now be presumed to have—the detailed knowledge of almost everything we planned."[29]

But over the following days the bodies of every intelligence officer were found, even though hundreds of other corpses were never recovered. It was "one of those amazing miracles which characterize war."[30] Overlord was still a secret, it seemed. But only on D-Day would Allied intelligence know for sure.

In Company A, one thing was certain: Captain Fellers had changed. Before Operation Tiger, he had been infectiously confident and self-assured. Now he was full of doubt.

8

The Sausages

A<small>T LAST, ON</small> M<small>AY</small> 18, 1944, the Bedford boys climbed into trucks and were driven to containment camps in preparation for Operation Overlord. The camps were called "sausages" because they were located alongside roads and actually resembled sausages on maps. By D-Day they would contain over two million men, the greatest gathering of personnel in the history of war.

The Bedford boys' "sausage" was code-named D-1 and located ten miles north of Dorchester, a half-hour truck drive from the English Channel. "Its tents contained the entire 1st Battalion, 116th Infantry," recalled Hal Baumgarten. "Company A was in the northeast corner of the camp . . . Foxholes were dug in the calcified English earth. There were outhouses with collecting pails. The collected excretions were regularly burned, and shipped away for fertilizer. The acrid odor of the smoke was very unpleasant."

At the southwest corner of D-1 stood an old English ancestral home, Doulish.

The Bedford boys were now sealed off from the outside world. The only way out would be on a truck bound for Weymouth where the boys would board the *Empire Javelin* and then cross to France. No passes would be issued to anyone for any reason. "Sentries were posted everywhere to keep us from escaping," recalled John Barnes. Barbed wire curled along high perimeter fences, giving D-1 the look of a POW enclosure.

At first, the men were kept busy with final kit preparations. Every square inch of their uniforms had to be gas-proofed, waterproofed, and then camouflaged. That done, they sat for hours, speaking little, nursing their own thoughts, writing letters to loved ones. They could not write a word about Overlord but many hinted in letters that they were about to see action.

Captain Fellers ordered his officers to be especially attentive when censoring the men's mail. John Barnes remembered that "any attempt to pass on news of the upcoming invasion was censored by cutting out the offending words. Any slight reference to any person, place, or thing was deleted. I'm sure our letters looked more like ribbons than anything else."[1]

"It was my turn to read the boys' letters home and censor them," Lieutenant Nance recalled. "Once, I came across a suspicious-looking letter, with illegible words repeated over and over. It looked like some kind of code, which we'd been warned to look out for." Nance called the private who wrote the letter into his office. "This doesn't make sense," Nance said. "Well, my wife knows what it means," said the private.

I LOVE YOU were the only words the private had almost learned to write.[2]

Earl Parker wrote as often as he had promised, at least once a week, never failing to tell Viola about the latest "flick" on base, as the Brits called films. He had seen his first castle in Scotland and other sites around England. He asked about Danny, now over a year old. Viola had kept the boy's name because she thought it would make Earl happy.

Dickie Abbott had always written "cheerful letters" to his grandmother. He hadn't realized how much he loved her and his parents until he got to England. When he came home, he wrote, "I would like to work on the farm with Uncle Jerry." But in his most recent letter, he was "sad, blue and all down in the dumps."[3] His grandmother wrote back expressing so many other grandparents' hopes: "I pray our Dear Lord to be with you, protect and help you and bring you safely home. God bless and be with you, and each dear child in the service of our country. Dear God, be with dear little Dickie is the prayer of Grandmother and all the folks back home."[4]

On May 24 Raymond Hoback wrote to his parents. He had been in the hospital with severe nosebleeds, a medical condition that ran in the family, and had consequently been offered a discharge but had refused it. Nothing was going to separate him from his brother and friends.[5]

John Schenk asked Ivylyn to send him a new billfold and a belt, and then added: "Only God, a lot of luck and a deep foxhole can help me now."[6] He hoped she would not be disappointed when she saw him: His hair had turned gray.[7]

That spring, Schenk had also had the opportunity to avoid the invasion—he had been offered a commission in a different outfit. "Ray Nance and John [Schenk] were buddies," recalled Ivylyn Schenk. "They shared packages we sent from home—candy, good cookies, fruitcake, canned ham and chicken. Ray tried to get John to take the commission [as a second lieutenant]. But John thought it would mean he would take a lot longer to get home, and he wanted to stay with the Bedford men."[8] Leaving Company A would have felt tantamount to desertion.

On May 27, Sergeant Grant Yopp celebrated his twenty-first birthday. Two days later, Captain Taylor Fellers assured his family all was well and that as "soon as we take Hitler, we'll be back." He was looking forward to his thirtieth birthday on June 10.[9]

Back in Bedford, several wives shared news from the boys over coffee in Green's drugstore. Some joked that Company A had an official letter writer who mimicked each man's handwriting and repeated the same message. Many had read a poem their men had sent in letters as a jibe against the censors:

> Can't write a thing
> The censor to blame
> Just say I'm well
> And sign my name
> Can't say where we're going
> Don't know where we'll land
> Couldn't inform you
> If met by a band.[10]

In their letters from America to the men in Company A, the wives were just as careful as their men about what they wrote. The U.S. Government's Office of War Information had warned citizens in the "interior zone" not to unsettle the men overseas. They should be as positive as possible. "Dear John" letters, announcing the end of a relationship or even marriage, could send men over the edge.

The news from Bedford was mixed. Several men had been prosecuted for black market activities. There was widespread concern about the drafting of many fathers in Bedford that March. But there were also signs that severe shortages might be coming to an end. On May 3, the Office of Price Administration in Washington ended meat rationing except for choice cuts of beef.

May is often the most beguiling month in Bedford. Evenings are scented with jasmine, the Peaks of Otter blaze with rhododendrons, the days are mild without too much humidity. Ivylyn Schenk knew spring and early summer was John's favorite time, as with any keen gardener. He had planted white pines around his parents' home before the war as a windbreak, and Ivylyn often wrote describing how the trees and other plants were flourishing. Despite a drought she and other "victory" gardeners were confident of eventually producing even more food than the year before.

President Roosevelt had urged Americans to cultivate plots wherever they could and by 1944 "practically every home with even a small plot of ground" in Bedford had a victory garden. In a report to the Commonwealth of Virginia Conservation Commission, Bedford native Mrs. George Parker noted that "experience has taught [townspeople] what to plant, how to cultivate it, and how best to save their 'truck.'"[11]

While vegetable patches sprang up all over town, Bedford's farmers had battled to stay solvent. By summer 1944, finding local men to plant and harvest crops was nearly impossible. The previous fall, German POWs had been trucked into the county to pick apples and other fruit crops. But the largest pool of "captive labor" came from the old CCC camp at the foot of the Peaks of Otter, where Earl Newcomb had worked in the thirties. In early 1944, the camp had started to house 153 conscientious objectors, more than half of them members of the Church of Brethren, Mennonites, or Quakers. Of over ten million American men drafted in World War II, approximately 43,000 became conscientious objectors, three times the total in World War I, but still a tiny minority. Six thousand were sent to prison but most ended up in work programs like the one at the CCC camp in Bedford.

News of the arrival of conscientious objectors had incensed many locals. There had been a paid advertisement denouncing these men in the *Bedford Bulletin*, and several vitriolic letters to the newspaper's editor. Clippings had found their way to men based in England. Two Bedford soldiers, Lloyd Ayers and Jesse Jones, wrote from their base "somewhere in England:" "[We] hate to think we're fighting for these fellows, who, able-bodied and perhaps in perfect condition, (except in mind) are shunning what a really true American must endure so that in years to come we can return home. It's going to be a great day when it's over and we can say 'did my part.' Don't forget the yellow flag pointing toward the foot of good old Peaks of Otter."[12]

Bedford native Rebecca Lockard, a perky eighteen-year-old, worked in a "five and dime" store in Bedford that was popular with many of the objectors. "They would come into the store and be seen elsewhere around town," she recalled. "They weren't thought of that highly, and you didn't want to associate with them, but some women didn't mind them being objectors. Men were scarce around here. There was a girl who worked as maid in town who even married one and had a child."[13]

By May 1944, the Bedford boys were not the only absent sons. Over two thousand men from the town and surrounding Bedford County were also in service, roughly one in every fifteen inhabitants.[14] Mrs. George Parker noted: "Gasoline scarce—not a drop to be had at times. Workers have doubled up, shared rides, walked when possible, and somehow reached their places of work. No industrial plants have been forced to close, though in many instances labor shortage is acute. Women are replacing men where possible."[15]

Every week, there was news of another Bedford man's death overseas. The *Bedford Bulletin* commented: "Those who have lost sons or husbands in this war inevitably resent comments that the casualties are only a fraction of what some extravagantly pessimistic people predicted they would be. In the homes that have been darkened by the death of a soldier, or have welcomed back the shattered remnants of youth, the burden of war's tragedy is little lightened by the reassurance that it might have been worse."[16] By May 1944, gold stars signifying the death of a son were displayed in two dozen Bedford homes. By war's end, there would be another hundred—so many that it "seemed as if every house had a star in its window."[17]

Despite the death notices appearing in the *Bulletin* every few days, boys still volunteered, eager to serve. And by 1944, Bedford girls were also joining the women's wings of the armed services in droves. On April 15, twenty-seven women were named on an incomplete list of locals who had joined up. "They would rally in front of the courthouse," recalled Bettie Wilkes, "say their goodbyes, and off they would go in military buses. . . . Most had similar backgrounds—untraveled, unsophisticated, and certainly unprepared."[18]

Mrs. George Parker also noted that the town's morale was still high. Bond drives continued to be well supported, and collections at local churches exceeded all precedents. Whatever people could spare, they gave to the war effort. Parker proudly informed the state authorities that after many bond drives, Bedford "responds conscientiously to all government appeals—war bonds, scrap metals, waste paper, fats, etc."[19] News of Japan's inhuman treatment of American prisoners had "infuriated Bedford people to white heat, and has helped to boost the Fourth War Loan Drive which was launched January 29 by the Lions Club in an auction sale of bonds which brought more than $50,000."[20]

One local campaign, funded by several Bedford businesses, asked ominously: "How many of our boys from Bedford won't come back? Nobody knows the exact number. Nobody. But the number who do come back—on their own two feet instead of in a flag-draped box—will be in exact proportion to the job we do here at home."[21]

Several Bedford wives suspected their husbands were about to be involved in an imminent invasion of France. The radio and newspapers reported on the possibility every day. When not at factories, they spent evenings trying to stay busy, knitting, canning goods, and preparing care packages for their men—anything to keep them from worrying for an hour or two.

Each Tuesday, Bettie Wilkes joined other wives in the basement of the Bedford library to roll bandages for wounded soldiers. There was something of a competitive element to the work, with ambitious targets set. The wrapping was sometimes interrupted by air raid sirens, sending families to their basements and reminding them to pull blackout curtains over windows. A bell rang at 9 P.M. to warn children of the wartime curfew.

Many of the wives, reported Mrs. Parker, had returned to their "parental homes or doubled up for companionship, convenience, and conservation of fuel."[22] More than ever they relied on each other, helping haul wood to each others' homes, sharing rides in horse-driven buggies, which had made a comeback because of gas rationing, caring for children while friends worked at Rubatex or Hampton Looms, pooling resources to send Bedford boys special care packages for their birthdays.

Like other wives, twenty-year-old Viola Parker tried to stress the positive in her letters, although life was increasingly hard without Earl, what with trying to get by and support Danny. By day, she worked on her parents' farm, where she and Danny were living. Viola slept in her childhood bedroom, Danny in a small crib in an adjoining room. Every night that May, Viola drifted off to sleep with the low whisper of a radio close to her ear. After a few restless hours, she would wake up and lean closer. The dial was set to a station in Washington, D.C., that was usually first with breaking news.[23]

When they weren't writing letters and watching movies at camp D-1, the Bedford boys relieved their tension through physical exercise and games of baseball and tackle football. Frank Draper Jr. and Elmere Wright threw curve balls at Hal Baumgarten, who had been a first-rate catcher at college. "Whenever we had spare time, I put a glove on and they pitched to me," Baumgarten said. "Wright was fast. I had to put a double sponge in the glove. He was big too, about six foot three, and he had a large, prominent nose like the guy in the cartoon—Dick Tracy."[24]

John Barnes recalled playing a game organized by Jack Powers, the ex-Ranger, that was meant to instill confidence in one other. "We were to put our trust in our buddies by leaping upon their open arms and bounce down the line. When my turn came, I was so light that I flew in one bounce over the line and landed straight on my head. I was knocked out."[25]

A few days after arriving in the containment camp, section Sergeant Allen Huddleston, now in charge of two squads of machine gunners, practiced unarmed combat with another Bedford boy, Sergeant Robert Goode, a jeep driver in Company A. "The aim was for the other guy to take you down without using a weapon. We both went down and fell badly, breaking my ankle," Huddleston said.[26] He would sit out the invasion.

Close by the famous *Life* photographer, Robert Capa, entered a similar containment camp, or "sausage." Capa had volunteered to land in the first wave with the 1st Division's 16th Infantry. Before long, he recalled, "we were all suffering from the strange sickness known as 'amphibia.' Being amphibious troops had only one meaning for us: we would be unhappy in the water before we could be unhappy on the shore. . . . There were different degrees of 'amphibia' and those who were scheduled to be the first to reach the beach had it worst."[27]

"Amphibia" affected everyone differently. Some men became serene, having seemingly made their peace with fate. Others regressed, letting off steam as if they were at high school again. One incident caused a few minutes of panic throughout the 116th Infantry's 1st Battalion. Someone threw a clip of M-1 .30-caliber bullets into a burning barrel. Bedford boys ran for cover as the bullets exploded, ricocheting in all directions. Fortunately, no one was injured, but many men's nerves were set on edge.

There were many last-minute changes to boat teams. "On May 20, sixteen men were blown up in training in Company B of the 116th Infantry [and] I was transferred from Company A to Company B to bring them up to strength," recalled Hal Baumgarten.[28] John Barnes was surprised one morning when Second Lieutenant Edward Gearing came into his tent. Gearing asked Barnes to join his boat team. He needed an assistant to his flamethrower. "Do you have any objections to using this weapon?" Gearing asked. Barnes said he'd give it a go. In a nearby field, he managed to light the fuel spitting from the flamethrower and pointed the jet in the direction of some haystacks. They were quickly ablaze. He then met the other members of his new boat team.[29] They included Bedford boys Harold Wilkes, Charles Fizer, Clyde Powers, and Sergeant Roy Stevens, Gearing's second in command.

Bob Slaughter had spent several months training with British commandos in the Scottish Highlands. Conditions in the "sausages" were a pleasant surprise. "We ate the best food," he recalled. "[It was] easy living: go to the range and fire all the ammunition you wanted to, play football, cards, movies—good times. The Red Cross women were there, too. For breakfast you could tell them how you wanted your bacon, and of course they had powdered eggs, and flapjacks or whatever. They gave us lemon meringue pie. We hadn't seen that since the States."[30]

The "good times" ended when the 1st Battalion's company commanders were called to a briefing on their specific role in Overlord. The battalion's four companies, plus a company of Rangers, would land on "Dog Green," one of eight sectors of a beach codenamed Omaha, somewhere across the channel.

Omaha was one of five beaches targeted by the Allies for D-Day, and by far the most heavily defended. In all, five divisions of men would land on a sixty-one-mile front. The Americans would seize the westernmost beaches—Utah and Omaha—and the Canadians and British would seize Gold, Juno, and Sword beaches to the east. The overall plan for D-Day, "Operation Neptune," detailing all but the air assault, was three inches thick. Essentially, it entailed loading 185,000 men and 20,000 vehicles onto ships that would cross the channel under cover of darkness. This force would then be landed on the beaches in successive waves after H-Hour, scheduled for 6:30 A.M. on the American beaches, forty minutes after sunrise.

Before the landing craft headed for the beaches, an airborne force of 20,000 would arrive over "drop zones" inland in a thousand transport planes and gliders. These paratroops would secure vital communications, German defensive installations, junctions, and other objectives, thereby aiding the rapid establishment of a beachhead.

Before Allied troops actually stormed the Calvados coastline, a massive bombardment would soften beach defenses. It was widely believed throughout the 29th Division that this would be the heaviest bombing ever made just prior to an assault. On Omaha, from H-30 to H-5, 280 B–24 bombers would drop 1,285 tons of bombs on thirteen target zones that covered every strongpoint in the Germans' beach defenses. Many generals believed that the Allies' superiority in air power—the Luftwaffe had been largely crushed by May 1944—would be the decisive advantage of D-Day.

Naval fire would begin forty minutes before touchdown on Omaha. The battleships *Arkansas* and *Texas* would fire from 18,000 yards off shore; from a tenth of that distance, eight destroyers would throw 2,000 rounds at German defensive installations. Various smaller ships would also open fire until just a few minutes before H-Hour. When the first wave of troops was three hundred yards from Omaha, nine LCTs armed with rocket-launchers would fire a thousand rockets at the Germans. If any of the defenders, thought to be inexperienced elements of the German 716th Division, were capable of action after this firestorm, they would surely not put up much resistance.

The invaders would also be aided by specially designed amphibious vehicles. Five minutes before H-Hour, "floating" DD tanks of the 743rd Tank Battalion would swim ashore, having been launched 6,000 yards out to sea, and then provide covering fire from the water's edge for the first wave. The DD tank was an Anglo-American development that, like the coalition it symbolized, had strengths and weaknesses. Designed to use a propeller to power it from a LST [landing ship tank], the DD was basically a Sherman tank fitted with special exhaust vents and a bulky canvas "skirt," pneumatically raised, which covered most of the tank and protected it from the seas. The tanks were highly effective in calm waters but tended to swamp with potentially fatal results in heavy seas.

It would not be machines, however, but men who would determine success or failure on D-Day. On Omaha, the 1st Division, commanded by Major General Clarence R. Huebner, would land to the east of Gerhardt's 29th Division. During D-Day, the 29th Division's 115th and 116th Regiments would be under Huebner's control until Gerhardt resumed command of them on the day after the landings. Two companies of specially trained Rangers would attack a series of cliffs, Point du Hoc, marking the far western limit of Omaha Beach. The Americans would, meanwhile, land companies of 200 men in waves of seven boats on each of eight sectors. Company A would land on Dog Green first and spearhead the 116th Infantry's ground assault. Colonel Charles Canham would command these "Stonewallers" on the beach.

The Bedford boys' first challenge would be to cross Dog Green at low tide—a journey of five hundred yards dotted with defensive obstacles. With covering fire provided by sixteen DD tanks, the Bedford boys would engage the German defenders concentrated in emplacements and a concrete pillbox at the mouth of a crucial draw codenamed D-1. At the same time, they would provide covering fire for demolition experts from the Special Engineer Task Force who would clear lanes through beach defenses to allow LSTs to deposit thousands more men and vehicles.

The crucial D-1 draw led up 150-foot bluffs to the village of Vierville sur Mer. Once the Bedford boys had secured it, aided by the other companies in the 1st Battalion and Rangers, they would move inland, taking Vierville sur Mer, six hundred yards from the beach, and then liberate their final objective, the town of Isigny, eight miles away.

It was a hugely ambitious plan. For it to succeed, the Bedford boys would have to overcome formidable obstacles.

The Germans knew that the Allies were coming and had prepared accordingly. If Overlord succeeded, their eventual defeat was inevitable. And so, given the enormity of the threat, Hitler turned to his most brilliant general, the maverick "Desert Fox"—Erwin Rommel. "The war will be won or lost on the beaches," Rommel had declared upon first visiting the beaches in January 1944. "We'll have only one chance to stop the enemy and that's while he's in the water, struggling to get ashore. The first twenty-four hours of the invasion will be decisive. . . . For the Allies, as well as Germany, it will be the longest day."[31]

Intelligence reports and aerial photographs made clear that Rommel had ordered the placement of ingenious and lethal obstacles along the entire Normandy coastline. A waist-high stake with a mine attached to it, and covered by water at high tide, was Rommel's own invention. Huge iron crosses covered with limpet mines were scattered across beaches to stop amphibious vehicles and tanks. Tank traps, defensive walls, thickets of barbed wire, and acres of minefields were also spread along the entire coastline from Brittany to the Pas de Calais and beyond.

On Omaha, the most heavily defended sections of the beach bristled with the full range of German mines, traps, and obstacles. Because the only clear exits from the beach, other than by infiltrating up steep bluffs, were four gullies, these areas were the most heavily fortified. At each gully, or draw, the Germans had set up a Stutzpunkt (strongpoint) manned by at least seventy men who operated MG-42 machine guns, mortars, and armor-piercing howitzers.

The most formidable Stutzpunkt was at the base of the Vierville draw, designated as D-1, overlooking Dog Green, where the Bedford boys would land at H-Hour. It was vital that bombing and DD-tank fire neutralize the D-1 Stutzpunkt and especially its MG-42 machine gun nests which had a panoramic view of Dog Green and could provide an arc of continuous fire along three hundred yards of water line.

The MG-42 would kill more Americans than any other weapon in Normandy. It fired three times faster than any American equivalent, was far more durable and easy to maintain, and was so essential to German combat tactics that many German riflemen were loaded down with extra ammunition for the MG-42 rather than for their slow-firing standard issue rifle, the Mauser Karabiner 98k, which was bolt-action, unlike the superior American M-1.

The Bedford boys could fire the M-1 as fast as they could pull the trigger and then slam a new clip of eight rounds into the gun in just a few seconds. But in combat, they would soon realize, it wouldn't matter that the gun allowed them greater firepower than any German rifleman. In a firefight against German squads armed with MG-42s, a rifle platoon armed only with the M-1 would be cut to ribbons.

During their briefing by 29th Division intelligence experts, Captain Fellers and other officers, including Lieutenant Ray Nance, examined a model replica of Omaha Beach built to scale and set up on a so-called "sand table." They were not told the date of the invasion. Nor were they told where Omaha was in Normandy, "only that it was in France across the channel."[32]

The briefing deeply troubled Fellers. According to Nance: "When the company commanders were called and the battalion commander told them where they were going, what they were going to do etc., my company commander, Taylor Fellers, told me later that he said, 'Colonel [Canham], I can take one Browning automatic rifle and get on that cliff and deny that beach to any infantry group.' And he wasn't a fellow who normally talked like that, [but] later he said, 'Ray, we'll all be killed!'"[33]

Fellers and other skeptics were assured that inexperienced troops of the German 716th Division were holding Omaha. Besides, heavy bombing would quickly decimate these inept defenders and destroy pillboxes and other obstacles. Others were told that "there would be no living things on the beach . . . it would be a piece of cake"[34] and that "the battleships would blow everything off the map—pillboxes, artillery, mortars, and the barbed wire entanglements. Everything would be blasted to smithereens—a pushover."[35]

Several of the 29th Division's most senior officers shared Fellers's reservations. Brigadier General Norman Cota, the 29th Division's assistant commander, would lead the Blue and Gray assault on Omaha. He had studied in great depth various amphibious landing plans and firmly believed that bombing the beach, even in daylight, would be ineffective. The best time to attack, he argued, was at night when the enemy could not see and surprise could be maximized. "The beach is going to be fouled-up in any case," insisted Cota. "Darkness will not substantially alter the percentage of accuracy in breaching—not enough to offset the handicaps of a daylight assault."[36] Cota's views were ignored.

After the officers had been briefed, platoon leaders were assembled and their roles outlined in detail. Roy Stevens studied the sand table with the replica of Omaha for a long time, memorizing every contour, every possible place for cover, and particularly the Germans' defensive positions. Stevens noted that at low tide there were some three hundred yards of flat sand between the water and the first cover, a sea wall. From training, Stevens knew how long it would take a fully loaded GI, with over sixty pounds on his back, to sprint to the sea wall—about a minute but an eternity if he was constantly under fire. But if the beach was bombed, creating protective craters, the going might not be so tough, especially if DD tanks led the advance and the pillboxes and machine gun nests dotting the flanks of the draw had been bombed effectively.

Stevens listened carefully as an intelligence officer pointed to a "promenade" road that ran parallel to the beach and then sloped steeply towards Vierville sur Mer. Before the road left the beach at the D-1 draw, there was an old house just to the east. This would be the first objective for Stevens's boat section. The briefing over, Stevens assembled his men and explained what lay ahead. "I wasn't too keen to tell them what we were facing. We were really going to have to do something now all right. That was for sure."[37]

Company B's Bob Sales would land sixteen minutes after Company A. By now, he recognized many of the Bedford boys after eighteen months of drinking in some of the same pubs and tramping around moors and parade grounds. When Sales asked about the threat of harrowing machine gun fire, his company commander, Captain Ettore Zappacosta, replied: "Don't you worry about that. The naval bombardment and air force will take care of all that."[38]

"They also told us," recalled Bob Slaughter of Company D, "that where we were landing, there was going to be twenty-two strong points, but only one or two of them would be manned. . . . Then we had to be dug in real well because there would be a counterattack afterwards that we had to be worried about. We would have to use the armor, and the German Panzers would try to drive us back into the sea."[39] But the counterattack would fail. Victory was not in doubt. Company A rifleman Murphy Scott recalled being told he would be in Paris in a week and then Company A would be shipped back to the states to train other units.[40]

Among America's most senior generals, there was no such optimism. General Omar N. Bradley, commander of American forces on D-Day, recalled that "Overlord represented both [Hitler's] greatest danger and his greatest opportunity. If the Overlord forces could be repulsed and trounced decisively on the beaches, Hitler knew it would be a very long time indeed before the Allies tried again—if ever. . . . The Third Reich might yet prevail."[41]

Bradley's superior, General Eisenhower—overall Allied commander— was "seething with the gravity of the invasion," according to a recent biographer, Carlo D'Este. "His health again deteriorated from a plethora of ailments. . . . As D-Day neared his smoking had increased to four packs a day."[42] At the end of April, V Corps commander General Gerow had written to Eisenhower outlining serious reservations about cooperation between the British navy and American assault troops and defensive obstacles on the beaches. Eisenhower rebuked Gerow, an old friend, for his skepticism. Gerow replied that he was not being "pessimistic" but simply "realistic."[43]

Britain's Prime Minister, Winston Churchill, was also full of doubts, telling a senior Pentagon official, John J. McCloy, that he would have liked to have had "Turkey on our side, the Danube under threat as well as Norway cleaned up before we undertook [Overlord]."[44] The British General Sir Alan Brooke, chief of the Imperial General Staff, had faced the Germans in Normandy in 1940 before the British Expeditionary Force's narrow escape at Dunkirk. Only hours before H-Hour he wrote in his diary that he was "very uneasy about the whole operation. At the best it will fall so very very far short of the expectation of the bulk of the people, namely all those who know nothing about its difficulties. At the worst it may well be the most ghastly disaster of the whole war!"[45]

It was essential that the 29th Division and other invading Allied armies have complete confidence in Overlord even if some of its architects did not. And so in late May every general of standing with the invasion forces appeared at various "sausages" to rally the troops. "In the final days before we embarked," recalled Bradley, "I made a point of visiting as many American units as I could, both to allay the growing rumors that we would suffer heavy casualties and to give the men some final words of encouragement."[46]

On May 30, Bradley visited the D-1 containment camp holding the 29th Division's 116th Infantry. Some 3,500 men stood around a small wooden platform on a windswept hillside. Bradley spoke slowly into a single microphone. "You should consider yourselves lucky," he concluded. "You are going to have ringside seats for the greatest show on earth."[47]

Private Hal Baumgarten stood listening to the final pep talk. "Our helmets shined with oil. Our bayonets gleamed. The 29th Division band played. I had had my head shaved. We had been given a lot of new equipment, including new assault jackets for D-Day. I didn't wear mine. My best buddy told me not to—'don't wear it Hal, it's going to drown you.'"[48]

When Roy Stevens tried on his assault jacket, he found it was too loose around his shoulders so he had it altered for a closer fit—a decision he would soon bitterly regret. Like every other Bedford boy, Stevens was also issued a $10,000 life insurance policy. Frank Draper Jr. made his out to his mother even though back home he had a fiancee, Nellie McKinney, whom he wished he had married before leaving for England. Finally, men checked their weapons and kit for the last time. Company A Private Thomas Valance recalled lining up to sharpen his bayonet on a large whetstone. "We were also issued some French francs, script it was called at the time," he said. "There was no explanation exactly where we were going to spend it."[49]

Colonel Canham ordered that a message be read to all the men before they left the containment camp: "There is one certain way to get the enemy out of action and that is to kill him. War is not child's play and requires hatred of the enemy. At this time we don't have it. I hope you will get it when you see your friends wounded and killed. Learn to take care of yourself from the start. Remember the Hun is a crafty, intelligent fighter and will not have any mercy on you. Don't have it on him. . . . To each one of you Happy Landing and come off those craft fighting like hell."[50]

At a meeting of his staff officers, a cautious Brigadier General Norman Cota warned: "This is different from any of the other exercises that you've had so far. . . . The air and naval bombardment and the artillery support are reassuring. But you're going to find confusion. The landing craft aren't going in on schedule and people are going to be landed in the wrong place. Some won't be landed at all. The enemy will try, and will have some success, in preventing our gaining a lodgement. But we must improvise, carry on, not lose our heads."[51]

On June 2, Company A was ordered to break camp the following morning. To their dismay, the Bedford boys learned that Captain Fellers was lying in a cot on the second floor of Doulish, the ancestral home converted for military use at the southwest corner of their "sausage." He had a bad sinus infection and would not be fit to lead them on D-Day. Morale plunged. That night, Fellers had trouble sleeping. Sweating profusely, with a bright rash on his face from the infection, he knew that in a matter of hours Master Sergeant Wilkes would order thirty-four of Bedford's sons to fall in and then board trucks bound for a channel port.

At some point in the night, Fellers struggled to his feet. A medical officer tried to get him to go to a military hospital. Instead, Fellers discharged himself and returned to his company. "He'd been with those men a long time and trained with them," explained his sister, Bertie. "He wanted to see it all the way through."[52] Grant Yopp was also laid up in the sick bay. He too got to his feet and returned to Company A against the advice of medical personnel. According to Yopp's sister: "[Grant] had some kind of respiratory illness. When he heard about the boys leaving, he went AWOL and rejoined his buddies. I've always thought: 'Oh, gosh, why did he do that?' He just wanted to be with his buddies."[53]

Company A's mess sergeant Earl Newcomb and two of his cooks, Bedford boys George Crouch and Cedric Broughman, had been frantically busy for several hours, checking that all the equipment and supplies needed to feed Company A were in order. Fellers suddenly appeared in the mess. Newcomb was shocked by his appearance: "He looked so sick—he should not have gone."[54] As Newcomb prepared Company A's final meal on dry land, he overheard Fellers confide in a fellow officer: "I want to go in [with the Bedford men]. If I don't and something happens to those boys, I'll never be able to go back to Bedford again."[55]

Roy Stevens recalled seeing Fellers appear before the men early that morning: "It really lifted our spirits. We had our leader back again."[56] Fellers said, "I've trained you. I'll die with you too if it comes to that."[57]

Company A loaded into trucks and then joined a huge convoy trundling south towards the sea. "Hedges that lined the narrow, winding roads were green and fragrant," reported the *Baltimore News-Post*. "Gorse splotched the broad and rolling moors with gold. From the tops of hills, irregular patches of farms spread in kin-folk shades of brown and green."[58]

In towns and villages, crowds soon formed, lining the road as the drab olive gray trucks sped along with MPs directing traffic at every junction. Children were held up for soldiers to kiss when the trucks dawdled, waiting to move closer to the coast. Every few miles, the men gaped at huge stockpiles of weapons, trucks, explosives, and endless rows of jeeps and artillery. They were part of an invasion force so vast it had filled most of southern England with troops and supplies. Thirty-nine divisions were leaving the crowded "sausages." Over 175,000 men would be involved with Overlord on D-Day. Standing by were 11,000 planes other than strategic bombers, and 6,939 boats were assembled along the coast—the greatest invasion armada in history.[59]

Company A finally arrived in Weymouth and formed up on the dockside. Again, Colonel Canham prowled the wharves, barking orders.

Company A marched towards its troopship, the *Empire Javelin*.

"Are you ready, men?" asked General Gerhardt, as he stood watching on the dockside.

"Yes, sir, general!" replied Bedford Hoback. "We're sure ready."[60]

9

The *Empire Javelin*

OMPANY A FILED UP THE gangway of the HMS *Empire Javelin*. From the main deck, British Sub-Lieutenant Jimmy Green watched as the Bedford boys and their fellow Stonewallers of the 116th Infantry came aboard. Green was in command of the flotilla of six landing craft that would deposit Company A in Normandy in a matter of hours.[1] Company A was scheduled to land at 6:30 A.M.—"H-Hour." Green and other British naval officers had already dubbed Company A "the Suicide Wave"—the men under Fellers looked so young and naïve, somehow sacrificial. "Actually, we also referred to ourselves as the suicide wave," recalled Green, "and to be honest we were all quite proud of the label."[2]

Green had already met Captain Fellers during maneuvers near Slapton Sands. Their conversations had been brief and mostly limited to logistics and landing procedures. As the *Empire Javelin* now prepared to leave harbor on June 4, Green and Fellers got to know each other better. "It was Fellers's first action. He told me his troops were National Guard, and he was worried how they would react under fire. He asked if I could put them ashore as quickly as possible when we got near the beach, and then fire over their heads to give them some encouragement. He said they'd need all the help they could get to get them moving forward."[3]

Green was surprised that Fellers would ask him to place covering fire above his men. It betrayed a lack of confidence. During exercises, Fellers had been composed and friendly, if a little too serious for the Brits. "He regarded us navy chaps as rather lighthearted in our approach.

111

Although we were serious and professional, we talked about Wrens and [soccer] matches rather than what we were going to do." For some reason, Fellers had changed since they had last met in April. In Green's eyes, Fellers now seemed very reserved and enormously burdened. It was as if he "had a premonition of doom."[4]

As the Bedford boys settled into their berths aboard the *Empire Javelin*, at Allied Headquarters General Eisenhower faced the most momentous choice of his life. "Low clouds, high winds, and formidable wave action were predicted to make landing a most hazardous affair," he wrote later. "The meteorologists said that air support would be impossible, naval gunfire would be inefficient, and even the handling of small boats would be rendered difficult."[5]

Should Eisenhower order a postponement or proceed as planned? General Montgomery, who would command all land forces in Normandy, said the invasion should go ahead. Eisenhower deliberated and then decided it would have to be postponed one day, until June 6. The question now was whether the largest armada ever assembled could reform and land as planned within twenty-four hours? Many ships were already in the Irish Sea, where gale forces had caused considerable problems and confusion. All Eisenhower could do was hope and pray that his staff would be able to reorganize in time.[6]

That afternoon, Company A learned of Eisenhower's decision. "Word came that the invasion had been changed from June 5," recalled Captain Robert Walker of the 116th's regimental headquarters staff. "We also heard, along with every kind of rumor imaginable, that in the U.S. it had already been broadcast that the invasion had begun. There was surprisingly little reaction among the troops, as if everyone was already numb to the situation. Or maybe it was just because they were good soldiers."[7]

The eternal wait resumed. Roy Stevens tried to stay busy, sharpening his bayonet and dagger and visiting the *Javelin's* canteen. He didn't like the British food aboard—too much fish. So he bought plate after plate of cookies. He shared some with his equally nervous brother and a jittery Earl Parker. A young man who had been an acrobat distracted them by walking down steps on his hands. "We knew somebody was going to die," recalled Stevens, "and it wasn't going to be long."[8]

At 9:30 P.M., RAF Group Captain James Stagg, chief meteorological officer for Supreme Headquarters Allied Expeditionary Force, stood just inside the entrance to the library at SHAEF headquarters, Southwick House, near Portsmouth, England. Before him, the leaders and architects of Overlord settled into couches and armchairs.

"Gentlemen," Stagg said, "some rapid and unexpected developments have occurred over the North Atlantic. In particular a vigorous cold front . . . is approaching Portsmouth now and will pass through all channel areas tonight or early tomorrow. . . . There will be a brief period of improved weather from Monday afternoon. For most of the time the sky will then be not more than half covered with cloud and its base should not often be below two thousand to three thousand feet. Winds will decrease substantially from what they are now. These conditions will last over Monday night and into Tuesday."

Stagg answered several questions concerning how long the window of relatively good weather would last and whether he could predict conditions reliably beyond the next three to four days.

Air Chief Marshal Trafford Leigh-Mallory looked grave. "With the cloud conditions Stagg has given us," he said, "there's certain to be difficulty getting markers down accurately, and the bombing will therefore suffer."

Eisenhower's deputy, Air Chief Marshal Sir Arthur Tedder, also looked anxious. Air power, he believed, would win the war and make all the difference on D-Day. He and Mallory had fought hard to secure enough bombers from RAF Bomber Command and the United States Strategic Air Forces in Europe. It was only after their boss, Eisenhower, had threatened to resign that they had been given the requisite planes that April.

Tedder agreed with Leigh-Mallory: "Yes, the operations of the heavy and medium bombers will probably be a bit chancy."

Eisenhower looked over at General Montgomery.

"Do you see any reason why we should not go on Tuesday?" he asked.

"No," replied Montgomery without hesitation. "I would say go!"[9]

Late into the night the question of whether to launch Overlord or not was debated. Just about 4:15 A.M. on June 5, Eisenhower again paced back and forth slowly at another meeting of Overlord's top generals in the library at Southwick House. "His head was slightly sunk on his chest, his hands clasped behind his back," recalled Major General Kenneth Strong. "From time to time he stopped in his stride, turned his head quickly and jerkily in the direction of those present and fired a rapid question at him . . . then resumed his walk."[10]

Montgomery looked impatient as Eisenhower walked over to a sofa and then sat down for five minutes, still weighing whether or not to launch the invasion. At 5 A.M. Eisenhower finally said: "OK, we'll go."[11]

By mid-afternoon on the 5th, the *Empire Javelin* was heading out to sea. Men gathered nervously on the ship's main deck to watch the vast armada dotting the horizon. Typically, to ease the tension, Master Sergeant John Wilkes joked that every man in Company A would get the Bronze Star after landing in France.[12] Hal Baumgarten made his way to the bow. On the back of his field jacket he had painted a large Star of David using his standard issue "Eversharp" blue ink pen. He'd etched "The Bronx, New York" around it. At the bow, Baumgarten struck up a conversation with Morris Saxtein, a balding, overweight forty-five-year-old fellow Jew from New York who had just joined the headquarters staff for Company A.

"Why are you here?" asked Baumgarten.

Saxtein puffed on a pipe.

"All I want is one German . . . You, Hal, will be a hero tomorrow morning—whether you like it or not."[13]

Baumgarten would never see Saxtein again.

Earl Parker stood at the *Empire Javelin*'s rail with the Stevens twins. "It was a solemn thing," recalled Roy Stevens. "We sat around and talked about what we would do when we got back home."[14] Suddenly, Parker pulled out a picture of his sixteen-month-old daughter, Danny. "If I could just see her once," Parker said, "I wouldn't mind dying."[15]

It was a bright evening with dusk beginning well past 10 P.M. Groups of officers huddled, cracking Mark Twain jokes about the weather, gossiping, signing each other's 100-franc notes, trying to control their fear. But it showed in many of their eyes. They were as afraid of death as they were of not being equal to facing it.

As the *Empire Javelin* and hundred of other ships crossed the English Channel, General Eisenhower visited Newbury airfield, a launch area for the 101st Airborne, the "Screaming Eagles," who would be the first American paratroops to land behind enemy lines in France, shortly after midnight. Eisenhower was not expected. Taking his time, he wandered among the young men, their faces blacked up, hair shorn in Mohican haircuts, chutes, and packs neatly stacked at their sides. He asked several where they came from. Texans, Missourians, Californians, and many others cheered as they heard their home state named.

After wishing the men good luck, Eisenhower stood and watched them board gliders and leave Newbury on their way to the blackness of occupied France. There were tears in his eyes. In his wallet was a draft of a press release in case things went terribly wrong:

> Our landings in the Cherbourg-Havre area have failed to gain a satisfactory foothold and I have withdrawn the troops. My decision to attack at this time and place was based upon the best information available. The troops, the air and the Navy did all that Bravery and devotion to duty could do. If any blame or fault attaches to the attempt it is mine alone.[16]

Meanwhile, Captain Fellers visited the *Javelin*'s operations room several times to consult maps etched with red and blue lines and to examine photographs of Omaha Beach. When he and other officers returned to the deck, they could not help but notice that the evening sky was clouding over. The wind was rising.

At 11 P.M., darkness enveloped the *Empire Javelin*. A gale was now blowing. Every officer now had the same concern as their generals—bad weather could destroy the invasion just as it had destroyed the Spanish

Armada. A strict blackout was imposed and smoking banned on deck for fear that even a lighted stub might alert German E-boats and the disaster at Slapton Sands would be repeated.

Below decks, the 116th Infantry attended religious services. John Barnes went to what he thought would be his last mass. "I was deeply conscious that my parents' (especially my mother's) great prayer was that [their] son would grow up to become a priest. When I graduated from high school, I had to tell her that I didn't think I was cut out to follow religious life. It was a great disappointment to her. As I prayed that night, I thought I would make a bargain with God. My life spared tomorrow, and I'd become a priest. Then I thought that was a bad deal, and especially a bad bargain, either for Him or me, so I said I'd take my chances."[17]

The crossing got rougher as the night wore on. Many men became terribly seasick. It is thought that John Schenk lay groaning in his bunk, clutching a sick-bag, courtesy of the British navy, when he wasn't up on deck vomiting over the ship's rail with dozens who had also taken their standard issue seasickness pills. British sailors working the decks briskly reminded the green-gilled Yanks to puke "to leeward, mate—leeward!"

Hal Baumgarten was also feeling under the weather as he talked with Company A's Private Thomas Mullins, a medic from Worcester, Massachussets. Mullins gave him some "APCs"—Aspirin Phenacidin Caffeine—not realizing the aspirin would make Baumgarten bleed more profusely if wounded. Mullins was one of two medics who would go in with Company A's headquarters boat led by Lieutenant Nance. The other was Cecil Breeden, a soft-spoken and unflappable man from Iowa who called Colorado home.[18] During training, Master Sergeant John Wilkes had pointed at Mullins and Breeden and then told the rest of Company A: "Be nice to them! You may need them one day."[19]

At 4 A.M., the Bedford boys stood on deck ready to climb into the British LCAs that hung over the sides of the *Empire Javelin* suspended from

davits. For a few moments, they stood in silence. It seemed that whatever each man was thinking formed part of some communal prayer. The
silence was broken as an officer read Eisenhower's final words of encouragement over the *Javelin*'s public address system:

> Soldiers, sailors and airmen of the Allied Expeditionary Force! You are
> about to embark upon the Great Crusade, toward which we have striven
> these many months. The eyes of the world are upon you. The hopes and
> prayers of liberty-loving people everywhere march with you. In company
> with our brave allies and brothers in arms on the other fronts, you will
> bring about the destruction of the German war machine, the elimination
> of Nazi tyranny over the oppressed peoples of Europe, and security for
> ourselves in a free world.[20]

Company A went to its boat stations. Groups of thirty men were assigned to six boats. An additional seventeen men, including Lieutenant
Ray Nance, went to a seventh boat that would land nineteen minutes
after the others with vital communications equipment. Boats with even
numbers would go in to the right of the odd ones. Captain Fellers
thanked his men for their hard work during training and asked them to
be careful. "This is it," he added. "This is the real thing."[21]

Roy Stevens's boat was number five of the seven. His brother Ray's
was number two. Roy looked around, trying to spot his brother. He was
desperate by now to wish him good luck, slap him on the back, buoy his
spirits, tell him they'd be back in Bedford soon working their farm together. Roy knew that now, more than ever, Ray needed all the encouragement he could get.

Nearby in the darkness, Roy saw an obviously distressed Jack Powers,
the powerfully built, normally unflappable ex-Ranger whose brother
Clyde was in Roy's boat team. Roy was surprised by Jack's behavior. Jan-
gling nerves had gotten the better of him: "He was just carrying on, all
nervous. Things were very tense. Everybody was ready to go, ready to do
something at last."[22] Stevens looked around. It seemed that the men fell

into two groups. Those who had already decided they were "going to die," and those who hoped "to make it through."[23]

Roy suddenly stumbled into his twin, Ray. All the other Bedford boys were shaking hands, wishing each other luck.

Ray stuck out his hand for Roy to shake.

Roy refused it.

"I'll shake your hand in Vierville sur Mer," he said, "up at the crossroads above the beach, later this morning sometime."

Ray bowed his head and held out his hand again.

"I'm not gonna make it."[24]

Of course he would. Roy still refused to shake Ray's hand. He'd do it later . . . after they'd crossed Omaha Beach.

Since Company A would land on Omaha Beach first, its men were first to leave the ship. Their British-made landing craft hung above the choppy water, at the same level as the deck. They did not have to climb down nets and ropes as later waves of troops would do. On command, the men formed up in their boat teams and simply walked across a narrow metal gangplank, a yard in length, and then clambered into the boats that would deliver them to the most heavily defended beach in history.

Twenty-year-old Second Lieutenant Edward Gearing and Roy Stevens stepped into their craft, LCA 911. "Gearing was just a kid with a buzz cut but you never realized it," recalled John Barnes, a fellow member of their boat crew. "He had been to a military academy in Virginia and was the kind who just took charge, was sympathetic to all the men, a very good officer."[25] The kind of officer thirty older men would follow, possibly to their deaths. "[Gearing] didn't stand back and tell you what to do," recalled Roy Stevens. "He did it. He was a leader."[26]

Roy directed the boat team to its positions. His buddy, Clyde Powers, took a position on one of the three rows of benches for the men to sit down. Powers's uncle, Sergeant Harold Wilkes, lumbered aboard, his assault jacket crammed with a quarter pound of TNT, K rations, and a medical kit containing morphine. John Barnes went to the back of the boat and took his seat beside the flamethrower, a normally cheerful and slightly built young man from Tennessee named Russell Pickett. "Guys were hollering back and forth at each other once the boats were hanging out there," Barnes remembered. "The men just stepped over the *Empire Javelin*'s rail into their boats. I think Roy Stevens shouted out to his brother. Everybody had buddies in different boats."27

Sub-Lieutenant Green stood in LCA 910, giving orders to his coxswain. Captain Fellers stood a few feet to his left side. As more men boarded, Green was struck by how they struggled to even stand upright in the swaying boat, their packs stuffed with over sixty pounds of kit. "They had far too much weight. I don't know why the first wave did not go in light. We had worked before with British commandos, and they would not have gone in so heavily weighed down."28

A gale was blowing. At 4:30 A.M., winches began to lower the craft into the water. Suddenly, boat number 911 hit Green's astern.29 There didn't appear to be any damage. It was difficult in the swells to unhook the craft from the mother ship. "We didn't want to get bashed against the ship's side or capsize," recalled Green. "It was straightforward in calm conditions but not in the dark in a gale."30

A landing craft carrying a group of the 116th Infantry's senior officers would later get stuck for thirty minutes just below the *Javelin*'s sewage outlet. "During this half-hour," recalled one of the officers, "the bowels of the ship's company made the most of an opportunity that Englishmen have sought since 1776. Yells from the boat were unavailing. Streams, colored everything from canary yellow to sienna brown and olive green, continued to flush into the command group, decorating every man aboard. We cursed, we cried, and we laughed, but it kept coming. When we started for shore, we were all covered with shit."31

As Company A's landing craft formed up, Jimmy Green's coxswain in LCA 910 suddenly heard a beep through his voice pipe. The stoker down below had bad news. They were taking on water—the earlier collision had damaged the boat after all. Green scrambled along the deck to have a look. Water gushed into LCA 910's engine room through a small hole. Green alone had Company A's course and other vital landing instructions. He decided to continue, confident that his signalman could keep them afloat, using a hand pump, long enough to make the beach and get back.

John Barnes stood a few feet from Roy Stevens in LCA 911. "Once we were in the water and away, we all waved at the men in other boats, and they waved back. We were confident that we would get across that beach."[32] From the *Empire Javelin*'s deck, the seas had looked cold and choppy. Now, as Roy Stevens hunched down in 911, the slapping waves felt violent and ominous: "I never saw water that bad. [The seas] were just rolling and rolling, and there were white caps way out where we were, [12 miles] from the coast. It was really, really rough."[33]

Other Bedford boys began to wonder whether they would get to France, let alone across Omaha Beach.

10

The First Wave

THE 116TH'S 1ST BATTALION headed for the beach in waves
of LCAs. In each LCA, a British coxswain steered the craft from a
cockpit that had light armor-plating. Sub-Lieutenant Jimmy Green stood
right beside his coxswain in LCA 910.[1] "The coxswain was connected by
a voice pipe to the stoke hold, where a stoker operated two powerful
petrol engines. The stoker had to be small and extremely agile to get into
the hold through a small hole on the aft deck. There were two other
crew members—one forward and one aft—to unhook the boat from the
main ship, and the other to lower the landing-craft doors and work the
boat's anchor."

Green had been ordered to keep radio silence until he landed Captain Fellers and his boat team. As his flotilla formed up, he checked his
watch. H-Hour for Company A was 6:36 A.M.; he had just over two
hours to get to Omaha Beach.

The direct route to the beach was approximately twelve miles but
Green had to steer a "diagonal course," making the total journey close to
twenty miles. The LCAs could move at about 10 knots in good conditions but now the seas were, if anything, rougher than when Eisenhower
had postponed the invasion. Nevertheless, Green was confident he
would get Company A to Omaha on time.

Green gave the order for Company A's six boats to approach the beach
in two columns of three craft. Whenever he looked over his shoulder, he
could see Fellers and his men sitting in tense, glum silence. "They were
just boys, pleasant, fresh-faced country boys. They looked like nice lads

on a trip around the bay. The rest of [the British seamen in] our flotilla also thought they were a nice bunch. But not assault troops in the sense that they were heavily laden with 60 pounds of equipment."[2]

The two columns of three boats ploughed ahead. Green kept his eyes fixed on a landing-craft control boat guiding him towards France. So long as Company A's craft followed the control boat, it would stay on the right course. Green had taken a tour of the boat and been impressed by its state of the art navigational devices, including one of the first radar sets: "a magnificent piece of equipment that even showed the contours of land."

Five miles from France, the control boat broke away, signaling: "You're on the right course. There it is." Company A was on its own. Green checked his course as the flotilla plowed forward, bucking in the swells, men now puking into paper bags and even their helmets.

Suddenly, Green came upon a group of LCTs [Landing Craft Tanks] carrying tanks destined for Omaha Beach. In the heavy seas, they were making very slow progress.

"What are they doing here?" asked Green.

"They're supposed to go in ahead of us," replied Fellers.

"But they won't get there in time for six thirty," said Green. "I think we might have to go ahead of them. Is that all right?"

"Yes. We must get there on time."[3]

The tanks were supposed to lead the first wave up the beach and were essential to destroying resistance and providing Company A with cover: The men could cluster behind them as they advanced and fired on German positions. Without the tanks, Company A would have only craters blown in the beach from air and naval bombardment for protection.

In the far distance, Green spotted what looked like land. A few minutes later, Omaha Beach started to take form. In the murky light, the tidal waters off the beach looked as unforgiving as those out in the channel. Company A still cruised forward in two columns of three. It occurred to Green that the legendary British Admiral, Horatio Nelson, had employed the same formation at the battle of Trafalgar in 1805, the greatest naval engagement of the Napoleonic Wars.

Eleven miles out at sea, a troopship carrying the second wave from the 29th, USS *Charles Carroll*, pitched and rolled in heavy swells. Colonel Charles Canham and Brigadier General Norman Cota struggled down a cargo net slung over the boat's side and boarded LCVP 71 (landing craft, vehicles and personnel). They were scheduled to land at 7.30 A.M. on Dog White, several hundred yards to the east of the Vierville sur Mer draw.[4]

Three miles from the beach, Company A heard a massive explosion. The men looked to their right, westward. The battleship *Texas* was firing at Omaha; when the ship's enormous fourteen-inch guns erupted, shock waves threatened to swamp the boats. By now, severely seasick men, including John Schenk, barely had the strength to bail with their helmets. Some had collapsed with exhaustion.

Just after 6 A.M., Lieutenant Ray Nance peered through a narrow slot at the bow of his LCA. A pall of smoke hung like a storm cloud over the beach, obscuring many of the bluffs. Nance closed the slot, keeping his head down. A few feet from Nance, John Clifton struggled to repair his radio set. The antenna had broken off in heavy seas. Should he abandon it? Nance told him to bring it along and they would repair it later on the beach. Without radios, there was little chance of setting up Company A's first command post. Clifton shouldered the broken set. Medic Cecil Breeden, broadfaced, five-foot-ten-inches, 180 pounds, sat nearby. A red cross was emblazoned on an arm-band and a canvas shoulder bag that was crammed with medical supplies.[5]

In LCA 911, Roy Stevens watched a volley of rockets flash overhead.

"Take a good look!" a man shouted. "This is something you will tell your grandchildren!"

"Sure, if we live," thought John Barnes.[6]

"There was a lovely firework display," recalled Jimmy Green. "The rockets went up in the air and then down in the sea about a mile off the shore, nowhere near the coast. They killed a few fish but that was about it. I was furious. They'd come all that way just to misfire. Doing, doing, doing! Bang, bang, bang! It woke those Germans up who didn't know we were already coming, but that was it."[7]

The question as to whether or not the planned naval bombardment with rockets and shells was woefully inadequate remains highly controversial to this day. Many after-action navy reports confirmed that the bombing did have an effect. Guns had been identified all along Omaha and in some sections were destroyed. But in the most heavily defended areas most Germans had survived.

Out at sea, a British coxswain gunned LCA 911's engines.

"We're on our way in," someone said.

Stevens said a prayer. Most of the men beside him were so seasick they did not seem to care if they lived or died. Mortars and artillery fire began to drop into the seas. In Stevens's boat were fellow Bedford boys Harold Wilkes, Charles Fizer, and Clyde Powers.

"We're sinking!"[8]

Water gushed into LCA 911. Stevens whipped off his helmet and began to bail frantically. John Barnes glimpsed the spire of Vierville sur Mer's church. Then the front of 911 disappeared beneath the waves. Barnes felt the craft fall away below. He squeezed the CO-2 tubes in his life belt but as he did so the belt flew away. The buckle had broken. He turned and grabbed a man nearby and managed to keep himself from going under by climbing on the man's back.[9]

At the head of the flotilla, Jimmy Green heard a man shout for help and turned around just in time to see LCA 911 go under. His orders were not to stop and pick up men from the water. In any case, his boat did not have space for the men from 911. "I'll be back," Green shouted.[10]

Roy Stevens could barely swim and was soon struggling to keep his head above water, weighed down by sixty pounds of kit as well as his assault jacket, sodden and crammed with ammunition, which now fit so well he couldn't get rid of it. Stevens gulped sea water between desperate breaths and then grabbed hold of a Bangalore torpedo. Somehow, he managed to stay afloat.

Clyde Powers was a good swimmer, having spent many summer days as a boy plunging into swimming holes and on the shores of Bedford

County Lake, a few miles from Bedford: "It was quite a bunch of the thirty that couldn't swim. I would say it was eight or nine who couldn't swim [despite having tried to learn in England]."[11] Those who could swim, like Powers and his uncle Harold Wilkes, did their best to prop up those who couldn't. Every man wore an inflatable Mae West but their assault jackets and packs were so heavy when soaked that even men who could swim had to kick hard simply to keep their heads above water.

"I'm drowning!"[12] one of the men suddenly shouted. Stevens turned and saw his boat team's radio operator, Private James Padley. A wave slapped Stevens in the face. He wiped salt water from his eyes. Padley was gone.

Aboard LCA 910, men could now see vague outlines of defensive installations and other landmarks. Jimmy Green spotted some "nasty looking pillboxes along the coast." One looked particularly lethal, positioned on the beach at the bottom of the D-1 Vierville draw. "If there's anybody in there," Green thought, "we've had it."

Green turned to Fellers.

"This is where we're going to land, is that OK?"

"Yes. Land me this side [west] of the draw and the others on the other side."[13]

Green gave the command to approach at full speed. He still couldn't see any Germans but everybody knew they were now ready and waiting in some strength because mortars started to splash around them with much greater frequency.

Suddenly, off to Green's left, an LCA was hit by an antitank rifle bullet which ripped through just above the water line, tearing off Frank Draper's upper arm as he sat in the middle of the craft. "I was later told that the other men tried to get Frank to lay down he was bleeding so bad," recalled Draper's sister, Verona. "But he wouldn't do it. He kept trying to stand."[14] Finally, Draper fell to the floor awash with vomit and dirty sea water and began to lose consciousness.

Jimmy Green looked at the pillbox looming at the mouth of the D-1 draw. He checked his watch. It was 6:25 A.M. He then saw something moving along the top of Omaha Beach. "It looked to me like a steam train going along say from Vierville to Cherbourg—along the coast. I thought: 'That's strange—in the middle of all this lot, they're still running a train!'"

There was a loud bang in Green's right ear. He turned to see an LCG (landing craft gun) with 4.7-inch guns. It suddenly let rip with a barrage that hit the pillbox at the base of the D-1 draw and appeared to damage it significantly. "If there's somebody in there," thought Green, "they've had it."[15]

The LCG fired again and then disappeared as fast as it had arrived. After the ear-splitting naval barrage and the rocket display, it was suddenly eerily quiet. There were the steady plops of mortars landing in the water and the odd antitank round but little else. It seemed they were still out of range of rifle and machine-gun fire.[16]

Several hundred yards behind Green, out at sea, 911's boat team were struggling to keep from drowning. "Our heads bobbed up above the surface of the water," John Barnes recalled. "We could still see some other boats moving on to the shore."[17] Barnes grabbed for anything that might help him stay alive—an M-1 carbine wrapped in a flotation belt, and then a flamethrower that was floating around with two belts wrapped around it. The water was freezing, numbing his hands and feet.

Barnes hugged the flamethrower for dear life. He heard the shouts of other men. Then Lieutenant Gearing was at his side, a fierce look of determination on his face. He grabbed Barnes by his assault jacket, whipped out a bayonet, and cut the straps to Barnes's pack. Others swam over and helped free Barnes of over sixty pounds of deadly ballast. Barnes kicked his legs and found that he was now able to keep his head above water.

There was a head count. Just one man was missing—Padley, the radio operator. He'd gone down with a forty-pound SCR 300 radio strapped to his back. Roy Stevens still clutched at his Bangalore torpedo. At the crest of waves he could see Omaha Beach and the remaining five landing craft carrying Company A. They were closing on the beach.

In LCA 910, Jimmy Green scanned the fast approaching sands. He had expected to see craters blown all along the beach—the result of the bombing that was planned to precede the landing. But there were none, and the bluffs above looked unharmed.

Three hundred twenty-nine Liberator bombers had indeed dropped 13,000 bombs between 05:55 and 06:14 A.M., but because of thick cloud cover and fear of hitting incoming troops, their bombs landed well inland. The bombs killed plenty of cows and some local French residents but left the sands of Omaha and its defenders unscathed. Indeed, Omaha was as "flat as a pancake," in Green's words.

The Bedford boys' hearts sank.

Even if the bombs had hit the beach, there would have been no craters for shelter: Most of the bombs were 100-pound devices designed for high fragmentation and had "instantaneous fuses" that would "prevent cratering of the beach and consequent delay in the movement of traffic across it."[18] Yet the Bedford boys had been assured that there would be craters.

Green gave the hand signal for Company A to make the final run to the beach. His craft touched bottom about thirty yards from the shoreline and then bucked up and down in heavy surf. He opened the doors, lowered the ramp, and then turned to Fellers: "Good luck."

Fellers thanked Green for getting the men in on time.

The armor-plated door leading onto the ramp opened. Fellers stood, exited, and then clambered down the ramp. The middle row filed after him. "They went out in very good order," recalled Green. "They didn't need to be ushered out and about—they knew what they had to do."[19]

It took over a minute for the other two rows to get out of the boat. The enemy still held their machine-gun fire. Green watched as the tall figure of Fellers and his men waded, guns above their heads, through the water, snaking onto the beach in a long line.

Green examined the bluffs above the D-1 draw. "They looked menacing, dark. You knew the Germans were there. It was creepy, especially because of the silence. We'd been expecting the Germans to open up as soon as we arrived. But they didn't. It was the calm before the storm."[20]

Green saw Fellers and his men lie down on a slight incline. Green went back to work, ordering his coxswain to pull off the beach and head back to pick up LCA 911's crew still in the water. It was H-Hour: The Bedford boys had arrived on the shores of Fortress Europe exactly on time.

11

Dog Beach

CAPTAIN FELLERS LAY WITH his boat team two hundred fifty yards from the D-1 Vierville draw. Jimmy Green had not been able to provide covering fire because his landing craft had bucked up and down too much in the heavy seas. There was only one thing to do—they would have to run for the nearest cover, making sure they did not bunch together to minimize casualties.

All along the bluffs above Omaha, veterans of the German 352nd Division lay in wait. They had moved into the area in recent weeks, relieving the inferior 716th Division. They totaled two regiments, almost two thousand men.

As Fellers and his men started to advance, German officers finally ordered their men to fire. Above the Vierville draw, the 352nd opened up with at least three MG-42 machine guns, firing over a thousand rounds per minute, and several mortars. Two dozen snipers lurked in nearby trenches. The slaughter was fast and merciless. Fellers and the twenty-nine men in his boat died in a matter of minutes, riddled by machine-gun bullets from several directions.

No accurate record exists of the boat roster for Company A on D-Day. It was probably lost with many others in the chaos and carnage after H-Hour. But it is thought that the following Bedford boys may have been among those who died within yards of their captain: twenty-two-year-old Sergeant Dickie Abbott; twenty-six-year-old Clifton Lee, the shy but fiercely patriotic private whose eyebrows arched dramatically above his pale face; twenty-three-year-old Gordon Henry White

Jr. who dreamed of his mother's cooking; the well-mannered Southern "gentleman" Nick Gillaspie; and the ace dice player, Wallace "Snake Eyes" Carter.

Less than fifty yards away, another LCA had also approached the beach. On board were George Roach, Thomas Valance, Gil Murdock, and the Bedford boys Dickie Overstreet and Master Sergeant John Wilkes. "We're going to drop this ramp and as soon as we do, we're going to back out," shouted a British bowman, "so you guys better be ready."[1]

The ramp slammed down into the surf and then the metal door swung open. Lieutenant Alfred Anderson exited, closely followed by Valance and seconds later by Roach and then Wilkes. Instantly, the Germans found their range. Men began to fall in every direction, picked off at random, while others miraculously staggered unscathed through a hail of bullets and shrapnel.

John Wilkes was one of the few who managed to get out of the shallows and onto the sand, where he and George Roach started to fire towards the base of the D-1 Vierville draw. Neither Wilkes nor Roach had yet seen a German.

"What are you firing at?" asked Wilkes.

"I don't know," said Roach. "I don't know what I'm firing at."

Wilkes and Roach spotted Lieutenant Anderson, thirty yards in front of them. He waved for them to follow him across the beach. Then Roach was knocked down. The next thing he knew, the sea was licking at his heels. There was no sign of Anderson or Wilkes. According to some eyewitnesses, Anderson was cut in two by a machine gun. It is thought that Master Sergeant John Wilkes was shot and killed as he fired his M-1 Garand rifle at the defensive installations at the base of the D-1 draw.

Dickie Overstreet also made it to the sands. He had dumped his flamethrower and picked up a dead man's rifle as he waded ashore. He then took cover behind one of two American tanks that had landed at the mouth of the D-1 draw. Suddenly, the tank took a direct hit, possibly from a mortar. Overstreet realized the Germans were zeroing in on any spot where men clustered—burnt out landing craft and immobilized vehicles—knowing entire platoons could be huddled behind them, frozen with shock and panic. The ammunition in the tank started to explode. Overstreet ran for cover. "I took off, started running, criss-crossing," he recalled. "That was when I got hit."[2]

Machine gun bullets wounded Overstreet in the stomach and leg but he finally made it to the sea wall running along the top of the Dog Green sector assigned to the 1st Battalion. "I called for first aid," Overstreet remembered. "I finally got a guy to come to me. He was so nervous he couldn't open the first aid kit. I had to do that for myself."[3] Overstreet would lie beside the sea wall until 4:30 A.M. on June 7, when he would finally be taken to a hospital ship and then to England, where he would spend six weeks recovering from multiple bullet wounds. "He wouldn't talk about the war with me when he came home," recalled his sister Beulah Witt. "He suffered from stomach problems for the rest of his life."[4]

Boatmate Gil Murdock had plunged into nine feet of water in one of the many tidal runnels on Omaha, and had then fought to get back to the surface, weighed down by his kit, punching the CO-2 tubes on his Mae West and even filling his gas mask casing with air to help him get buoyant. Finally, he had surfaced and gasped for air. Murdock had then made it to the shallows and was now crawling up the beach. Two men lay wounded, unable to fire a mortar. A sergeant ordered Murdock to operate it instead. Murdock got to the mortar and fired a couple of rounds but they didn't explode.

"Murdock, you dumb bastard," shouted the sergeant, "you're not pulling the firing pins!"

Murdock managed to get off several more rounds, which actually exploded, then began to crawl towards the sea wall. He tried to fire his rifle but it was jammed with wet sand. Then he came across a soldier with a gaping wound in his arm. The soldier asked for a shot of morphine. Murdock gave it, wished him luck, and kept crawling, this time towards an antitank obstacle. Murdock found two men already cowering behind the obstacle. To advance seemed suicidal but to stay where they were only marginally less fatal: Men were now being picked off by a score of snipers along the bluffs.

Murdock suddenly spotted George Roach crawling towards them.

"What happened?"[5] said Roach.

It looked like all A Company's officers were dead, and every sergeant either dead or wounded.

They tried to catch their breath. Suddenly, tracer fire sputtered towards them: A German machine gunner had spotted them. Fortunately, the tracers crackled above their heads. Every few seconds, another burst went high by just a few feet. Murdock couldn't understand why the German wasn't lowering his aim. Then he looked up and saw the German's target—an antitank mine strapped to the obstacle. A direct hit would blow anything within several yards to pieces.

They had better get the hell away, thought Murdock, before that German finds his mark. As the group left the obstacle, Murdock noticed that one soldier's left leg was soaked in blood. "You're hit!" he shouted.

"You damn fool," the soldier replied. "So are you."[6]

Murdock looked down. Two machine-gun bullets had pierced his leg and ended up in his right ankle.

"Look, I'm a good swimmer and you're not that badly hurt," said Roach. "Let me swim you out to that knocked-out tank in the water out there."

Murdock kept a photograph of his fiancée in the liner of his helmet. He looked at it. Roach grabbed the helmet and threw it away angrily.

"Let's get going."

Roach propped up Murdock as they swam out to sea. They finally got to the knocked-out tank. A few yards away, three men's heads bobbed up and down. They looked closer. It was the tank's crew, their faces disfigured by powder burns.

The tank commander sat behind the turret. His left leg was missing from the knee down. His shin bone dangled in the water. His men were useless. They wouldn't carry out orders. Could they give him a morphine shot?

Murdock crawled inside the tank turret, found a first aid package, pulled out some morphine and gave the commander the shot.

The commander said he wanted to get to the beach. It would be safer there. Murdock and Roach disagreed. But the commander was insistent. Finally, he persuaded his crew to do what he told them. They helped him into the water and began to swim in a group towards the beach. The tide was coming in.

Murdock watched as they got closer to the shore. Suddenly, the current snatched them, pulling them eastwards and then under.

Murdock and Roach sat alone on the tank. Shells started to land nearby. To make matters worse, the tide was starting to submerge the tank. Soon, they stood behind the turret, and then actually on the turret to avoid drowning.

Roach insisted he could swim out and reach a landing craft. Murdock shook his hand, wished him good luck, and thanked him for getting him off the beach. He watched Roach swim furiously away and then lost sight of him. Murdock would soon be picked up by a landing craft from a later wave. Roach would also be rescued, by an army control craft, and would also survive the war.

Back in the shallows, their boatmate Sergeant Thomas Valance cowered in knee-high water, scanning the bluffs. He couldn't see a single German. But the enemy was there, hidden in bunkers and trenches all along the bluffs. The air crackled with bullets. It seemed as if Company A had walked onto the wrong end of a firing range. Suddenly, tracer fire spat from the concrete pillbox at the mouth of the D-1 draw. It had not been immobilized by the naval barrage after all. The pillbox actually faced eastward, allowing machine gunners a clean sweep across the mouth of the draw and the entire length of Dog Green beach.[7]

Valance fired at the pillbox and several beach houses shrouded in smoke. They too were supposed to have been flattened by American bombers. All around Valance, Bedford boys were dying. In some spots, the sea ran red. Valance struggled to keep his balance. As he threw off his kit and sodden pack a bullet pierced his knuckle and exited through the palm of his hand. Valance felt only a small sting but his adrenaline surged as blood spurted from the wound.

Not far away, Company A's Private Henry G. Witt rolled over in the surf and faced Valance. "Sergeant," he cried hopelessly. "They're leaving us here to die like rats. Just to die like rats."[8] Valance didn't feel abandoned. He was determined to get out of the water, to push forward, to find cover, and then get Company A's objectives achieved, whatever the conditions. There was still a job to be done.

Valance crawled towards the sea wall at the western edge of the beach, where he finally collapsed, blood gushing from several bullet wounds. He would lie there for the rest of the day along with a small group of other badly wounded Company A survivors.

Back in the shallows, the few dozen men from Company A who were still alive were having a hell of a time simply keeping afloat or moving forward without exposing themselves to withering fire. The smartest lay with their nostrils just above the water so they could breathe but with every other inch of their bodies submerged. Now the Germans were shooting at anything that resembled a body, exploding the heads and bellies of the prostrate, turning areas of the beach into a bloody slaughterhouse.

By 6:45 A.M., the first wave boats had deposited Company A on the beach and pulled away.[9]

The next wave to approach the shore included an LCA carrying Lieutenant Ray Nance and seventeen other headquarters staff, including the medic Cecil Breeden and Bedford boys John Reynolds and John Clifton. They came in exactly as planned, nineteen minutes after the rest of Company A.

Nance's craft hit bottom. The British bowman, standing a few feet to Nance's right in a steel compartment at the front of the craft, pulled a lever to let the ramp down. The ramp lowered but then stopped. "Get it down!"[10] shouted Nance.

The bowman yanked the lever again and again. Finally, the ramp started to fall. Nance gave it a shove.

"Up and at 'em mates,"[11] cried the bowman.

Nance took two steps down the ramp and jumped into the water. A wave crashed down, almost submerging him. He began to wade forward, his sodden pack pulling him down, rifle above his head. The next thing he knew, he was lying winded on the cold sand. Nance looked around. He couldn't see any other men from Company A. Feeling terribly isolated, he struggled on up the beach. Soon he realized what had happened to Company A—corpses lay strewn across the sands and bumped against each other in the shallows.

Suddenly, he was not alone. Men appeared nearby. To the right: one of Nance's runners; to the left: his radio operator, John Clifton—Company A's Cassanova—crawling, his radio still on his back. The radio was useless, and it made him a sitting target. He should dump it fast, thought Nance.

"Keep moving, keep moving," shouted Nance.

"I'm hit," cried Clifton.

"Can you move?" asked Nance.

Clifton didn't answer.

Nance ducked and then looked up again. Clifton had disappeared.

Nance spotted four other men huddled down behind a steel tank obstacle. "Spread out!" shouted Nance. The words had barely left his mouth when a mortar round landed, killing three of the men and severely wounding the other.

Nance couldn't see a single German. He fired a few rounds towards the bluffs but then another mortar shell exploded nearby. A piece of shrapnel took a chunk out of his rifle, just a few inches from his face. "The Germans were so accurate with those things," Nance recalled, "they could put one in your back pocket if they spotted you."[12]

Tracer fire spurted towards Nance, kicking up sand, ricocheting off the stones, stitching the hard beach with bullets. The Germans had spotted him and were zeroing in. The machine gun snarled again. He was definitely the target. The fire came from a bunker just to the right of the draw, half way up the bluffs.

Nance positioned his body so he was facing the machine gun head on, providing less of a target. If he did get hit, it would be over quick—a shot to the head. He looked at his rifle; it was useless. Wet sand had gotten into the workings.

Nance held his breath as the sound of the bullets got louder. Then his body began to shake with terror. Another burst of bullets. He looked to his right—a Company A rifleman was up on his feet and sprinting, trying to escape the machine gun volleys. Nance recognized the runner. It was twenty-two-year-old John Reynolds. Reynolds stopped, knelt down and raised his rifle to return fire. He never got to pull the trigger. Nance saw him fall dead.

Finally, the bullets stopped spitting across the beach towards Nance. Perhaps the Germans had found another runner. There was no retreat for any man on D-Day—he had to push on. Nance crawled forward, aiming for a cliff-face three hundred yards away. Suddenly his right foot felt like Frank Draper Jr. had hit it with a baseball bat. Part of his heel had been shot away. Bullets again stitched the sand, again heading in his direction. "They came so close," recalled Nance. "Then, suddenly, when I thought there was no more hope, I looked up in the sky. I didn't see anything up there. But I felt something settle over me. I got this warm feeling. I felt as if somehow I was going to live."[13]

Nance lay as still as he could, hoping the machine gunner would think he was dead. But even corpses were now targets for the Germans above Dog Green. "That machine gunner just wouldn't let me be. He'd send a line of bullets my way, pass on to another target then come back for me again, like he was playing cat and mouse."[14] Nance tried in vain to dig a shallow foxhole in the sand and shingle with his hands. Then he spotted a tidal pool. It looked deep enough for a man to disappear beneath its surface.

Nance crawled as fast as he could, slithering into the pool's tepid waters. He filled his lungs and ducked down. Suddenly, a bullet pierced the strap on his World War I binocular case. Nance ducked down again and again. Some time later, when he came up for air, there was a soldier from

New York not far from him. The machine gun bullets returned. Nance again turned to face them head on. He told the New Yorker to do the same. The bullets moved away.

Nance and the New Yorker scrambled across the last yards towards the cliff. At last, they felt shingle beneath them. Nance collapsed, blood pouring from his foot. But at least he was safe. He looked out to sea. "I recognized two [dead] officers. They were face up, lying in the water. A lot of men were caught by the tide. Had we been on dry land, a lot of men would have made it."[15]

The tide had crept up behind Nance, drowning Company A men who no longer had the strength to crawl. Among them, it is thought, was Raymond Hoback. Nance had trained them. He had tried to be good to them. He had read their last love letters. As he now lay on the blood-stained pebbles below Vierville sur Mer, he still felt responsible for them, every last one. "I was their officer. It was my duty. . . . They were the finest soldiers I ever saw."[16]

12

"Medic!"

OTHER THAN NANCE, it is thought that just one man survived from Company A's headquarters boat—medic Cecil Breeden. As soon as he reached the sands, he stripped off his pack, shirt, helmet, and boots. Then he stood up. He wanted other men to see him, and to follow his example. They must get up and free of the kit that could soon drown them.

"Medic! Medic!"

Breeden walked back into the water to pull wounded men up the beach, away from the advancing tide. Slowly, a few others shook off their packs and began to help.[1]

The Germans had cut Company A to ribbons but they were still not satisfied. They now riddled wounded men with arms outstretched in supplication. They peppered soldiers who could not crawl and American teenagers risking their own necks to save them. The lazy machine gunners shot rescuers in the back. Snipers aimed for the forehead. By some miracle, Breeden wasn't hit.

As Breeden "[stayed] with his work indomitably,"[2] Company A's Private Russell Pickett came to and found himself lying on wet sand. Just before his craft had landed, he had heard a "low rumble" and had then been knocked unconscious. A dead man, whom he guessed had pulled him up the beach, now lay twelve feet away. The tide lapped at Pickett's feet. He couldn't move his legs. He didn't know how long he'd been unconscious. All he had was a combat knife. Someone had pulled off his pack. "I began to think I'd been hit in the back and I worked my arms around to feel but I couldn't find anything wrong."[3]

Petrified he would drown with the incoming tide, Pickett desperately grabbed for Mae West life preservers among macabre flotsam nearby. He put one under each arm and another around his chest and began to float ashore. He saw a replacement from Ohio nicknamed "Whitey"—he only knew a handful of men in Company A by their real names. "He got shot and it knocked him down and he got up again and they hit him again, in the leg, and spun him around," Pickett recalled. "Then he crawled away, out of my sight, even after he'd been hit twice."

Pickett recognized another man, a Lieutenant Fergusson, a recent replacement who had played football for the U.S. Army. "He was huge. I knew him pretty well because he'd sneak around and play poker with us guys in training. He'd been hit real bad. The top of his head was down over his face. You couldn't see anything but a mass of bloody flesh. It was like his scalp had peeled down over his face."

"I can't see," shouted Fergusson.

"Turn left and go!"4

Fergusson turned left but was cut down within a few yards by a machine gun.

Pickett fought to keep his head above water as he floated towards the shore with the tide. Eventually, he would be fished out of the water and taken back to the *Empire Javelin*.

The Americans kept coming, Company B arriving at 7 A.M. Radio operator Bob Sales stood a few feet from Captain Ettore Zappacosta, Company B's commanding officer. As their craft came in "on target," right at the base of the Vierville draw, Zappacosta told Sales to "crawl up on the edge and see what you can see."5 The beach was a stone's throw away but Sales couldn't see anybody from Company A fighting, just corpses. Where were the Bedford boys and their buddies? Had they landed elsewhere?

"Captain," shouted Sales, "there's something wrong. There's men laying everywhere on the beach!"

"They shouldn't be on the beach."6

Sales hadn't seen a living soul on the beach but it was obvious that plenty of machine gunners were in the bluffs: Bullets sprayed back and forth, tearing up the beach in puffs of sand.

A British bowman said he was going to drop the ramp. Sales ducked down again. Zappacosta was the first out. MG-42 bullets riddled him immediately. "I'm hit, I'm hit," he called out. Every man who followed Zappacosta down the ramp met the same fate, caught in a relentless crossfire.

Sales would have been killed too but he stumbled as he exited, lost his balance, and fell into the water off the side of the ramp. He was still wearing his radio. He struggled under water to release it; if he didn't get the damned thing off his back, he knew he would never fill his lungs with air again. Sales finally ripped the pack free and surfaced. He was several yards in front of the craft. The machine guns were now enjoying open season. Men were still exiting, still dropping the instant they appeared on the ramp. "Everybody was getting cut down as soon as they came off," Sales said. "Those German machine guns—they just ate us up."[7]

Up above on the bluffs, triggers of the Germans' MG-42 machine guns were hot to the touch. "It was the first time I shoot at living men," recalled one German in 1964. "I don't remember exactly how it was: The only thing I know is that I went to my machine gun and I shoot, I shoot, I shoot."[8]

Sales spotted one of the 1st Battalion's surgeons, Captain Robert Ware, a fellow Virginian with a flaming red buzz cut: "He had brought himself in on an early wave rather than later in the day because he knew there was going to be a lot of wounded. When that ramp went down, they opened up and they got him. Just cut the boat to pieces. He'd got me a three-day pass to London. Treated my knee after a river crossing in England, came from near my home in Lynchburg."[9]

Sales looked around again. He couldn't see any other survivors from his boat. A mortar shell exploded, stunning Sales. Some time later, feeling "very groggy," Sales grabbed onto a log that had been part of a beach defense. A live mine was still attached to one end. Suddenly, another soldier was at his side, helping strip off his heavy assault jacket so he wouldn't drown.

Sales used the log as cover, pushing it in front of him, his face pressed to the wood. Finally, he got to the beach, where he spotted his boat's communications sergeant, Dick Wright, who had jumped off after Zappacosta. He was badly wounded and had been washed ashore. When he saw Sales he tried to raise himself up on his elbows to tell him something. But before he could utter a word, a sniper hiding in rocks along the bluff shot him.

"It looked like his head exploded. Pieces just fell about in the sand. And I lay there, just figuring I'd be next. I said to myself: 'That sniper done and seen me, too.' And evidently something distracted him, another boat maybe, a bigger target, because he didn't get me. I buried my head in the sand as far as I could, put my arms over my head, and I just waited. I reckon I lay there thirty minutes.[10]

"I'd seen a wall, maybe 150 feet away. I thought: 'If I can get to that wall, I got a little protection. And maybe I can get another gun or something.' I had fifty yards to go—a long way, especially when you're expecting a man to kill you. So I started using dead bodies. I would crawl to one, and then real easy, I'd move to another one. That was the only protection."[11]

All around Sales, Company B men were being picked off as they crawled forward. Those lingering on the water line were raked by continuous machine-gun fire. "Man," thought Sales, "I have to be awful careful here."[12] Sales inched forward. The corpses of Bedford boys and others dotted the beach, every ten yards or so. Some faces were familiar. They'd smiled at him across bars. They'd passed him on cold parade grounds.

"I never talked to a living soul from A Company that day," recalled Sales. "But I saw their bodies. I don't remember the names. I was so scared to death. But there was quite a few of them. It was definitely A Company I crawled around—there was nobody else that could have been dead that quick. There'd be a body with legs off, sometimes just a leg, mangled parts. I heard later that Captain Fellers and Captain Zappacosta—couple of great buddies—were washed up on the beach within thirty feet of each other."[13]

Suddenly, Sales saw another Company B man, Private Mack Smith, by a cluster of rocks—at the base of the sea wall. Sales crawled over. He'd made it. Smith had been hit three times in the face. An eyeball lay on his cheek. Sales gave him a "morphine jab," popped the eye back into its socket, and then bandaged him.[14]

"Them's failed, man," said Smith. "We gotta get off this beach. They gotta send boats in for us."[15]

The pair stayed at the sea wall, both in shock, for what felt like an eternity. Sales would be taken off the beach that afternoon but would return before nightfall after persuading a doctor to allow him to join a launch going back for wounded on Omaha. "There wasn't a man off my boat who lived, except me. Not one. Every one of them got killed that day,"[16] he said.

Some men from Company B in Private Hal Baumgarten's landing craft did live, but not many. As his boat neared the shore, slightly to the east of the D-1 draw, icy water crashed in and was quickly up to Baumgarten's waist. Company B's Lieutenant Harold Donaldson leaned against the door of the landing craft. "Well, what the hell are you waiting for?" he shouted. "Take off your helmets and start bailing."[17] Bullets ricocheted off the LCA. To Baumgarten's left, another of Company B's landing craft suddenly exploded, hit by an 88mm shell. Fragments of men and wood showered down.

They moved forward, the thunder of explosions growing louder and louder. Then the ramp was down. Men exited as fast as they could—into the crosshairs of yet another MG-42 machine gun.

Baumgarten jumped, rifle above his head. A bullet skimmed his helmet. He landed in six feet of water, bright red from men mown down in front of him, including Donaldson—killed as soon as he exited.

Baumgarten spotted the sea wall, three hundred yards away. Barbed wire curled along the top. Beyond, a bluff rose a hundred feet or so and

was veined with trenches linking snipers, mortar crews, rocket launch-
ers, and several MG-42s.

Baumgarten waded ashore, bullets spattering around him. There were
two waterproofed tanks to his left. Men huddled against them. One
fired its 76mm cannon at the Germans along the bluffs, now some two
hundred yards away. The other was disabled. A dead man hung from its
turret. The rubber flotation skirts had fallen off both.

Where were the other tanks scheduled to land at the D-1 Vierville
draw?

A machine gun opened up, just above the sea wall, slightly to Baumgarten's left. A bullet hit his rifle. There was a "clean hole in its receiver
in front of the trigger guard. The seven bullets in the receiver had
stopped the German bullet from penetrating the rifle to hit [his]
chest."[18]

Another Company B man, nineteen-year-old private Robert Dittmar,
fell on his back about ten feet away.

"I'm hit—Ma, Mother,"[19] he cried and then lay dead.

Baumgarten dropped to his knees behind a defensive obstacle called
a "Czech hedgehog:" four iron girders welded together to form a star-like
shape. Bedford Hoback lay thirty yards to his left. Hoback looked
wounded. Three others from Company A lay motionless beside him.

"There was a pillbox built into the bluff to my right," recalled Baumgarten. "It appeared to be camouflaged as a seaside cottage. The pillbox's machine gun could sweep the beach laterally with its deadly fire.
What miracle kept me from being hit? I removed the protective latex
condom from the mouth of [a] rifle, and fired at the shine of a helmet
on the bluff slightly to my right . . . after my shot, the gunfire from that
area ceased."[20]

Fighting back felt good. But the feeling didn't last long. Fragments
from an 88mm shell hit Baumgarten in the face, shattering his jaw and
slicing his upper lip in two. "The roof of my mouth was cut up, and teeth
and gums were lying all over inside," he would recall. "Blood poured
freely from the gaping wound."[21] The same shell also hit Bedford

Hoback square in the face. "His head dropped—he was done for. Next to him lay Elmere Wright. I was certain it was him because of his nose; it was just like Dick Tracy's in the cartoon."[22]

Baumgarten washed blood from his face. He was in severe shock yet still able to stand. His limbs were unharmed. He quickly threw off most of his kit and then slithered forward using corpses and "hedgehogs" as cover. There were no reinforcements landing behind him to divert the Germans' fire. Because beach obstacles had not been cleared on Dog Green, Companies C and D had veered far off course and were landing two beach sections to the east. The Germans above the D-1 Vierville draw had nothing to do but pick off anyone who so much as twitched.

Meanwhile, a thousand yards from the beach, John Barnes and Roy Stevens managed to keep their heads above water. They could hear a fierce firefight around the Vierville draw. As they bobbed up and down in the heavy swells, they also heard twenty-year-old Second Lieutenant Gearing's calming voice. He urged them to keep close together. That way they could help the weakest stay afloat.[23]

Sergeant John Laird, a small Scotsman whose family hailed from near Greenock in Scotland, thought they should swim ashore and help Company A fight its way off the beach.

"Let's swim in," he called out.

"No, let's wait here," replied Gearing.

Laird wanted to know how far it was.

At least a thousand yards, someone replied, but no one really knew.

"We can't make it," Gearing insisted. "Too far. We'll wait and get picked up by some passing boat."[24]

Muscles cramped. Men clung to their buddies desperately, hypothermia setting in. Boats passed but none stopped. Then, as men started to die, as their grips on floating objects and each other grew weaker, they heard the "friendly shout of someone with a Limey voice"[25]—Sub-Lieutenant Jimmy Green. As promised, he had returned in LCA 910.

Green and his crew started to pull the men from the water. It was back-breaking work: Some men were twice their normal weight. Green and his crew used their seamen's knives to cut away leaden packs and soggy kit.

Roy Stevens was jarred awake. He saw Clyde Powers clambering aboard Green's boat.

"Clyde, can you help me here!" Stevens cried.

"Sure."[26]

Powers reached out and slowly hauled Stevens into the craft. For most of the time they had spent in the water, Powers had helped Stevens stay afloat.

Stevens fell to the floor and vomited sea water. He shook and shivered. The next thing he knew, a Brit was removing his assault jacket and Mae West. Another handed out cigarettes. Jimmy Green broke out a carton of 200 Capstan duty-free "fags." He apologized as he handed them around. "Sorry, chaps, they're only British, no Camels or Lucky Strike on this boat."[27]

LCA 910's engines gunned. They were heading out into the channel. Many seemed surprised. Others were upset: They were leaving Roy's brother and their buddies to fight it out alone.[28] Under no circumstances, Green said, would they return to the beach. They were in no fit state to fight. They were going back to the *Empire Javelin*.

John Barnes tried to get warm. He recognized two A Company men lying nearby: Russell Pickett, shocked but conscious, and Sergeant Frank Draper Jr., covered in blood.

"Draper was still alive but unconscious," recalled Pickett. "[The] antitank rifle bullet had gone through his left shoulder and upper arm. You could see his heart beating."[29]

Draper was bleeding to death. He had less than an hour to live. "He didn't get to kill anybody," his sister Verona later said. "I'm glad of that."[30]

"How about the others [in Company A]?" someone asked.[31]

Green said they had all landed safely on the beach, unaware of what had then happened when the German machine guns opened up.

Around the same time, Company D's Sergeant Bob Slaughter was approaching Omaha in the fourth wave. A few hundred yards from the beach, he stood up to get a better look at the bluffs, careful to keep his head down: Bullets ricocheted off the boat and whizzed by. There was no sign of the Vierville sur Mer church steeple, the landmark to guide them onto Dog Green. Had it been bombed? Instead, Slaughter saw a fierce brush fire and a pall of black smoke hanging over the bluffs of the Dog White sector of the beach straight ahead. The Germans seemed to be zeroing in on select craft, pouring down every kind of caliber.

The ramp came down. Slaughter froze. The craft bounced up and down in the surf, so violently it was as if he were "riding a bucking bronco." He rose and fell with the ramp two or three times. The men behind him couldn't move. He was blocking their exit. Slaughter jumped off to the side, waded ashore then looked back at his landing craft—several buddies from Roanoke had been hit. They were bleeding badly, some flailing around in the water. One man got caught up in the craft's motor. Slaughter watched him spin "like a top" as he died.

The craft started to pull out to sea. But as it left the beach, ramp still down, it was hit and quickly sank, taking two British sailors with it.

Slaughter could see tanks. A landing craft ablaze. A GI running towards him.

A shot cracked out.

The man went down, stumbling, screaming.

"Medic! Medic!"

A medic rushed over. The Germans got him too, "just drilled him."[32]

Slaughter finally got to the sea wall where he tried to catch his breath.

Several hundred yards to Slaughter's west, Hal Baumgarten was now consumed by rage. It was all so monstrously unjust, so one-sided. He grabbed a dead man's M-1 carbine and quickly flopped back into the water, pretending to be dead, joining a raft of corpses bobbing towards the sea wall with the incoming tide. Baumgarten finally got to the water line. Then dry sand. But there were still another hundred yards before the wall. From some unknown reserve, he found the strength to crawl to it. To the east, Baumgarten saw a group of men from Company A, lying on the sand, dying from their wounds. He recognized a couple. It broke his heart to watch them, scarcely out of their teens, crying for their mothers, calling for their brothers.

"Medic! Medic!"

But where the hell were the medics? Had they all been slaughtered too?

Baumgarten got up and ran east along the sea wall. He tried to pull the wounded a few feet closer to the wall, out of the path of MG-42 bullets and sniper fire.[33] But he could only help a few. There were so many of them. So many young Americans with arms outstretched, only feet from survival.

Baumgarten finally reached the D-1 Vierville draw. A Sherman tank stood at its base. It was knocked out.

The invasion looked like it had failed.[34] A V Corps operational report summed up the situation: "Assault units in state of dissolution. Heaviest casualties. Enemy fire preventing leap across beachline. Disembarked units crowded together within narrowest space. Engineers unable to clear passages through minefields or to demolish foreshore obstacles. Armor and vehicles immobilized on the narrow beach."[35] Of the assault units in dissolution, Company A had suffered most. It was now "inert, leaderless . . . a forlorn little rescue party bent upon survival and the saving of lives."[36]

Baumgarten spotted a good buddy, Private Robert Garbed of Newport News, Virginia. Garbed was dead, facedown. He too had reached the vital D-1 draw. Along the way, he'd paid the ultimate price, as had 102 others from Company A.

13

Every Man Was a Hero

BY 7:30 A.M., THE GERMANS above Dog Green thought they had won the day. They were about to do what Rommel had ordered: Drive the enemy back into the sea. The few Americans still alive were simply target practice. There was no sign of reinforcements.

The commander of the Wilderstansnest (defensive emplacement) 76 telephoned the 352nd Division Headquarters. "At the water's edge at low tide near St. Laurent and Vierville the enemy is in search of cover behind the coastal obstacles," he reported. "A great many vehicles—among these ten tanks—stand burning at the beach. The obstacle demolition squads have given up their activity. Debarkation from the landing boats has ceased, the boats keep farther seawards. The fire of our strong points and artillery was well-placed and has inflicted considerable casualties among the enemy. A great many wounded and dead lie on the beach."[1]

Meanwhile, an increasingly concerned Brigadier General Norman Cota and Colonel Charles Canham approached Dog White beach, seven hundred yards to the east of the D-1 draw. Their boat carried the 29th Division's headquarters staff, including Lieutenant Jack Shea, Cota's aide. Two hundred yards from the shore, they neared a series of timbers set at an angle in the water. Engineers from the 146th Special Underwater Demolition Battalion were supposed to have cleared these deadly obstructions but they had landed over a mile to the east.[2] About a third of the timbers had Teller mines attached to them with rusted, barbed wire.

The boat's coxswain cut the throttle as they prepared to land. A three-knot crosscurrent and the surf swept them against a timber several times, forcing the Teller mine free of the obstacle. To their relief, the mine did not explode. "The coxswain gunned his motor, maneuvered the boat free, and dropped the ramp," recalled Shea. "Moderate small arms fire was directed at the craft as the ramp was lowered."[3]

Cota, Canham, and their staff crossed under fire through three-foot-deep water. Suddenly, they came to a runnel, five feet deep and thirty feet wide. As they waded across it, a Major John Sours, the 116th Infantry's S-4 intelligence officer, was hit in the chest by machine gun fire and fell face down, dead, in the water.[4]

The first available cover was a DD tank of C Company, 743rd Tank Battalion. It and seventeen others stood a few yards past the water line. The tanks had landed six minutes before H-Hour and many had already been immobilized. Two of them, in front of the D-1 draw, were on fire. One was C-5, another DD tank of C Company. It had been hit with rounds from an 88mm gun firing from the concrete pillbox at the base of the D-1 draw. Cota and Canham realized the landing of crucial tanks had been a disaster. There was no covering artillery fire from the beach itself, and this left men exposed to emplacements and machine gunners all along the bluffs.[5]

The Germans were now firing flat-trajectory rounds, watching for where they splashed down and then adjusting their fire. In a couple of minutes, they were able to zero in on landing craft as they ground against the shore. By the time ramps had lowered, most craft were under direct fire. Cota and Canham ran forward and reached the Dog Beach sea wall, five feet high.

The sea wall had small timber fences every fifty yards or so which jutted twenty or thirty feet into the sea. All along it, men formed bedraggled and paralyzed jumbles of several different companies. Engineers cowered next to medics, men from the 2nd and 5th Rangers, and navy personnel. They all shared the same plight. In Lieutenant Shea's words, they were firmly "pinned down!"[6]

Cota and Canham crouched behind the sea wall as German Nebelwerfer and mortar fire increased. Most rounds landed in the sand beyond the sea wall but some exploded among the groups of Americans, causing horrific injuries and heart-stopping panic. The Nebelwerfer rounds broke into very large hunks of shrapnel, commonly the size of a shovel blade, which sliced men in two if hit in the stomach or small of the back. The Nebelwerfers were less fatal than the mortars, however, which sprayed far more fragments over a wider area, and caused most of the deaths on Omaha after the MG-42 machine gun.

The longer men stayed behind the sea wall, the greater chance they stood of being blown to pieces. Shortly after H-Hour, squads from Company C had made their way up the bluffs of Dog White by way of a path marked clearly on their officers' invasion maps. Somehow, the men still pinned down behind the sea wall would also have to find a way off Dog Beach if they were going to live.

But time was running out. Medics were already overwhelmed by the extent of the slaughter, working furiously with limited supplies—often just bandages and morphine spikes and a few capsules of sulfa. Everywhere men lay with severe head and stomach wounds. The limbless died quickly from blood loss unless comrades applied tourniquets, which many did, using strips of rope, belts, and even torn pieces of uniform. Intestines and internal organs had to be pushed back into men struck dumb by terror. There were so many wounded, so many severe cases of trauma, noted Shea, that "gaping head and belly wounds were bandaged with the same rapid efficiency that was dealt to the more minor wounds."[7]

Lieutenant Ray Nance had lost all sense of time as he lay bleeding on the shingle below the sea wall near the Vierville D-1 draw. At some point, he spotted what looked like a German panzer tank. It seemed as if the battle had been lost: The Germans had counterattacked and were driving the 116th Infantry back into the water.

"This thing is a failure," Nance thought. "They're mopping us up."[8]

But then the sun caught the side of the tank. Nance saw the "prettiest white star" placed on all American vehicles. It was a Sherman. He stared at the star. Looking at it made him feel better.[9]

Then, all of a sudden, a navy medic wearing green overalls was leaning over him. Nance was soaked and covered in oil and grease. The medic looked immaculate, dry as a bone. He knelt at Nance's side and started to examine him. He had been in combat before. That was clear from the way he handled himself under fire.

"This is worse than Salerno," he told Nance.

The medic gave Nance a shot of morphine, opened up his hobnailed boot and dressed his heel wound. At some point, Nance had also been shot in the hand and again in his foot. He was one of the very lucky. He had "million-dollar" wounds serious enough to put him out of the war but not life-threatening.

"Good luck," said the navy medic.

Then he was gone. Wounded men around Nance hadn't seen him: Nance was delirious—the man was a figment of his imagination. But Nance knew he was real. He just knew it. Heaven-sent, the medic had saved him and moved on. Only God knew where.[10]

Nance looked around, the morphine starting to kick in. He saw two dead men lying face up. He recognized both. One was an officer from D Company. Suddenly, he was aware of another man beside him: Cecil Breeden.

Breeden checked Nance's dressings and said he had seen the bodies of Captain Fellers, John Schenk, and John Wilkes. All of them had probably been killed by machine-gun fire within minutes of arriving on the beach.[11] As far as Breeden knew, Nance was the only living officer from Company A and therefore in command of what was left of it.

Meanwhile, Cota and Canham were moving from one group of men to another, urging them to arm themselves with whatever weapons they could scavenge and then get up and off the beach. Suddenly, Canham was shot through the left wrist. He continued along the beach, toting a Colt .45 in his good hand, blood gushing from his wound.

"Medic!"

Cecil Breeden arrived, wrapped a bandage around Canham's wrist and then quickly moved on. Cota suggested Canham be evacuated.

Canham refused and set off along the sea wall, looking for a gully, a weak point, anywhere to get up to the bluffs. His bodyguard followed closely behind, reloading Canham's Colt .45 every few minutes.

Behind the sea wall at the base of the D-1 draw, Hal Baumgarten looked east and saw a figure, back straight, walking along the beach, "an angel of mercy,"[12] bending down here and there to comfort the dying and patch up others. . . . When Cecil Breeden finally got to Baumgarten, he handed him twelve sulfa tablets and told him to drink some water. He was badly dehydrated. Shells and mortar rounds began to land all around them. Breeden leaned over, seemingly oblivious to the heavy fire, and put a pressure bandage on Baumgarten's face.

Baumgarten tried to pull Breeden down, out of the line of fire, but he slapped his hand away.

"You're hurt now," said Breeden. "When I get it, you can take care of me."[13]

In Baumgarten's eyes, Breeden was "probably the single greatest hero of D-Day."[14] Breeden would survive the war, accompanying Company A all the way to Germany, and would not receive a scratch. Despite long and concerted efforts by many survivors, notably Baumgarten, Breeden died without receiving a military honor in recognition of his heroism on Omaha Beach—a heroism that sustained hope among those who were a breath from dying.

According to a subsequent report by the United States Army Medical Department, because of the "actions and example of men like the medic Breeden, [Company A] survivors found the will to rescue many of the wounded from the advancing tide and move off the beach to a sheltered position where the remnants of the company rallied. Were it not for Breeden all of them might well have died on the beach."[15]

"Every man was a hero, [I] never saw a coward," Breeden later said with typical self-effacement. "When I found Baumgarten, he had his cheek about over his ear. I patched him up and went on my way. I glanced now and then at the boys trying to take that damned pillbox [at the base of the draw]. As I remember, it took six or more to do it. As far as I know, none of them lived. I couldn't tell you who any of them were. I was just too busy to know what was going on around me."[16]

Breeden left Baumgarten at about 8:15 A.M. All along Dog Green, men were starting to organize, terror and determination on their faces. They included "Big Bill" Presley, Master Sergeant of B Company.[17] Breeden saw Presley walking along the beach, seemingly oblivious to the bullets and shrapnel hissing all around.

"What are you doing?" asked Breeden.

"Looking for a damn rifle that will work," said Presley, pointing up to the bluffs. Some of his men had moved past the sea wall.

"Get down or you'll get hit," Presley ordered.

"What the hell are you talking about?" replied Breeden. "You're a damn sight bigger target than me."

Presley grinned and walked on. Before long, he came back, toting an M-1 carbine, waved at Breeden, and then joined his men.[18]

By 8:30 A.M., approximately five thousand troops had been landed on the 6,500 yards of Omaha Beach. Out at sea, naval commanders realized something had gone terribly wrong. According to the Overlord plan, the 1st and 29th Divisions should be inland by now. But when observers peered through binoculars and telescopes, they saw wave after wave of soldiers jammed together on the beach. Along the surf line lay a gruesome jetsam of dead men, body parts, and vast quantities of equipment essential to forcing exits from the beach: TNT packages, boxes of ammunition, wire-cutters, and countless Bangalore torpedoes. The loss of communications equipment was especially grave. Three out of four radios among the 116th Infantry battalions were useless.[19]

Realizing that covering fire was essential, given that most of the amphibious tanks were out of action or sunk, U.S. Navy and British Royal Navy commanders brought their boats as close to the shore as possible, a couple actually scraping the sea bed, and trained their five-inch guns on the bluffs. But where were they to fire? Only a couple of the men fighting for their lives along the sea wall had radios to direct the ships' salvos. Nonetheless, the warships opened up. At one point, desperate men had to use flag signals to stop a heavy barrage of their sector. But for most men, such as Bob Slaughter, the shelling was a much-needed boost to morale.

Since coming ashore, Slaughter had crouched down behind the sea wall. Suddenly, he saw several officers moving towards him. Slaughter recognized Canham, his arm in a sling, a Colt .45 in his good hand.[20]

"They're murdering us here!" Canham shouted. "Let's move inland and get murdered!"

"Who the hell is that son of a bitch?" asked one GI.[21]

Every Stonewaller would know before the day was out, for Canham seemed to roam everywhere. "We'd have shot him in training," recalled Company A's Russell Pickett. "But once the fighting started, he was a true soldier."[22] Few veterans disagree that Canham was the most outstanding regimental commander on D-Day.

Brigadier General Norman Cota was just as brave and inspirational. He also gave men hope when there was none. Some found the will to fight on simply by looking at him as he strode about defiantly, back straight, chewing his unlit cigar, mumbling ditties to himself when he wasn't cursing the Germans.

Hal Baumgarten would never forget seeing Cota's rangy figure approach him that morning. It was as if he was immortal; from the outset, officers had been first to be picked off by snipers. "He was coming from the west with a major, had a pistol in one hand, and the fellows were all yelling for him to get down. He looked very similar to the actor Robert Mitchum with his slanted eyebrows. He was very, very brave."[23]

All along Dog Beach, others watched as Cota still moved from one group to another, now urging the Rangers to lead the way off the beach. Inspired by Cota, officers began to organize their men for an advance.

Cota had spotted a section of the sea wall with a low mound of earth five yards beyond it. He ordered a Ranger to place a Browning automatic rifle on the mound. He then crawled after the man and ordered him to provide covering fire. Next, Cota organized the blowing of an opening in a thick barbed wire fence that ran along the far side of a ten-foot-wide promenade road beyond the sea wall.

Smoke from a grass fire now partly obscured the beach. Cota seized the opportunity to move while the German gunners' view was obscured.

"Rangers, lead the way!"

The first man to run through the opening was cut down by an MG-42. "Medic," he yelled. "Medic, I'm hit. Help me."[24]

A few minutes later, he sobbed "Mama" over and over and then died.

Many of the men around Cota were again paralyzed by fear. Cota once more led by example, dashing through the opening. Troops followed him across the promenade, through the gap in the wire and into a field of marsh grass. Cota, his aide Shea, and several squads wormed their way along shallow trenches and finally reached the base of the Vierville bluffs.[25]

"A single file of troops, composed of rifle men of the 116th 1st Bn, and headquarters, Rangers, and some members of the 82nd Chemical Mortar Battalion (armed with carbines) then ascended the bluffs, diagonally and to the right," Shea later wrote. "They reached the crest at a point about 100 yards to the west of a small, concrete foundation (evidently a summer house) which lay twenty-five yards below the crest of the bluff. A few anti-personnel mines were detonated during the ascent, but they were not in great number."[26]

It was now about 9 A.M. Canham had set up the 29th's first command post at the base of the bluffs. He tried but failed to make contact with the 1st Division on the eastern half of Omaha Beach. Suddenly, several rounds of very accurate two-inch mortar fire landed on the post. The mortars killed two men three feet from Cota and seriously wounded his radio operator, throwing him thirty feet up the bluff. Cota's aide, Lieutenant Shea, was blown seventy-five feet below but only slightly hurt.

Cota carried on climbing, urging men on. Again, the advance stalled, this time just below the crest of the bluffs. Someone yelled out that they should take a look below. A lone American rifleman walked along the promenade road. "Before him marched five German prisoners who had been stripped of their weapons and who held their hands above their heads. Inasmuch as they were the first Germans the men had seen, they caused particular interest."[27]

An MG-42 snarled. Two prisoners were cut down. The American dived towards the sea wall. Two other prisoners fell to their knees, as if begging the German machine gunner to spare them. "The next burst caught the first kneeling German full in the chest," recalled Shea, "and as he crumpled the remaining two took to the cover of the sea wall with their captor."[28]

Cota finally reached the top of the bluffs. Another machine gun was firing from a hedgerow three hundred yards inland across a level field. Men huddled out of sight below the crest of the bluffs. Cota asked who was in charge. No one replied. "In the face of the fire," Shea reported, "[Cota] passed through the men, personally led them in a charge across the field instructing them to fire at the hedgerows as they advanced. . . . The machine gun fire stopped as soon as the troops started to move across the fields towards it."[29]

Cota then led his men along the perimeter of the field, using the hedgerow as cover, until he reached a narrow lane 600 yards from Vierville sur Mer. As he advanced along the lane, Cota saw other survivors from the 116th's 1st Battalion and Rangers who had also fought their way off the beach. There was minimal opposition as Cota and these men entered Vierville sur Mer and then headed for the crossroads where Roy Stevens was supposed to meet his brother Ray in the center of the town. At the crossroads, about noon, Cota reunited with Colonel Canham.

The remnants of the 1st Battalion would advance further west to assist Rangers assigned that morning to knocking out gun positions on cliff tops at Point du Hoc at the far end of Omaha Beach. It was also essential, before the Germans counterattacked, to open the D-1 draw so that vehicles and troops could move inland and establish a beachhead. Cota formed a patrol with three officers and two enlisted men and set off towards the D-1 draw.

The tide was turning in favor of the Americans at last. By now, other groups had also broken through the beach defenses and were fighting their way up the bluffs all along Dog Green and other sectors of Omaha. Hal Baumgarten joined eleven other men, most of them wounded. Now they were scrambling along a trench midway up the Vierville bluffs, stepping over dead Germans. One had his head blown off. Baumgarten wondered if it was the man he'd fired on earlier that morning.

A machine gun fired from a beach house nearby. Despite his wounds, Baumgarten was feeling "remarkably strong."[30] Adrenaline coursed through him. He spotted a German, took aim, and fired. It was only the second time he'd done so that day. A small redhead tossed a grenade and the machine gun fell silent. Baumgarten's group was now down to eight men. All afternoon, Baumgarten would fight on with the remnants of Company A and B. By 5 P.M., his group would be down to seven men and have killed at least ten more Germans.

More and more men were getting off Dog Beach and moving inland. Captain Robert Walker of the 116th Infantry's headquarters had swum ashore around 7:30 A.M. By 12:30 P.M., he was "about halfway to the top" of the bluffs. "I rested for awhile in a small gully," he recalled. "After awhile, I heard the sound of someone groaning nearby and calling for help. It was about fifteen or twenty feet away. Cautiously I went over to investigate and saw it was a German soldier, gravely wounded in his groin. He had already been treated by a medical aid man. He had a bandage loosely fixed over the wound, sprinkled with sulfa powder. He was gasping, 'Wasser, wasser'—German for water.

"I assumed he had been given a sulfa pill which causes great thirst. In German I told the man I had no water with me and didn't know where to get any. He then said there was a spring. He called it 'ein born,' about fifty feet away. I didn't believe him but I made my way over to the area he indicated. Incredibly, there actually was a spring, a sort of water hole with apparently clear water in it. I filled my helmet with water and brought it to him. After drinking thirstily, he thanked me profusely. I left him some water in his canteen cup. Later on his groans became weaker and he soon died."³¹

Twelve miles out at sea, John Barnes, Roy Stevens, and other survivors from their landing craft boarded the *Empire Javelin*. Most were near naked beneath blankets. Some had even lost their dog tags. Their shock had given way to a deadening exhaustion. They ached for sleep but could not. The battle for Omaha was still raging.

The *Empire Javelin* was unnervingly quiet. Only a few hours ago, its decks had been crammed with anxious men. John Barnes salvaged his wallet from his drenched kit. He took out his invasion currency, laid out the notes on a bunk to dry, and then went on deck. Some time later, he returned to the bunk to lie down. The money was gone.

Several men wanted to re-arm and take the next landing craft back to the beach. They were told this was not possible. The surviving LCAs were not fit for further use on D-Day. Most were badly damaged and covered in gore and vomit. The flotilla had to return to England for essential repairs. Besides, the men were too exhausted to fight effectively. "We were to stay on board, go back to England, get re-armed and make our way back to the company," recalled John Barnes. "Gearing had picked up a spare rifle and said he would hitch a ride on a passing U.S. craft. He ordered us to stay together and left Sergeant Stevens, our NCO leader, in charge. There was no doubt that Stevens would get us back since he was concerned about his brother, Ray."³²

Bedford boys Roy Stevens, Charles Fizer, Harold Wilkes, and Clyde Powers could hear a constant barrage, especially intense between midday and 1 P.M. when several American and British destroyers, now directed by shore observers, pounded the pillbox and trenches around the D-1 draw.

The explosions knocked several men in Cota's patrol off their feet. "The concussion from the bursts of these guns seemed to make the pavement of the street in Vierville actually rise beneath our feet," recalled Lieutenant Shea.

"I hope to hell they cut out that firing," said one of Cota's men.

The batteries of the *Texas* battleship fired four salvos of four rounds each. Fellow destroyer *McCook* then radioed shore that Germans were fleeing the pillbox at the base of the draw and other strong points.

As Cota and his patrol entered the draw from Vierville, the naval barrage stopped. Smoke cleared, revealing a road frosted with concrete dust and shrouded in bitter-tasting cordite fumes. The road led down to Dog Beach.

"That firing probably made them duck back into their holes," warned Cota. "But keep a sharp eye on those cliffs to your right."

They moved down the draw. "There were a few scattered rounds of small arms fired at the patrol, but a dozen rounds of carbine and pistol fire sufficed to bring five Germans down from the caverns in the east wall of the draw," recalled Shea. "They were stripped of their weapons as they reached the road, and herded before the patrol as it proceeded to the mouth of the draw."[33]

The Germans led the way through a minefield at the entrance of the draw and then Cota and his patrol walked out onto Omaha Beach.

Near the base of the draw, and at an aid station on Dog Beach, there were a cluster of Rangers and dozens of badly wounded and dog-tired Company A and B survivors. Among the wounded were Bedford boys Dickie Overstreet, Anthony Thurman, Lieutenant Ray Nance, and the 116 Yankee baseball player, Tony Marsico.

Staff Sergeant Anthony Thurman had been hit in the arm and the shoulder; his nerves were also shot to pieces. He would never fully recover from the psychological trauma caused by D-Day.[34] Sergeant Marsico had been hit in the leg and shot through the arm by a rifle bullet as he crossed the sands. "I thought [the invasion] would be pretty hot but I didn't know it was going to be like that," recalled Marsico, who would soon be evacuated to a hospital in England along with his surviving comrades from Bedford. "I'm no hero. I know that. The heroes are the ones who didn't make it."[35]

There was one last obstacle blocking the road from the beach to Vierville—an antitank wall at the mouth of the draw. An engineer placed a TNT charge beside it and the wall was blown around 1:30 P.M. Then Rangers moved up the draw and started to mop up last pockets of German resistance along the bluffs.

At enormous cost, the 116th Infantry and Rangers had secured the D-1 draw. The challenge would now be to keep it. Wanting to check on progress at the other end of the 29th Division's section of assigned beach, Cota walked off along the promenade road leading to the next village to the east, Les Moulins.[36]

Later that afternoon, after securing Vierville, men began to return to the beach for medical aid. Twenty-seven-year-old Private Warner "Buster" Hamlett of F Company managed to hobble down to the sands. "Thousands of bodies were lying there. You could walk on the bodies, as far as you could see along the beach, without touching the ground. Parts of bodies—heads, legs, and arms—floated in the sea. Medics were walking up and down, tagging the wounded. As I stepped gently between my American comrades, I realized what being in the first wave was all about."[37]

Lieutenant Ray Nance lay at an aid station on the beach. A sergeant had carried him that morning on his shoulder several hundred yards along the sea wall. "Late that afternoon," recalled Nance, "Second Lieutenant Gearing landed by himself. . . . He came over to me and I got him up on what I knew. I said: 'Hey, I think you're it—company commander.' I never felt so sorry for a person when he left. He didn't know what he was getting into."[38] Gearing was the only officer from Company A who had not been killed or wounded. Of the five officers in Nance's berth on the *Empire Javelin* that morning, only Nance and Gearing were still alive.

At 7 P.M., Ray Nance spotted another familiar figure—General Gerhardt, commander of the 29th Division. He looked as immaculate and confident as ever as he came ashore, his shiny twin revolvers at his waist. By nightfall, Gerhardt would have set up a command post in a quarry near the Vierville draw.

For Hal Baumgarten, the battle was not yet over. Towards evening, he had penetrated all the way to the top of the bluffs and was headed towards a village to the west of Vierville called Maissey le Grand. As Baumgarten crawled along a road he tripped a "castrator mine." A bullet shot through his foot.

"When I turned [my] shoe over, blood poured out like water from a pitcher," recalled Baumgarten. "Using my first aid kit, I powdered with sulfa and dressed my foot, which had a clean hole through it."[39] Suddenly, Baumgarten came under heavy shellfire. He tore off the dressing and crammed his foot back into his boot and jumped into the cover of a hedgerow. He stayed there with seven other GIs until darkness fell and then took off across the road to find fresh cover. The German shelling had gotten more accurate—Baumgarten suspected they'd been observed.

As Baumgarten and his group moved forward, an MG-42 opened up, hitting every man. "I was shot through my left lip and lost part of my right upper jaw, teeth and gums." Nearby, one of the men shouted: "Help me, Jesus!" The others moaned in pain. Baumgarten drifted into a "hallucinatory dream state":

I pictured a box of goodies from my mother that I was opening back in Camp D-1. The homemade cookies, cake, and salami were shared with my Company A buddies. They were cooking the green mold covered salami (result of the long shipping time from the States), stuck on their bayonets over an open fire.[40]

Back on Dog Beach, Thomas Valance—one of the few survivors from Master Sergeant John Wilkes's boat—watched darkness fall around 11 P.M. He had been placed on a stretcher in a clearing surrounded by barbed wire. Sometime after dark, litter-bearers moved him onto a LST loaded with wounded and emergency medical equipment. He was headed back to England. After three months in various hospitals, he would return to Normandy and then fight on through Germany before going back to America in December 1945.

"I've wondered over the years about one thing," Valance wrote on Veteran's Day 1987, "and that is why we, in A Company of the 1st Battalion, 116th Infantry, 29th Division, were chosen to be the American equivalent of stormtroopers. Was it because we had such potential? We had no combat [experience], and the other troops that were around and with us in the invasion, such as the 1st Division, were highly trained. Or was it simply because we were considered expendable?"[41]

Finally, the longest day drew to a close. There had been an estimated 2,500 casualties on Omaha, and less than a tenth of that number on Utah, the other American beach. Total casualties—dead and wounded—for the entire Allied invasion forces approached 10,000, a loss of 10 percent given that just over 100,000 men were now in Normandy, and far less than the 25 percent that Allied generals had predicted for infantrymen.[42]

All along the bluffs and hedgerows that had cost so many lives, the 116th Infantry dug in for the night. Most men had not slept in well over two days. Many barely had the strength to scoop out shallow foxholes. "We started to dig a foxhole," recalled one private, "but the ground was rock hard and we were both totally exhausted by the time the hole was about three inches deep. Finally, standing there in the dark, aware that it was useless to continue, my sergeant said, 'Fuck it. Let's just get down and get some rest.' And so, D-Day came to an end with both of us sitting back to back in the shallow trench throughout the night."[43]

Sometime near midnight, Hal Baumgarten awoke on the road above Omaha's bluffs and saw German fighter planes above. All the men in his group lay dead from their wounds. Baumgarten felt as if he was dying. There was little pain—just a cold clamminess, and pins and needles all over. To fend off the agony from four wounds received in twenty hours, he had continually injected himself with morphine. To prevent dehydration, he drank from his dead buddies' canteens.

Company D's Bob Slaughter saw the same belated attack by the Luftwaffe. "An enemy ME-109 fighter plane flew over the entire Allied fleet, from right to left above the barrage balloons. Every ship in the English Channel opened fire on that single airplane, illuminating the sky with millions of tracer bullets. The heroic Luftwaffe pilot defied all of them—not even taking evasive action. I wondered how he ever got through that curtain of fire."[44]

Company B's Bob Sales and several exhausted Virginians settled down to snatch desperately needed sleep. "It was very cold," recalled Sales. "I never dreamed it could be so cold in France in June. So I traded a bunch of K rations with an old woman for a blanket and slept with my gun right beside me, back to back with another guy. I woke up suddenly and I thought it was Bob Slaughter poking me awake but he wasn't moving. It was the old French woman trying to steal the blanket back. I pointed my gun at her and she ran off."[45]

Around 3 A.M. two medics lifted Hal Baumgarten into an ambulance. His uniform was dripping with the blood of his fellow Stonewallers, men who "gave above and beyond, and [would] never be cited for their bravery."[46] The ambulance took Baumgarten down to Dog Beach where he was placed on a stretcher besides other wounded.

Incredibly, the battle was still not over for Baumgarten and the men around him. "While I was laying on the beach on a stretcher, around 10 A.M. on June 7th, a sniper shot one of the aid men right through his red cross. Then he shot me in the right knee and started picking off all the wounded next to me. The next shot would have gone through my head. But the destroyer *McCook* offshore blasted away the sniper before he got to kill me."[47]

Baumgarten's longest day was finally over. For the few who had survived unscathed, the nightmare of Normandy had only just begun.

14

Bedford's Longest Day

JUNE 6, BEDFORD, VIRGINIA. Viola Parker dozed next to her radio. At 2 A.M., a stern voice interrupted a broadcast: "German radio says the invasion has begun."[1] It was 8 A.M. on Omaha Beach, ninety minutes after Company A had landed.

Just after the 2 A.M. newscast, Elva Newcomb woke up in her log cabin. She instinctively checked on her three children: Nancy, Bill, and Garland. They were sleeping soundly. "I had been worried about Earl for some time," she recalled. "His mail had been held up for some reason. I turned on the radio and heard about the invasion. Then I was really worried because they were saying we might have to pull out because it was so rough. I couldn't sleep after that."[2]

At 3:32 A.M., Viola Parker's radio announced that the Supreme Headquarters of the Allied Expeditionary Force in London was confirming German reports of an invasion. Viola finally stirred at 4 A.M., turned up the volume on her radio, and heard: "Under the command of General Eisenhower, Allied naval forces, supported by strong air forces, began landing Allied armies this morning on the northern coast of France."[3]

As the sun rose, the bells of Bedford's central Presbyterian Church began peeling.

Bells rang all across the United States that morning, from Alaska to Florida. The great crusade had finally begun.

In Philadelphia, mayor Bernard Samuel tapped the famous Liberty Bell for the first time since 1835.

In New York, a two-minute silence marked the opening of markets on Wall Street and then the money men and war-profiteers returned to their war efforts. The Dow Jones would rise 142 points that day to a new high for the year. In many factories and stores, workers were told to go home. Broadway shows were canceled, as were all baseball games. Newspapers cleared advertising and features to make space for blanket coverage of the invasion. In Times Square, somber crowds craned their necks to watch news bulletins flicker across message-boards high in the clear summer sky.

In her parlor in Bedford, Ivylyn Schenk sat with her mother close to an old radio. "Mama brought me what she thought I would enjoy eating, and she sat there with me most of the day as we listened to all the reports," recalled Ivylyn. "I knew that John would be involved in the invasion. He had not told me anything directly but in a round-about way I knew."[4]

Across town, other wives and parents also rose early; many, like Elva Newcomb, worked the day's first shift in several of Bedford's factories producing war supplies. Bettie Wilkes switched on the radio while eating breakfast. At 7 A.M., she had to be at the Belding Hemingway plant, where she made material used for parachutes—the same parachutes used by the 101st Airborne on D-Day. "I caught the early news. I thought John might be involved but I hoped he was not. We were just hoping to get through the war, begin our lives together. . . . In his most recent letter, John had said: 'I probably won't be able to write for a while, but I will as soon as I can.'"[5]

Twenty-year-old Bertie Fellers prayed that morning for her brother, Captain Fellers, and for her husband, Clarence Higginbotham, who was serving with the Engineer Corps in England. "The previous evening," she recalled, "my mother and my sister and I had attended a prayer service at Oakland Methodist Church near our home. We knew something was going on even though we had not yet had news."[6] Bertie had just sent her brother a birthday card. He should have been thirty on June 10.

At 7:30 A.M., over a hundred conscientious objectors boarded trucks at the former CCC camp at Kelso. They would spend all day working on local farms before returning to the camp at 5:30 P.M.

As other Bedford residents went to work, they picked up the *Bedford Bulletin* from their mailboxes or in stores.

That week's paper contained an eerily prescient full-page advertisement for war bonds: "America—this is it! Don't let them down! Do your part as they are doing theirs . . . This is America's Zero Hour—Civilization's Zero Hour!"[7] It was also reported that a plaque honoring servicemen in arms had been erected at Hampton Looms with names added as employees left for service. It already held the names of Frank Draper Jr. and Clifton Lee.

Election season was well under way in Bedford on June 6, 1944. Sergeant Allen Huddleston's former boss, Dr. W. L. Lyle of Lyle's drugstore, was running hard for mayor against incumbent J. W. Gillaspie, who had been challenged only three times during a fourteen-year-term. Lyle hoped to turn Bedford into "THE tourist town of the State, perhaps of the South."[8] The vote would be on June 13, exactly a week after D-Day. A turnout of over 90 percent was expected.

The *Bulletin* also mentioned that parents throughout Bedford County were worried about an outbreak of infantile paralysis. Medical authorities had begun to urge them to keep their children away from crowded places until the epidemic was over. Nevertheless, local Girl Scouts were still going from house to house canvassing for a forthcoming bond rally organized by the town's undertaker, Harry Carder.

It was a beautiful morning, warm but not too humid. Up on the Peaks of Otter, ramblers noticed that the dogwood blossom had passed. Rhododendron and laurel were still in bloom, and monks' hood and May apple had taken the place of trillium and ladies' slippers. Cherry trees promised a bumper crop. Down in the valley, in Bedford's Mud Alley, trains crammed with war supplies and troops passed Frank Draper Jr.'s home. His mother and sister, Verona, worked in Frank Sr.'s garden, harvesting the season's first vegetables, which they had planted in March. Canning had started in earnest. Tobacco farmers throughout the county were also starting to harvest, hoping they would receive even higher prices at the Bedford Tobacco

Market than they had the previous year. Prices had risen significantly since before the war.

Local stores advertised Father's Day gifts for June 18. "Shop early for Fathers in the service!" they declared. Brightly striped broadcloth pajamas, sizes A,B,C,D, were a bargain at $2.98. It was also bargain day at Liberty cinema—adults were charged just twenty cents to see the musical extravaganza *Trocadero* starring Rosemary Lane.

Around mid-day, Bedford native Eleanor Yowell sat down and wrote to her husband, a pilot based in England:

> The big news came this morning, and my heart has been so full all day it's been hard for me to get anything done. I know it is a big show, probably the biggest that has ever been staged in the world for that matter, but it still is so damn unnecessary that it makes your blood boil when you think that a few people whom money and power control started the whole business. They are not the ones who have to pay for it either; it is the innocent masses of people who do. We are having a prayer service over here at 2:30 this afternoon, and Dr. Grey is coming over to lead it. All the churches everywhere are having services all day long. Let's hope that these prayers will be heard for the good of everyone.[9]

One man from Company A was actually in Bedford on June 6. In October 1943, Sergeant Pride Wingfield had been accepted for training into the Army Air Force and was now on furlough from a camp in Missouri. He listened to the radio with his mother in their 1933 home on Oak Street, a block from Bedford High School, which had graduated its 1944 class the week before.

Wingfield had recently started dating a pretty nineteen-year-old, Rebecca Lockard, who worked in a beauty shop, Modernique, above Green's drugstore. They would marry on October 22, 1945. "I was always running down there, getting change or sandwiches," recalled Rebecca. "It was a focus for women in the community, especially us women who had been left behind. When word got back about D-Day, we all finally knew what the boys had gone over to England for."[10]

At the back of the drugstore, twenty-one-year-old Elizabeth Teass worked at the Western Union counter. Her hours were from 9:30 A.M. to 5 P.M. All morning she watched as townspeople came in and sat and talked over lunch, a Coke, or fresh coffee. There was just one topic of conversation—D-Day.

Three thousand miles away in England, Bedford boy Sergeant Allen Huddleston heard about the invasion on a radio in a rehabilitation center where he was nursing his ankle back to full strength. It would be several weeks before he realized how lucky he had been to avoid D-Day: "Somebody was looking after me."[11]

In town centers across the rest of Britain there was no dancing in the streets. Silence that morning seemed to blanket much of the island: Everybody was caught up in his or her own thoughts, thinking of relatives involved, reflecting on the long years since Dunkirk. That afternoon, King George VI addressed his subjects via the BBC: "This time the challenge is not to fight to survive but to fight to win the final victory for the good cause. . . . At this historic moment surely not one of us is too busy, too young, or too old to play a part in a nation-wide, perchance a world-wide, vigil of prayer as the great crusade sets forth."[12]

All along Britain's south coast, doctors and young nurses prepared to receive the first wounded from the invasion beaches. John Reynolds's "sweetheart," the American nurse Kathleen Bradshaw, worked in a hospital in Plymouth. Now she knew why John had been unable to see her for several weeks.

Another nurse, Mary Verrier, worked at the Queen Alexandra's Hospital in Portsmouth. Early that afternoon, she went down to the Victorian South Parade Pier to help transport badly maimed men to the hospital. Two days earlier, Portsmouth harbor had been packed with boats and landing craft. Now gray boats slowly pulled into harbor, crammed with wounded. Verrier would later write:

It was a privilege to serve those lads. They never moaned or asked people to hurry up when they were laid on their stretchers waiting to come in. They lay there with patience, a joke and a smile. One chap who was badly burned said to me, "I'm quite good looking really, you know, nurse." I said, "Your eyes are not bad now, they're quite saucy." So he said, "You wouldn't like to give us a kiss, would you, nurse?" We weren't allowed, but I looked around and I bent down and kissed him on his horribly burned lips with the awful smell coming off his burns.[13]

Back in America, another nurse—Eloise Rogers—tended to the sick at a 128-bed hospital in Richmond, Virginia. She had started work at 7 A.M. in the busy civilian hospital, helping with the delivery of babies, taking temperatures, replacing dressings. She heard about the invasion over the radio and immediately thought of her brothers, Clyde and Jack Powers, as well as many of the other Bedford boys such as Harold Wilkes, with whom she had played as a young girl. "I then realized they were probably involved with the invasion. But I only understood what that meant later when I saw a newsreel. That day, I was twenty, getting on with my life. As far as I knew, the boys were still away on some big adventure."[14]

That adventure gave millions hope. In their cramped hideaway in Amsterdam, Anne Frank and her Jewish family heard of the invasion on their radio. Anne wrote in her diary: "The best part of the invasion is that I have the feeling that friends are approaching. We have been oppressed by those terrible Germans for so long, they have had their knives so at our throats, that the thought of friends and delivery fills us with confidence!"[15]

That afternoon in Bedford, journalists at the *Bedford Bulletin* prepared the following report:

News of the invasion brought a feeling of uneasiness to hundreds of Bedford county homes for many of them have sons, husbands and brothers in the army in England. Old Company A has been in training there for nearly two years and probably was among the first landing forces, and hundreds of other Bedford county men will ultimately be thrown into the fight, and among them some casualties can be expected.[16]

Mrs. George P. Parker also prepared a report that day which she would send to the Virginia state authorities:

Church bells and chimes, but no whistles, have announced the beginning of the invasion. A feeling of awe and extreme quiet is prevailing. One woman who has a brother with the Army in England said, with trembling voice, "I don't know how to describe my feeling. I can't cry and I can't laugh." A doctor, sitting in a home of illness, heard the announcement before day. The family seemed stunned. There were no comments by anybody—just a quiet tenseness. Churches have been open . . . with sad-faced worshippers going in and out constantly. Tears only occasionally.[17]

At around 2 P.M., many townspeople made their way through silent streets to a stately brick building with a high steeple, the Presbyterian Church. They filed quietly through double doors and took their places at dark wooden pews. Bright afternoon light streamed through tall, clear glass windows. Dr. J. H. Grey, a small, bony-faced man with a soothing voice, stood before them and asked them to pray. "The [service's] program [also] consisted of music . . . all marking the one theme of supplication to God for guidance and divine aid in the struggle in which the United Nations are engaged."[18]

So many attended—well over three hundred people—that dozens stood outside and listened to the service through the open doors.[19] Mrs. Parker reported: "A crowded house, extreme quiet, and rapt attention marked the simple, deeply spiritual service. So many young people in the congregation."[20]

As soon as they had returned from church later that afternoon, many families tuned to the news broadcasts on their radios. The United Press now reported that the invaders had "met surprisingly little opposition from the enemy land forces and practically none from the German air force, but at points on the beach losses were quite heavy from concentrated machine gun fire. A beachhead was quickly established, troops began pushing inland and within a few hours had gained a strong foothold."[21]

That week's *Bedford Bulletin*, read by many that evening after long shifts in the local factories, included a letter from a Mrs. H. M. Lane. It echoed the prayers of so many families that night as Bedford wondered what had happened to its sons and when news would arrive from Europe:

> Dear Father and Great Maker of all things: Beauty that dies the soonest, lives the longest. Who can fail to see the beauty and sacrifice our brave lads are making? Because they cannot keep themselves for a day, we'll keep them forever in memory and give them immortality.[22]

At dusk in Bedford, about fifty women—three times the usual number—sat in the Bedford County library rolling bandages. By midnight, they added another 9,000 bandages to the 68,300 they had prepared in May.

Finally, Bedford's longest day drew to a close. Families listened to President Franklin Roosevelt as he united all America in prayer:

> Almighty God: Our sons, pride of our nation, this day have set upon a mighty endeavor . . . These men are lately drawn from the ways of peace. They fight not for the lust of conquest. They fight to end conquest. They fight to liberate . . . They yearn but for the end of battle, for their return to the haven of home. Some will never return. Embrace these, Father, and receive them, Thy heroic servants, into Thy kingdom. . . .[23]

Three thousand miles away, as the lights went out in Bedford that night, nineteen of its sons already lay dead.

15

Bocage

EARLY ON JUNE 7, Roy Stevens and the twenty-eight men placed under his command landed in Plymouth, England. They included Bedford boys Charles Fizer, Harold Wilkes, and Clyde Powers, and New Yorker John Barnes. It was as if they were "on a secret mission to a foreign land" recalled Barnes. "We were told not to say where we had been or what had happened. We went to a Reppledepple, that is, a replacement depot. There we were re-armed and sent on our way.... We traveled by civilian train to Southampton. Though the news of the invasion was all over the English papers, we never spoke of anything military to the English people we encountered. At Southampton, we embarked on our second voyage across the channel."[1]

On June 11, Roy Stevens and his boat team returned to Dog Green on Omaha, landing without so much as getting their feet wet. In just four days, the beach had been transformed into a bustling port, through which tens of thousands of reinforcements and countless armored vehicles were now pouring. Most of the corpses had been removed from the beach, although here and there the tide had brought in new bodies that had been sucked out to sea on D-Day. The sun shone fiercely. Barrage balloons dotted the sky "like big white doves" as protection against air attack. The channel was dark blue and glistened in the sun. As Stevens and his men left the beach, they passed the ruins of a pillbox. An American flag had been draped across its encasement.[2]

Before joining Company A, Roy Stevens and Clyde Powers decided to visit a makeshift graveyard near the village of Colleville sur Mer. Not far from the graveyard, they came across a work detail of German prisoners. A few prisoners had passable English. Stevens struck up a conversation. It seemed the Germans had fled the American attack soon after H-Hour. "Why hadn't they stayed in their foxholes," asked Stevens, "and fought to the bitter end?"

"We got scared when we saw all the boats," one of them replied. "So we just got up and left."[3]

The graveyard was lined with several rows of crosses. From each cross dangled a dog tag. Bodies lay in neat rows ready for burial. German prisoners brought yet more in two-wheel carts from piles on the beach. "All they had to bury you in was a bed-sack. They didn't have no coffins or nothing like that. Just a bedsack tied up at the end."[4]

Stevens walked to a section for men with second names beginning with an "S." He scraped some mud from a dog tag. It belonged to his twin brother Ray. In shock, he walked on through the graveyard, looking at more dog tags on more crosses. One bore the name of Jack Powers—Clyde's brother. "We didn't know what to say to each other," remembered Stevens. "I felt like crying but couldn't."[5]

It could not be true. There could not be so many dead from Bedford: By the time Stevens and Powers had walked along each avenue of crosses, they had found all but six of the Bedford boys who had landed on D-Day. How many others had been blown to pieces or washed out to sea and would never be recovered didn't bear thinking about. Corpses discovered on Dog Green beach included those of Master Sergeant John Wilkes . . . Captain Fellers . . . John Clifton . . . Clifton Lee . . . Tony Rosazza . . . John Reynolds . . . Gordon Henry White . . . John Schenk . . . Bedford Hoback . . . Wallace Carter . . . Nicholas Gillaspie . . . Grant Yopp . . . Jack Powers . . . Elmere Wright . . . Ray Stevens. Of the thirty-four Bedford boys who had left the *Empire Javelin* in the early hours of June 6, nineteen were dead.

Stevens and Powers left the graveyard, overwhelmed and dumbstruck by the tragedy.

"How come it ain't me in the ground?" thought Stevens. "Why did my boat sink? Why should I be living when the rest of them paid the price?"[6]

Above all, why in God's name hadn't he shaken his twin brother's hand on D-Day before dawn?

Soon, the shock and guilt had turned to blind rage.

"Clyde, let's go," Stevens told Powers, still reeling at the discovery of his own brother's grave. "Let's get the men who did this."[7]

Later that afternoon, Stevens and Powers rejoined their boat team and headed inland in trucks. By nightfall, they were waiting nervously in tents as rain pelted down. Stevens spoke little, numbed by the deaths of so many of his buddies. The following morning, Stevens and his group boarded trucks again. Soon, they heard artillery fire in the distance. John Barnes began to get a "tight iron band of fear around [his] chest"[8] as the shelling grew louder. Others struggled to control their fear. For Stevens, there were no qualms. All he could think about was getting even: "I was gonna kill a German for every one of my buddies."[9]

The men got closer and closer to combat. "First we came to the 29th Division headquarters, then to regiment and finally, battalion," recalled Barnes. "At battalion we met some of our company cooks. Sergeant Newcomb and Sergeant Jack Mitchell who we called 'Mom' back in Ivybridge because he always took care of us like a mother."[10]

"What happened to Captain Fellers?" someone asked.

"Killed," they replied.

Just three officers from Company A's original nine had survived the landings. Only one was still fighting—Second Lieutenant Gearing. Bedford boy Leslie Abbott had been killed in fierce hedgerow fighting on June 9 as the German 352nd Division launched counterattacks. Now Company A was being brought up to full strength. All the officers except Gearing were new.[11]

"What about [my brother] Ray?" said Stevens.

"Don't know," replied Newcomb. "We haven't had much information. Haven't been able to keep up, it's a mess."[12]

Even though he had seen his brother's grave, Stevens refused to believe he was dead. There had been some mistake. He was missing in action, perhaps wounded. He would turn up some day, he was certain of it. It would be many days before he could accept the reality of his brother's death.

Newcomb explained that he and Company A's mess staff had landed on June 7 on Omaha, rolling out of a landing craft through the surf and up the beach in a ten-wheeled truck pulling a trailer holding a new stove and supplies. Newcomb had then been ordered to set up a temporary mess and take water in a jeep to what was left of Company A.

Jack Mitchell, Company A's supply sergeant, also of Bedford, had joined Newcomb and driven along a narrow road above the bluffs. Eventually, they had found a few dozen men dug in besides a hedgerow. When Newcomb had prepared that evening's meal, only eight men from Company A had arrived at the mess tent. None were from Bedford.[13]

In all, an estimated twenty men, approximately 10 percent of full company strength, had survived the landings and fought past the beach, led by Second Lieutenant Gearing. "[Then] on the fourth day after the landing," Barnes recalled, "[Gearing] had jumped into a trench during a firefight and landed on top of a soldier's bayonet. Both men were surprised, but he was able to shoot the Jerry with his pistol and was only slightly injured by the point of the bayonet."[14]

That evening, Stevens and his boat team were finally led up to the line. Foxholes dotted a thick hedgerow. They were to pair off. A lieutenant told them to dig in for the night. They dug three to four feet deep, and then managed a few snatches of sleep before dawn. Not long after first light, enemy shells started to explode nearby. "Get your ass down, or you won't have it very long," someone shouted.[15]

Few things in Normandy were as terrifying as finding oneself in the target area of an artillery barrage. Every sinew and synapse screamed for a man to run. But fleeing almost invariably meant death: Shrapnel from 88mm shells often shredded any living object within fifty yards. Finally, the barrage ended. Shaken, muscles taut with fear, Stevens and his men crawled forward to form a new line. They passed spent shells, dead Germans, and dead GIs. Cows had been blown to pieces. In nearby fields, they stood in rigor mortis, grotesque carcasses amid the endless "bocage"—the French word for the maze of hedgerows that dominated the landscape.

For hundreds of years, the Normans had cultivated the impregnable bocage. In some areas, its earth base was over three feet high, the hawthorn hedgerow above so thick with thorny branches that TNT had to be used to get through. For the Germans in retreat, by contrast, the bocage was an ideal natural defense. By placing MG-42s at strategic gates and corners of fields, they were able to slow even the boldest American assaults. American infantry companies sometimes fought all day to secure a single hedgerow.

Later that afternoon, the 116th Infantry received orders to secure the Elle River, one of the 29th Division's key objectives on its push towards the strategically vital town of St. Lô, where several important roads intersected. The 115th Infantry had been battered that morning trying to secure the river, losing seven officers and fifty-nine men. Twice as many were wounded.

That night, Company A jumped off and fought across the Elle, encountering heavy small-arms fire, and then set up bivouac for the night. At dawn, Stevens and his men advanced again. By 10:45 A.M. on June 13, Company A and the rest of the 1st Battalion had captured the small town of Couvains. A fierce counterattack was expected. According to the 29th Division official history, *"29 Let's Go!"*: "Patrolling was insisted upon. 29th Division Field Order No. 6 of June 13 instructed each front-line company to send one patrol two miles to the front every twenty-four hours, and each battalion to capture one prisoner in the same period."[16]

Stevens volunteered to lead a patrol. But in his foxhole later he had second thoughts: "I knew I had volunteered for something I should not have. I was sitting in that foxhole and I asked God to help me. The image of Jesus Christ came up on that dirt, and he says: 'Go, you'll come back.'"

Clyde Powers shared Stevens's foxhole.

"Do you want to come?" Stevens asked.

"If you're telling me I got to go, I'll go, but I'm not volunteering."

"If you ain't gonna volunteer, then don't," replied Stevens. "I want you to go of your own free will."[17]

Stevens blacked up with several other volunteers and then crawled towards the enemy lines. As the "getaway man," it was up to Stevens to make sure the enemy did not creep up from behind and surprise the patrol. Stevens suddenly heard a movement and then saw the silhouette of a figure. A private named Kessup had fallen out of position and lagged behind: "I nearly killed him. I would have if I'd remembered to bring a knife with me."

The patrol crossed a hedgerow into enemy territory. A group of Germans opened fire. Stevens dived for cover and returned fire. A sergeant close to him shot a German with his pistol. Stevens threw a grenade. Then he saw one of his patrol go down, badly wounded. He crawled to his side. The man's eyeball was dangling on his cheek. Stevens did his best to dress the wound. The squad regrouped. They had lost a man. He had been challenged by German lookouts and had replied in bad German, only to be instantly shot.

Stevens returned to his foxhole where he sat and prayed. "I had come back," he recalled, "just like Jesus had said. There and then I made a deal with God. 'If you let me get back home,' I asked him, 'I'll be your servant.'"[18]

While Roy chased Nazis at night, Clyde Powers huddled in their foxhole and mourned. Later that summer, he wrote to his parents about his dead brother: "[Jack] is buried on top of a hill, overlooking the English Channel, alongside of the rest of the boys he served with. It is a very pretty place, and the French people have planted flowers there. Just be glad, Mom, that he is not missing, for at least you know where he is now, and that is a lot better. He was killed instantly and there was no suffering on his part. I talked to the boy in the medics that saw him get hit and he said that he died instantly. Will tell you more about it when the war is over."[19]

Despite his close call, Roy Stevens's hunger for vengeance was just as great as the day he found Ray's grave. He joined other dangerous mis-

The Bedford boys leave Ivybridge bound for Omaha Beach, spring 1944.
Allen Huddleston.

Jack Powers, just before being selected to join the elite 29th Division Rangers, England, 1943. *Eloise Rogers.*

"God was looking after me." Allen Huddleston outside Company A's recreation room, Ivybridge, 1943. *Allen Huddleston.*

"What have I gotten into?" New Yorker John Barnes, who joined Company A as a replacement in early 1944. *John Barnes.*

"A first-class fighting force." Bedford boys from Company A after twelve months of rigorous training in England. Front row, right to left: Earl Newcomb beside Roy Stevens. Back row: right to left, John Wilkes, Andrew Coleman, Jack Powers, unidentified soldier, Gordon Henry White. *Elva Newcomb.*

Bob Slaughter of Company D, one of a miraculous few who landed on D-Day on Omaha Beach and was still fighting at the war's end. Photograph taken in Germany, March 1945. *Bob Slaughter.*

Boat Team Number Five, one of seven Company A boat teams that were scheduled to land on Omaha Beach. Photograph taken near the D–1 "sausage" a few days before D-Day. Standing in the back row, left to right: Clyde Powers, Harold Wilkes, unidentified soldier, Lieutenant Edward Gearing, Roy Stevens. Bottom row, fifth from left: John Barnes. *John Barnes.*

The top brass. Allied Supreme Commander General Dwight D. Eisenhower, pointing, and General Bernard L. Montgomery, far right, chief architect of Overlord, watching invasion practices in March 1944. *National Archives.*

"The greatest armada the world has ever seen." Landing craft similar to ones used by Bedford boys are shown in foreground, LSTs (Landing Ship Tanks) behind them, in an English port just prior to the invasion. *National Archives.*

HMS *Empire Javelin* at anchor before D-Day. The *Javelin* would transfer the 1st Battalion of 116th Infantry to within twelve miles of France, where the Bedford boys would then take the LCAs, visible hanging from davits along her sides, to the shores of France. *Bob Sales.*

"The Limey." Sub-lieutenant Jimmy Green, British naval officer in command of the flotilla of landing craft that took Company A to Omaha Beach. *Jimmy Green and Kevan Elsby.*

Russell L. Pickett, flame-thrower in Boat Team Number Five, from Soddy Daisy, Tennessee. *Russell Pickett.*

Wounded GIs from the first waves on Omaha Beach. *National Archives.*

One of an estimated 2,500 American casualties on Omaha Beach. *National Archives.*

"Dear Mom and Dad." A "V-gram" from wounded Clyde Powers to his parents in Bedford explaining where his brother Jack was buried in France. *Eloise Rogers.*

Right:
The enemy. German soldier killed by Bob Sales in Normandy on June 30, 1944—the day Roy Stevens was almost killed by a German "bouncing Betty" mine. *Bob Sales.*

Below:
The ruins of the French city of St. Lô. The prime objective of surviving Bedford boys after D-Day was finally liberated in late July, 1944, after huge losses by both Germans and Americans. *National Archives.*

IN REPLY REFER TO:

AG 201 Powers, Jack G.
    PC-N ETO 137

WAR DEPARTMENT

THE ADJUTANT GENERAL'S OFFICE

WASHINGTON 25, D. C.

emp

1 August 1944

. Mrs. Alice P. Powers
1020 Madison Street
Bedford, Virginia

Dear Mrs. Powers:

It is with profound regret that I confirm the recent telegram informing you of the death of your son, Private First Class Jack G. Powers, 20,363,657, Infantry, who was previously reported missing in action on 6 June 1944 in France.

An official message has now been received which states that he was killed in action on the date he was previously reported missing in action. If additional information is received it will be transmitted to you promptly.

I realize the burden of anxiety that has been yours since he was first reported missing in action and deeply regret the sorrow this later report brings you. May the knowledge that he made the supreme sacrifice for his home and country be a source of sustaining comfort.

My sympathy is with you in this time of great sorrow.

Sincerely yours,

J. A. ULIO
Major General,
The Adjutant General.

1 Inclosure
    Bulletin of Information.

"With Profound Regret." Letter from the War Department to Mrs. Alice Powers confirming that her son Jack Powers was killed on D-Day. *Eloise Rogers.*

"I can't remember whose name came first." Twenty-one-year-old Elizabeth Teass, who worked in Bedford's Western Union telegram office when news of the town's tragic loss came over the wires. *Elizabeth Teass.*

Dear MRS.Schenk
I am SORRY to hear
about youR husband.
I wish I could come
to see you. come to see
Me. I hope you will be
My teacheR Next
Fall.
with love,
BookeR

Booker Goggin
July 1944

"They gave me the will to go on." Letter from first grade pupil Booker Goggin to his teacher Ivylyn Schenk, sent in July 1944, a few days after Booker learned that his teacher's husband John was dead. The letter reads: "Dear Mrs. Schenk, I am sorry to hear about your husband. I wish I could come to see you. Come to see me. I hope you will be my teacher next fall. With love, Booker." *Ivylyn Hardy.*

"Some found happiness." Roy Stevens with his wife Helen in front of their new home in Bedford just after their marriage on Groundhog Day, 1946. *Roy and Helen Stevens, and Virginia Historical Association.*

"The daughter he never got to touch." Earl Parker's daughter, twelve-year-old Danny, in her scout uniform at the unveiling of Bedford's memorial stone in 1954. *Mary Daniel Heilig and Virginia Historical Association.*

Hal Baumgarten, left, and medic Cecil Breeden at the Colleville American Cemetery above Omaha Beach, 1988. Breeden saved many lives and treated Baumgarten and several Bedford boys on D-Day. *Hal Baumgarten.*

Fifty years later. Roy Stevens, center, returns to where his twin brother and so many friends died on Omaha Beach. Photograph taken on June 6, 1994. *Virginia Historical Association.*

Bob Slaughter with President George W. Bush at the dedication of the National D-Day Memorial in Bedford, June 6, 2001. *Bob Slaughter.*

They died that others might be free. The grave of John B. Schenk, one of eleven Bedford boys resting in peace at the Colleville American Cemetery in France. *John Snowdon.*

sions and even volunteered to run messages to artillery observers. He wanted every chance he could get to kill a German. Eventually, word about Stevens's apparent death wish got back to the 116th Infantry headquarters. Stevens was called in front of Colonel Canham.

"It's gonna take us all to win this war," Canham told him, "so you take it easy."[20]

Stevens saluted and returned to his squad. In England, Stevens had disliked Canham for his overly harsh discipline. Now he had a profound respect for him. Everyone in the 116th knew what the colonel had done on D-Day. "He walked it like he talked it," Stevens said. "He was a rough, tough dude. We all knew he'd refused to go to hospital when he got shot. We knew he was always going to be with his troops, whatever happened."[21]

Stevens cursed as well as any sergeant but was surprised by the constant stream of profanity and blasphemy that issued from Canham's lips. Stevens in fact worried that if he cursed the Lord like Canham, he'd be headed to hell: "The things he would say. . . . I wouldn't even want to say them up on the line—you didn't know what minute you gonna be gone."[22]

One day, Stevens returned from the line to pick up a group of replacements. Canham addressed the men before Stevens took them into combat for the first time.

"As sure as there is a damned heaven in the sky, we are going to kill these sonsabitches," Canham said. "Some of you will be heroes. Some of you will die. Some of you will die quickly."[23]

Other officers were even more to the point, telling men they were as good as dead so why not spend their last moments fighting with honor, getting the job done?

"D-Day was the longest day, there's no doubt about that," recalled Company B's Private Bob Sales, "but for those who survived, it was just one day. I had a hundred and eighty to go. I couldn't begin to tell you how many men right beside me got killed. The average infantryman survived a week, if he was lucky."[24]

As he waited to "jump off" on another attack, Roy Stevens received a letter from his parents wondering about him and Ray. "I didn't want to write back. I still didn't want to believe that grave was my brother's. I still hoped he might show up."[25] Roy finally wrote his parents. He was alive. He did not mention Ray, unable to tell them what he had only gradually come to accept—Ray had been cut down savagely with so many other Bedford boys, probably before he got to fire a shot, in the shallows of Omaha Beach.

By the third week of June, the 29th Division was meeting ever-stiffer resistance: The Germans were throwing everything they could into a desperate attempt to contain the Allies to a narrow beachhead. At all costs, they must be stopped from taking strategically crucial cities such as Caen and St. Lô.

Every day, it seemed, Company A lost another squad as it advanced. It looked as if there were only two ways out of the nightmare of Normandy—dead or on a stretcher. "That was all you could look forward to," said Stevens. "Hurt or killed. You looked forward to it."[26]

"Your best hope was for a million-dollar wound, nice clean sheets and a pretty nurse," remembered Company D's Bob Slaughter. "You didn't want to lie out there and bleed for a long time. I'd see guys on a stretcher, and they'd been shot through the leg and they would be smiling. 'I'll see ya buddy!' they shouted. You didn't want it in the groin or stomach but the legs, arms, shoulders, hands. That would have been wonderful. Fingers didn't count."[27]

Like Slaughter, Roy Stevens quickly came to recognize every sound of every weapon. The Wehrmacht's MG-42 machine gun, which had killed most of his friends and brother, sounded like a giant piece of fabric being torn close to one's ear. Company A at full strength—193 men— had just two machine guns, while a full German infantry company of 142 men carried fifteen MG-42s. Not surprisingly, Company A often found itself pinned down by MG-42s until artillery support made up for the imbalance in firepower.

The German 88mm guns, which had killed Bedford Hoback, fired shells at head height down lanes at nearly three times the speed of sound. At close range, flesh and blood targets never heard the shells coming. At a mile, men had perhaps a split second to react. "As soon as you heard an 88, you hit the ground," recalled Company B's Bob Sales. "If it caught you standing up, it would put some shrapnel in you. You knew what it sounded like because you saw so many men die because of it."[28]

Then there was the German Panzerfaust, again superior to the American equivalent, the bazooka. Its sudden "whoooosh" echoed in the fevered sleep of many American tank crews. But perhaps the worst sound of all was the wail of "Moaning Minnies," the bombs fired almost simultaneously by Nebelwerfers. The Germans nicknamed them "Stukas on Wheels" because the sirens with which the shells were equipped, like Stukas, were so terrifying that they sent many GIs insane.

"You never got used to combat," recalled Sales. "Every damn morning, you got up wondering if you were going to live through the day. You didn't sleep too damn much—the Germans would send out patrols, and they wouldn't shoot you because that would alarm everybody. They'd cut your throat. That's why most of the time we slept two to a hole. Neither of you were ever really sound asleep. Next morning, you got up, and if it had rained, you'd be soaked, and then you ate your cold mess breakfast, again wondering if you were going to live that day."[29]

Men became terribly numb to the death around them. Bodies lay for days within yards of foxholes, swelling in the sun, beside the carcasses of livestock. "After a couple of days, the smell became unbelievable," recalled Bob Slaughter of Company D. "Bodies would blow up into a purple balloon, and the smell would stay with you, always with you. . . . I was out there forty-two days without changing socks, without changing underwear. It was hell every day. You get up at 3 A.M., go after the next hedgerow, fight for that hedgerow, then get knocked back a hedgerow, lose half your company, and then get men straight from the states who couldn't fire a rifle. It just got worse."[30]

Roy Stevens also ate hastily prepared K rations only yards from the dead. When he looked at the corpses, he mostly felt pity and envy. One day, as Stevens crawled through a hedgerow, he came across a dead GI. Stevens looked at the man's face. "He doesn't have anything to worry about," Stevens thought. "Maybe he's the lucky one."[31]

Surviving the next firefight was now all that mattered. Nonessential weapons and kit were quickly dumped. Whenever possible, machine guns were salvaged from the battlefield—the Yanks needed all the firepower they could get against the Germans' MG-42s. The rule that chin straps be buckled was universally ignored.

Dead Germans lay everywhere, along every road, in every hedgerow. "I used to love to take pictures off the dead Germans—all of them had pictures of naked women," recalled Bob Sales. "The prisoners we took would say: 'Look, wife, wife.' They were naked most of the time. I'd take a look, give the picture back. But I'd always keep their watches. Man, I had a damn bag full of watches, and several pistols. That German technology! . . . Word got back one time I'd been hit. They were fighting over my bag back in the kitchen!"[32]

It was now impossible to tell officers from noncommissioned ranks. Even the greenest "ninety-day wonders" quickly learned to strip off insignia that made them prime targets for snipers. "Even Colonel Canham looked like the rest of us," recalled Roy Stevens. "The only way you could tell his rank was by looking at the back of his helmet."[33]

Just two weeks after D-Day, a 35th Division lieutenant, fresh to the frontlines, came across a group of 29ers. Their uniforms were barely recognizable, the Blue and Gray patches faded and often torn, their assault jackets slick with oil, dirt, and sweat. "We found all of the men wearing their field jackets reversed. The field jacket had a kind of shiny, almost sailcloth kind of material. It reflected a lot of light."[34] By turning the jacket inside out, the men had made themselves less obvious; some had then stained it with mud and grass.

Bob Slaughter's jacket was also unrecognizable. Since landing on D-Day, all but a couple of his buddies from Roanoke had been killed or wounded. Slaughter thought his number would also come up soon. One afternoon, he was ordered to take command of a defensive section badly exposed to enemy fire. He crawled forward and finally got to an observation trench on the frontline.

"Don't stick your head up," a sergeant warned. "There's a sniper. He's killed several riflemen."

"Goddamn," said Slaughter, "we got to keep a look out in case those Germans sneak up on us."

"OK, you go ahead and do it."

Slaughter had to prove he was not afraid. "So I stuck my head up and wham! God almighty! I felt like a baseball bat had hit me in the head. My helmet flew off. My eyes were all swollen. I'd not been up there twenty seconds and he drilled me. My ears were ringing. I saw a million stars. I'm on all fours down in that foxhole, and the blood is just pouring out."

Slaughter looked at the sergeant.

"Get me a medic!"

The sergeant's eyes bulged. He stared in disbelief, frozen to the spot.

"Never mind," said Slaughter. "I'll get him myself."[35]

The bullet had grazed Slaughter's scalp. Three days later, he was back on the line, his head so tender he couldn't wear a helmet.

The longer a man spent in combat, the more likely he was to die but also to break down with mental and physical exhaustion. One morning in late June, Roy Stevens came across a Company A man from his boat team: "Back in England, this little feller always had a smile on his face— he was a real nice guy. I'd get on at him for smiling all the time."

The boy no longer smiled. His nerves had been shot to pieces. "Can I go back to the kitchen?" he asked Stevens. "I don't feel good."

"You go back and rest a day or two," Stevens nodded. "Just go back."[36]

The man went back to the canvas tent where Company A's mess sergeant, Earl Newcomb, was now working day and night to prepare meals for the men. Newcomb knew how uplifting hot chow and a cup of coffee could be to shattered spirits. "So we always tried to set up as close to the boys as we could," he recalled. "If it was at all possible, we'd get hot meals up to them. They seldom had to eat hard tack."[37]

The boy who no longer smiled ate his first real meal in days, went outside, dug a foxhole, got into it and then shot himself to death. "He couldn't take it no more," recalled Stevens. "Don't remember his name. But I'll never forget his face, the way he smiled all the time. He was maybe nineteen—at most."[38]

Three weeks after D-Day, Yanks were shooting themselves in extraordinary numbers. As he dug in one evening, Stevens tallied up how many men in Company A had received SIWs (self-inflicted wounds) that day: at least five. The next morning, Stevens again found himself before Colonel Canham, this time being questioned about several men's wounds. "If you tell me it was intentional," Canham said, "I'll make an example of them."

Stevens told Canham the wounds had not been self-inflicted. "I knew he would have had those men shot," Stevens later maintained. "He'd have done it himself."[39]

Stevens believed that those who put a pistol or rifle to their limbs and then pulled the trigger were not cowards. They were to be pitied—they had taken more than their minds and bodies could stand. As Stevens saw it, they had reached a breaking point which he too would arrive at sooner or later: "A person's body can't but take so much. Those boys, they just couldn't take it any more."[40]

By June 30, 1944, Company A had fought to within a few miles of St. Lô, which had been devastated by weeks of Allied artillery and bombing. That morning, Major Thomas Dallas, the 116th Infantry's 1st Battalion commander, ordered Stevens's squad of twelve men to clear a machine gun nest blocking Company A's advance. The squad included Harold Wilkes and Clyde Powers, who had been in Stevens's boat team on D-Day.

Stevens's squad set off across a field of tall grass. Behind Stevens walked the squad's BAR man, a Private William Green, who was several years older than the rest of the men. Green had not used the vital submachine gun effectively; on a couple of occasions, Stevens had been forced to take the BAR from him to provide covering fire in the nick of time.

Many squads came to depend so much on the BAR's firepower that they often carried at least two of these light machine guns. They were as portable as M-1 rifles but had the power of a machine gun. Unfortunately, they could not fire for as long as the MG-42. The BAR expended all its ammunition, from a 20-round clip, within a few seconds after the trigger was squeezed. Like all bullets used by infantry squads, the BAR's ammunition created smoke and flashes, unlike the MG-42. Many squads became reluctant to open fire in case the telltale puffs of blue smoke gave away their position.

That morning, Green took his assigned place in the squad but then moved ahead of Stevens as they crossed the field. The squad's lookout man, a Private Brockman from Charlottesville, Virginia, suddenly saw a booby trap.[41]

"Wire!" he shouted.

But it was too late. Green stepped on a "Bouncing Betty" mine and died instantly. "That old boy Green took the load meant for me,"[42] recalled Stevens. The mine's ball bearings peppered several others, also killing them, and hit Stevens in "the shoulder, and through the neck and the jaw."[43] Stevens collapsed. Blood gushed from his windpipe. Rifleman Harold Wilkes rushed to his side and applied a pressure bandage. A few minutes later, Stevens was dimly aware of voices around him. His foxhole buddy Clyde Powers was kneeling at his side, undoing his wrist watch.

"You ain't gonna need that watch," said Powers, who then relieved Stevens of the watch and his pistol, figuring he wouldn't see action again.

"Clyde later had the watch engraved on the back," recalled Stevens almost sixty years later. "He finally offered to give it back but I let him keep it. Now I wish I'd taken it."[44]

By July 4, Powers would also be out of action, the victim of severe shell shock caused when an 88mm landed just yards from him. Wilkes was wounded later that month, hit in the shoulder and arm.

From seeing wounds similar to his own, Stevens knew he would die quickly unless he got to an aid station. Incredibly, just 3.5 percent of men who reached a battalion aid station died of their wounds, and almost three-quarters of men treated would return to duty. Eventually, medics arrived and Stevens was taken to an aid station, where his wounds were dressed, and then to the nearest field hospital—a series of tents shaped like a "T" ten miles from the front.

To his horror, Stevens was placed in a sick bay with men deemed unlikely to live. "I was still bleeding pretty badly out of my neck. I lay down in that place, and I looked over, and there was a soldier lying there—he was German. He wasn't moving. Then a nurse came by and I just grabbed her by the smock she was wearing. She was a nice-looking girl. I'd been away a long time: All of the nurses looked great by then."

Stevens told her he would live. He just needed some help.

"If you turn me loose," the nurse replied, "I'll see what I can do."[45]

Stevens let her go and waited. Finally, she returned. Stevens was operated on by a captain from Oklahoma, and then told he would be flown to a hospital in England to recuperate.

The day Stevens was wounded, the famous American war correspondent Ernie Pyle wrote from Normandy to a friend: "This hedge to hedge stuff is a type of warfare we've never run into before, and I've seen more dead Germans than ever in my life. Americans, too, but not nearly so many as the Germans. One day I'll think I'm getting hardened to dead people, dead young people in vast numbers, and then next day I'll realize I'm not and never could be."[46]

On July 6, 1944, Stevens was flown to England. He was one of 27,000 American casualties evacuated from Normandy since June 6. During his time in combat, 11,000 of his countrymen had been killed and a thousand more were missing in action. But what they had achieved was nothing short of miraculous. Over 71,000 vehicles had been brought ashore and then inland through draws such as the Vierville D-1 draw. Almost half a million GIs had crossed the channel. Throughout Normandy, the Germans were putting up a spirited and lethal resistance but were running perilously low of men, ammunition, and other materiel.[47]

The Allies enjoyed total air supremacy. Fortress Europe had been breached. "The weapons which alone could have enabled us to banish the danger—the Navy and Luftwaffe—were almost non-existent," recalled Generalleutnant Joseph Reichert, one of the senior German officers ordered by Hitler to repulse the 29th Division. "It was like pitting two people against one another, one with bows and arrows and the other with firearms."[48]

When Stevens landed in England, he was able to walk unaided off a plane carrying other wounded. "There was another boy with me who'd also been hit pretty bad. We both saw this beer joint—a mess or something—at the end of the runway. Well, I wasn't hurting that bad so we decided to take off, hoping maybe we'd get some whiskey. We started joking that if I did get a drink it would probably come out of the hole in my throat. But then some MPs grabbed us. When we told them what we had in mind, they got to laughing too."[49]

The MPs took Stevens and his friend to their assigned hospital in a jeep. A few days later, Stevens wrote a poem which he slipped into a letter to his mother back in Bedford:

I'll never forget that morning. It was the 6th day of June. I said farewell to brother. Didn't think it would be so soon. I had prayed for our future. That wonderful place called home, but a sinner's prayer wasn't answered. Now I would have to go there alone . . . Oh brother, I think of you all through this sleepless night. Dear Lord, he took you from me and I can't believe it was right. This world is so unfriendly. To kill now is a sin. To walk that long narrow road. It can't be done without him. Dear Mother, I know your worries. This is an awful fight. To lose my only twin brother and suffer the rest of my life. Now, fellas, take my warning. Believe it from start to end. If you ever have a twin brother, don't go to the battle with him.[50]

16

The Longest Wait

AFTER LEARNING ABOUT THE invasion, many of the Bedford boys' relatives and wives returned to work with renewed energy. The war effort meant more than ever: In the week after D-Day, Bettie Wilkes and other women rolled an astonishing 23,950 bandages in just two nights.[1] But however many bandages they rolled, the wives couldn't stop thinking about their husbands. "The wait to find out was so long," recalled John Schenk's wife, Ivylyn. "My mother and I visited other families. We took a flower or some treats and tried to comfort those who had lost sons in other parts of the world."[2]

Viola Parker still fell asleep listening to the radio in her childhood bedroom. "We knew the casualties were high, but we always hoped it wasn't ours. As time went on we had no letters. We were lucky not to have had televisions then because we would've seen what happened."[3]

By early summer 1944, at least two dozen homes in Bedford already had the saddest of decorations in their windows: a gold star and the words "Gold Star Mother," signifying the loss of a son. There were bound to be more, every mother in Bedford knew that. But they hoped to God they would be wrong. Throughout Bedford, parents began to cross themselves and pray when they heard or saw the mail carrier enter their street. Mothers fretted most. They wrung their hands when they weren't washing them over and over. They cleaned house obsessively, preparing their sons' rooms for when they returned. They quizzed others for every snippet of news as they worked long shifts in production lines at nearby factories. They re-read their sons' last letters. Every new day and every evening, they prayed.

In some homes, radios played news bulletins around the clock. Families were no longer so interested in the latest episode of the radio soap, *Ma Perkins*, or another hit show, *Amos and Andy*. Fathers turned the dial to every decent news station and paced back and forth, memories of waiting for loved ones to return from the last war suddenly flooding back. Broadcaster Walter Winchell had angered many in Bedford when he'd insinuated in 1941 that the Stonewallers were shirkers as they practiced maneuvers in North Carolina. But now everyone hung on Winchell's every word.

Ernie Pyle, America's most celebrated war correspondent, had written a chilling account of D-Day in his most recent Scripps Howard syndicated column. He had mentioned "many casualties" and described the "human litter" he had found on Omaha Beach: "It extended in a thin little line, just like a high-water mark, for miles along the beach. This was the strewn personal gear, gear that would never be needed again by those who fought and died to give us our entrance into Europe . . . There were the latest letters from home, with the address on each one neatly razored out—one of the security precautions enforced before the boys embarked. There were toothbrushes and razors, and snapshots of families back home staring up at you from the sand."[4]

Other newspaper reports repeated the official line that the invasion had entailed "considerable sacrifice." In a June issue, the immensely popular *Life* magazine contained photographer Robert Capa's astonishing images of the first minutes on Omaha. They were far from reassuring, showing men cut down in the surf and struggling to get ashore.

Tensions rose with the summer temperatures. Then, a fortnight after D-Day, letters from soldiers in Europe finally arrived in Bedford. Jack Harris, a military policeman from Bedford, told his parents that since arriving in Normandy he had met many men in the 29th Division who were full of admiration for what Company A had done. "That outfit sure made a name for itself in the invasion."[5] But he said no more.

On June 17, Earl Parker's mother received a telegram informing her that thirty-year-old Earl was listed as missing in action. The town doctor, Pete Rucker, dropped by to check on his mother and then volunteered to tell Viola, Earl's wife. She was stunned but refused to think the worst. For Danny's sake, she could not accept that Earl was dead. She would not until she received official word, however long that might take. "I went on looking after my baby," she recalled. "You do what you have to do."[6]

On July 1, Viola Parker spotted the mailman coming to her door. To her relief, he wasn't carrying a telegram confirming Earl's death. But he did hand her a distressing bundle—her recent letters to Earl. They had been returned to sender. Viola asked why. The mailman said he didn't know. Again, she refused to believe the worst.

On July 4, Bedford tried to put on a cheerful face for Independence Day. Lucille Hoback, who had celebrated her fifteenth birthday a few weeks earlier, visited nearby Bedford County Lake where other teenagers and families gathered for holiday picnics, swimming, and boating, and where Clyde Powers had learned to swim. That night, the town watched a rather muted firework display at the Bedford High School's athletic field.

Like her friends living on farms throughout Bedford County, Lucille worked every day from sunup to sundown, caring for chickens, picking berries, milking cows, tending to vegetables that her parents sold every weekend at market in Lynchburg. "Every evening, my parents listened to the radio," she recalled. "When Walter Winchell spoke, no one else could. We were just hoping to hear something, anything. We hadn't heard from Raymond and Bedford. My parents were anxious—the whole town was nervous."[7]

Melba Basham, niece of Nicholas Gillaspie, wondered why her uncle had not written to her for several weeks. Gillaspie was a prolific correspondent, writing to over a dozen friends and neighbors who had grown accustomed to receiving witty letters and postcards from England. "Neighbors would receive a letter from him and they were just tickled," Melba recalled. "They would come right over and tell us." But then came D-Day and the letters stopped. "I can remember several of the neighbors coming by and they would say they were really worried about Nicholas. Everyone was."[8]

Meanwhile, one of the Bedford boys was lying in a hospital ward in a converted hotel in West Virginia with other GIs who had been brought home from Europe. Andrew Coleman was so ill with Bright's disease that he was barely conscious. His body was filling with poisons because his kidneys had failed. Sibyle Kieth Coleman, the wife of one of Andrew's nephews, was deeply moved when she saw Coleman and the many other young Americans lying in cots, some close to death, at the elegant Greenbrier Hotel in Sulphur Springs. "I went to see Andrew with my husband," she recalled. "Andrew was just lying there, not able to talk. He had a lot of swelling. It was very upsetting to see him and all the other wounded men. They were so young. It was a shock."[9]

On July 6, 1944, the *Bedford Bulletin* revealed that the town's own Company A had landed in the first wave on D-Day and been commended for its role: "There have been no reports of fatalities, but as yet the government has given out no complete list of casualties. There has been considerable uneasiness about the fate of the men, as it seemed too much to hope that all of them could have come safely through the landing ordeal and subsequent fighting."[10]

Frank Draper Jr.'s younger sister, Verona, worked at the Belding Hemingway textile mill that summer. She had heard a radio report a few days after D-Day and had cried at reports of "significant" casualties. "For weeks, my mother couldn't eat or sleep. She was so worried about Frank she would sit and just look far out in distance."[11]

The first hard news of Company A in the *Bedford Bulletin* mentioned that they and the 116th Infantry Regiment had been "awarded a presidential citation . . . for the work of the 116th on D-Day and subsequent operations. This is the highest award a unit can receive and is given only when an entire organization has acquitted itself with exceptional valor in important operations." The newspaper added that Company A had been "continuously in the line throughout the French invasion and is at present engaged in the St. Lô battle, according to a dispatch from the front."[12]

Another news item caused widespread concern: "Mr. and Mrs. Charles Fizer have received a letter from their son, who has recently been made a sergeant in Company A, saying he was in France and O.K. He had quite an experience [on] Invasion Day. The transport on which he was, while traveling from England to France, was sunk. There were 2,500 soldiers on board and all were saved except five, 'Billy' being one of the fortunate ones who were rescued."[13] The report was incorrect of course. It was not a transport that sank with Fizer on board but a landing craft, and all but the radio operator, Padley, had been saved.

A month after D-Day, Bettie Wilkes wondered why John's letters weren't getting to her. "There were rumors that some of our men had died but this was secondhand information." Perhaps Company A's mail had been lost on a ship sunk by a U-boat? Or were regulations so strict that the men could not write until the battle of Normandy was over? There was a reason for no word. God only knew what it was. But soon enough John would contact her in some way to let her know he was all right. "Everybody went on about their business," recalled Bettie. "We all just stayed busy, busy."[14]

Whenever Bettie met another wife, relative, or girlfriend of one of the boys, the first question she heard was not the customary "how are you?" but "have you heard?" closely followed by "did you get any mail?"[15]

On Monday, July 10, Bettie finished her shift at Belding Hemingway and headed down Main Street towards Green's drugstore. "I had been preparing a package for John over the weekend—toilet articles, cigarettes and things like that. I had it all fixed—except one article I wanted to pick up at the drugstore. I had the package with me, ready to post."

She was about to enter the drugstore when she heard a familiar voice. "Bettie!"

She looked around. She saw a woman she knew. To this day, she won't give her name. Bettie stood on the corner of the street and waited for the woman to cross the road.

The woman asked Bettie if she had received any news.

Bettie shook her head.

"No. Have you?"

"Yes. I got a letter today."

"Well, good. What did it say?"

"John was killed."[16]

Bettie stared in disbelief and shock. She managed somehow to make her way back to the rooms she shared with her sister at Ramsey Apartments, the first new building in Bedford since the war started. The next few days were a blur but within a week, she recalled, "Family and friends had just about convinced me that the letter could not be true, and that I would have been notified by the government first. They insisted I wait until I got official word before I gave up hope. They kept telling me it was probably a mistake even though no letters or news was yet received from John. So I decided to go back to work and wait for official word."[17]

It was also on July 10 that Taylor Fellers's family heard of his death. That afternoon, they sat in the shade of a tree in front of their home in the foothills of the Blue Ridge Mountains. Taylor's youngest sister, Bertie, suddenly saw a car pull up in the dusty driveway. The local mailman, a Mr. McCauley, his wife, and dark-haired teenage daughter, Ellen, got out of the car. "The whole family had decided to bring a letter to us," recalled Bertie, "because they knew we were so anxious to hear the news."[18]

Bertie had sent her brother a card for his thirtieth birthday on June 10 but it had been returned to sender. She knew her mother and father had begun to suspect the worst. McCauley handed Taylor's mother a letter postmarked from England. She couldn't bear to open it so she handed it to Ellen and asked her to read it. The letter was from Taylor's friend in England, Mrs. Lunscomb. "Taylor had been to her home (shortly before D-Day)," recalled Bertie. "Several of the other Bedford boys went by her place too. She had kept in touch with my mother, sending her news."[19]

According to Mrs. Lunscomb, Taylor had died on D-Day. Ellen stopped reading. Bertie ran to her mother as she started to cry: "It was a long time before anybody could say anything. Later that night, I read the letter three or four more times."

The news spread fast. Families from neighboring farms dropped by to console and pay their respects. "Bertie, can you read the letter?" asked Taylor's mother. Bertie read it over and over again.[20]

Later that week, the *Bedford Bulletin* reported:

Mrs. Lunscomb stated that Lieutenant Bill Williams, of Company B, Lynchburg, had visited in her home at the same time as did Captain Fellers and that he was wounded sometime during the invasion and was returned to a hospital in England. He first called her by telephone and then wrote telling her Captain Fellers was killed in action. He said, however, that he had not seen Captain Fellers killed, but was told of it by a comrade who did see him. Since no official word has been received, there is still a chance that he was not killed but wounded too badly to send word home, although Mr. and Mrs. Fellers have been convinced of his death. Officials have warned that it is very risky to accept as final reports sent home by the men in battle since they can, during all the excitement and confusion, make many mistakes.[21]

On Saturday, July 15, the *Bedford Bulletin* contained the following lines:

I mourn for you in silence
No eyes can see me weep
But many a silent tear is shed
While others are asleep.
Never did I know that the gift that I sent
Would mean so little to you on your birthday, June tenth;
It will always break my heart and will cause many a tear
Just to know your burial day would have been your thirtieth year.[22]

The poem was from Naomi Newman, Taylor Fellers's wife.

Nearly six weeks had now passed since the invasion. Families and loved ones were frantic with worry. "We all knew something terrible had happened," recalled Helen Stevens, then a twenty-year-old factory worker. "It was like waiting for an earthquake."[23]

17

His Deep Regret

SUNDAY, JULY 16, 1944. Just about 9 A.M., Lucille Hoback was about to walk with her family to Center Point Methodist church, diagonally across the road from her house. The church was typical of many in Bedford: a small, white wooden building with one room that held a congregation of fifty people. Though just fifteen, Lucille sometimes taught a Sunday school class there. Her father, John Samuel Hoback, was the church treasurer.

Suddenly, there was a knock on the Hobacks' front door. It was Sheriff Jim Marshall, a good friend of Lucille's father. He had just pulled up in his car. He was holding a telegram.[1] A few minutes later, Mr. Hoback told Lucille and her sister to sit down at the kitchen table. "Mother was sobbing. Father said Bedford had been killed in the war, on D-Day."[2]

Perhaps half an hour later, there was another knock on the door. Outside were several members of the congregation, wondering why the Hobacks were not at church. The service was abandoned and instead the churchgoers gathered to pray at the Hobacks' home. Later that morning, others brought food over. It was also that morning that Lucille's parents drove to the home of his fiancée, Elaine Coffey. Somehow, they would have to break the news that she would not marry their son.

Elaine was getting ready to go to church when she heard the knock on her door. "Bedford's parents didn't say anything," she recalled. "They just handed me the telegram. I read it, turned around, and went back in my home. I couldn't cry. It was too much. I went to my room and lay on the bed. I didn't want to see nobody for a long time. I lay there all day. I didn't go anywhere for a week. Then I went back to work."[3]

When Mrs. Macie Hoback got home, she had to be put to bed. Her first child was dead. Her husband went to the barn to cry.

That night, news reached town of the death of another Bedford boy in Company A, thirty-four-year-old Andrew Coleman. He had passed away peacefully at the Ashford General Hospital in White Sulphur Springs in West Virginia, finally succumbing to the kidney disease that had kept him from joining his friends on Omaha Beach.

The next morning, July 17, 1944, just after 8 A.M., twenty-one-year-old Elizabeth Teass was dropped off near Green's drugstore on the corner of North Bridge and Main streets. She entered the store, passed the soda fountain and a couple of teenage soda jerks working there, then the prescriptions counter and finally walked through booths to her small Western Union office at the rear of the store, a polished wooden booth behind the cosmetics counter. Teass had worked at Green's since 1942 after graduating Bedford High School.

At several booths customers chatted and sipped freshly brewed coffee. "Many Bedford men gathered there every morning," recalled Teass. "Businessmen came by. And it was as if we were all a big family—lawyers, doctors, the town's undertaker, Harry Carder."[4] Several regulars browsed the morning papers and discussed the news. Coca-Cola had produced its billionth gallon of Coca-Cola syrup. Over a hundred children had died in a fire in Connecticut started by inept fire-eaters at a circus. In France, the 29th Division was fighting desperately in the outskirts of St. Lô after a month of deadly stalemate.[5]

Those reading reports about the battle of Normandy that morning could not know that hardly any men who had landed with Company A on D-Day were still fighting. On July 11, the last Bedford boy who saw action on D-Day, Charles Fizer, had apparently been strafed and killed by the Luftwaffe as he and several others lay sleeping: "They had been out on the front and had come back to rest. They were so tired and worn out they didn't dig in. They just lay on top of the ground."[6]

Of those who had trained with the Bedford boys in England, only medic Cecil Breeden, Sergeant John Laird, Gil Murdock, and George Roach remained in combat with Company A.[7] The previous morning, July 16, John Barnes had been wounded in the head by shell fragments a few hours before a reinforced Company A had "jumped off" for the final slog into St. Lô.

It was now 8:30 A.M. in Bedford. Elizabeth Teass switched on the teletype machine for receiving telegrams and then pressed a button that sounded a bell twenty-five miles away in the main Western Union office for central Virginia in Roanoke. All telegrams came to Bedford from this office. She then typed: "Good morning. Go ahead. Bedford."

Words emerged on a strip of paper chattering out of the printer. "Good morning. Go Ahead. Roanoke. We have casualties."

Teass's heart sank as she read the first line of copy: "The Secretary of War desires me to express his deep regret."[8] Teass had seen these words before. By July 1944, telegrams announcing the death of a local boy arrived on average once a week. She waited for the message to end, expecting the machine to fall silent. But it did not. Line after line of copy clicked out of the printer. Within a few minutes, as Teass watched in a "trance-like state,"[9] it was clear that something terrible had happened to Company A. "I just sat and watched them and wondered how many more it was going to be."[10]

The telegrams kept coming. Teass fed the ticker tape into a small barrel of water where the adhesive on the back of the tape was moistened. Using a large thimble, she then ran the tape onto pieces of Western Union stationery, snapping the tape every couple of inches to form a new line. The job required intense concentration and neatness, and Elizabeth took great pride in her work.

"Naturally, I was in shock," recalled Teass. "I was so afraid the news would be leaked before the addressees on the telegrams were notified. I didn't want somebody phoning up a relative, a mother say, and telling them before they'd gotten the telegram. That would have been just terrible."[11]

For a long time, the teletype machine clattered, spitting out telegram after telegram. When it finally stopped, Teass thought the messages of condolence were over but a few minutes later another stuttered out. "I don't remember who came first or when," she recalled. "But I do remember there were a lot of Johns—John Schenk, John Wilkes, John Dean. . . ."[12]

Green's caretaker, a "very kind"[13] man in his forties called Frank Thomas, usually delivered telegrams around town. But most of the messages that morning were for relatives who lived in surrounding areas on farms. Teass looked around the drugstore. She asked for help, explaining that she needed someone to deliver telegrams as soon as possible. Near the soda fountain sat the town's undertaker, Harry Carder, "a real small man with a quick step, very polite, always in a navy or black suit and white shirt."[14] He quickly left with a telegram.

Teass spotted Sheriff Jim Marshall and the local doctor, Pete Rucker, a bespectacled man in his sixties with thinning hair, who had been present at the births of several of the Bedford boys. He had an office nearby on East Main Street opposite the post office. "Back then, when you got sick, you called the doctor and he came to your house," recalled Teass. "Pete Rucker—he born me and my brother on my Daddy's farm. Lord have mercy, those were the good days."[15]

Teass gave Marshall and Rucker a telegram each. That left several more. Most were addressed to farms miles from town. She made a quick list of people in town still driving cars, picked up the telephone, and dialed Roy Israel at his office. Israel, a former cowboy from Texas, ran a taxi company and drove a Cadillac. He often came by Green's for a coffee and to chat when business was slow.

Israel took a telegram, got a signed receipt from a relative of the deceased, and returned an hour later to pick up another. "Elizabeth, don't look for anyone else to take them," he said. "From now on, I'll take all of them in the county. Just call me when another comes in and I'll use my taxi and take it out."[16] Israel would stay with family members if they were alone until relatives or neighbors could be found to comfort them. "I'm sure he was nice and compassionate to the families he de-livered them to. He was a wonderful, kind, dependable man," Teass remembered.[17]

Teass didn't want the whole town to panic because of rumors. But be-fore Israel had returned to pick up another telegram, news of the tragedy had spread like wildfire from street to street and factory to factory.[18]

Viola Parker may have received the first telegram. It confirmed that Earl was missing in action. "You're so hit that you don't cry, you don't do anything," she later said. "I thought, 'Well, I'd better dust.' . . . I dusted the whole house."[19]

Viola then took her daughter Danny in her arms, left the house and began to walk towards the Peaks of Otter where she and Earl had courted.

"Well, Danny," she finally said, "we're going to make it . . . we're going to make it."

But she wasn't sure, and the longer she walked, the more she began to wonder: "What in the world am I going to do?"[20]

Back at Green's drugstore, Teass was still snapping pieces of ticker tape and laying them on Western Union stationery. "I had a job to do and a responsibility," she recalled. "I don't remember crying, but it was shocking to get so many messages and keep them confidential and find someone to take them out to the families."[21] Teass took a break some-time that morning. A terrible pall had fallen over Bedford: "It was one quiet, still little town. Everybody's heart was broken. With a lot of the boys, if you didn't know them, then you knew members of their family. It was a very sad time. Fine young men had gotten killed."[22]

Across town, Elva Newcomb was working the first shift at the textile mill, Hampton Looms. The whole factory seemed to be on tenterhooks, a terrible anticipation filling the corridors and machine rooms. "Several of the boys' daddies and sisters and wives worked with me," Elva re-called. "There was a large door at the entrance, and that day they left it open."[23] Elva had only to glance up from her work to see who was com-ing and going. That morning, she could barely look away from the door.

At the Belding Hemingway factory, workers were also dreading the worst. At roughly 9:30 A.M. a manager approached a room where Bettie Wilkes sat opposite her sister, Mildred.

Mildred saw the manager and motioned him to stay outside.

"I've got to go to the bathroom," said Mildred.

"Okay," said Bettie.

Mildred left. One after another, Bettie's co-workers also got up and walked out until Bettie was left alone in the department. In the front office, Frank Draper Jr.'s sister Verona saw someone whispering about telegrams. Finally, Bettie went to see what was going on. In the hallway, she saw her sister rushing back to the department.

"We've gotta go home," Mildred blurted.[24]

Bettie burst into tears. The factory manager, Mr. Horne, drove Bettie and Mildred to their apartment. Nothing was said. "I knew if the news was good," Bettie recalled, "they would have said something right away."[25]

It was official. The love of her life was dead.

At the Rubatex factory, a few hundred yards from Green's drugstore, twenty-year-old Helen Cundiff worked in the shipping department on the second floor, not far from Frank Draper Jr.'s mother, Mary. "The minute [Mary] got a telegram, she was out of the place. She went home and never came back. Frank's father never got over it either."[26]

Back at her apartment, Bettie Wilkes heard crying. The sisters of two other Bedford boys shared rooms across the corridor. They had also received telegrams: John Dean, one of seven brothers in service, had fought with Company F and been killed a few days after D-Day; Dickie Overstreet had been wounded on D-Day. "So it was all around our small town and the surrounding farms as the dreaded messages kept coming," Bettie would later write, "all [twenty-two] of them, with each family receiving their own particular summons to grief and loss."[27]

At some point, Bettie collapsed, suddenly overwhelmed by the grief she had suppressed since hearing the rumor of John's death. Mildred called Dr. Rucker, who rushed over and prepared a sedative. Rucker had been present at Bettie and Mildred's births.

"This is going to make things better," said Rucker.

"I just hope you put me to sleep and I never wake up," Bettie replied.[28]

Back at Hampton Looms, Elva Newcomb prayed that she would not be called away from her loom. Suddenly, the foreman entered. He walked over to the sister of twenty-six-year-old Private Clifton Lee. It would be years before anyone in Lee's family would dare mention his death, so devastated were his parents.

It was also that morning that a friend of Verona Lipford called her away from her desk at Belding Hemingway and took her home to the Drapers' four-room house beside the railroad tracks. "By the time I got home," recalled Verona, "one of the neighbors had brought the message to my mother that my brother Frank was dead. He was her first born. . . . There was no conversation, just a lot of crying and carrying on. My mother [Mary Draper] was in bed. She had just given up."[29]

At Green's drugstore, Elizabeth Teass suddenly saw Harold Stevens, an older brother of Roy and Ray Stevens. He'd heard about the telegrams from customers at Smith's market, where he worked on the meat counter, and had rushed over. He was still wearing his white butcher's jacket, and now stood a few feet from Teass, concern creasing his handsome, tanned face.

"Elizabeth, if a message comes for my mother, can you call me?" he asked.[30]

Teass nodded. Of course she would.

Later that morning, a telegram arrived: Roy Stevens was listed as missing in action as of June 6. When Harold showed the message to his parents, they were just as startled and confused as he was, having read a letter from Roy in England postmarked after June 6. Had the War Department or some officer made a mistake? Had both their sons died, as had so many others in Company A? From what people were saying, it seemed that every boy from Bedford in the Stonewall brigade had been killed on D-Day. Perhaps their troopship had been torpedoed in the channel—how else could so many have been lost?

Harold comforted his parents. All they could do was pray and wait until further news arrived: another letter from Roy, or a telegram confirming either son's death.

Meanwhile, Ivylyn Schenk was driving across town with her mother. They were going to spend a few days with John's family. "Moma and I drove up into the yard at the Schenks' place," recalled Ivylyn. "Mother Schenk came out of the house to greet us. I knew right away that things were not right. She told us he had gone. . . ."[31]

Ivylyn and her mother stayed with the Schenks as planned. Instead of enjoying a short vacation, they grieved and prayed with John's two older sisters, two half sisters, and a brother. Later that afternoon, John Schenk's mother visited the Drapers to offer her condolences. Her husband stayed at home.

"Mr. Schenk was angry," remembered Elva Newcomb. "He thought his son should not have been killed, said John was supposed to be behind the lines like [my husband] Earl. He blamed people, wouldn't talk to boys who later came back. Mrs. Schenk later sent me a letter saying she was sorry he felt that way."[32]

Ivylyn discovered that John's parents had been in contact with one of John's cousins, who also belonged to the 116th Infantry regiment. The cousin had been able to prepare John for his burial in Normandy. The cousin did not know how John had died. But as a radio operator like John Clifton, Schenk was probably one of the first to be cut down as he struggled to get ashore weighed down by the metal target on his back.

As families throughout the county rushed to comfort each other, it seemed to Ivylyn that no one would ever be able to adequately express how much hope and joy had been destroyed so fast: "It was as if there was a big window wide open and then suddenly it was all shut down."[33]

At the Hoback farm that afternoon, Lucille and her sister Rachel were busy making peach ice cream as a treat for their mother, Macie. They thought it might cheer her up. Suddenly, they heard their father call them to the kitchen. He had just received another Western Union telegram. Raymond was missing in action.

"My parents were never the same," remembered Lucille. "I had never seen my father cry, but he did that day."[34]

At five o'clock that afternoon, Elizabeth Teass switched off the teletype machine and left work. That day nine telegrams had arrived declaring Bedford men dead or missing in action on D-Day.

As dusk settled on Bedford, several families walked in shock and tears to the white, two-story wooden home of Andrew Coleman in the heart of Bedford. His family had placed him in an open casket in their parlor. Sibyle Kieth Coleman was present as bereaved parents arrived to pay their final respects. "They were wailing, crying, grabbing for each other. They had lost their own sons and were coming into the room, emptied of furniture, and then, well, you can imagine, they see a dead boy lying there. . . . It was one of the worst things I've ever seen. Coleman's mother was in a room across the hall from where they had the casket. She was in bed, still very much crippled with terrible arthritis."

At some point during the evening, Dr. Grey from the Presbyterian Church in Bedford came over to pray with the families. "He had led the service on D-Day, and he had a soft voice," recalled Coleman. "He looked every inch a minister. Everyone admired him."[35]

Later that week, Anna Mae Stewart learned that her brother Grant Yopp was missing in action. She was still sharing an apartment in Washington, D.C., with Yopp's wife, Elsie. "I went down to the post office where we both worked. I had to call her outside and tell her what had happened. . . . Later, I was told that Grant had got to the shore but the paramedics couldn't get to him and a lot of the boys before they bled to death."[36]

On Wednesday, July 19, the *Bedford Bulletin*'s editorial brought fresh tears to many eyes:

> We can only point out that these Bedford men have given their lives in the same cause for which men in all ages have made the supreme sacrifice—the preservation of the ideals of liberty and justice toward which mankind has been struggling since the dawn of time. . . .[37]

On July 25, 1944, Bedford's Eleanor Yowell wrote to her husband, "Pinky," an American pilot based in England:

> Apparently, the 116th Infantry Division, Company A, really was "cannon fodder," as they were in the lead assaults to hit those heavily fortified Normandy beaches. The town has been in a state of shock. . . . I just hated to write you about it. The war is really hitting home now.[38]

Many Bedford boys had brothers in service. David Draper was a heavy equipment operator with the Navy Seabees on an island in the Asia-Pacific theatre. He was cleaning his eating utensils when his lieutenant commander took him aside and told him that his brother Frank was dead. "He said I could take two days off. I said: 'No, I don't want to.' I had a job to do beating the Japanese. . . . They weren't like us. They were brutal. But we got to be just like 'em in the end. Just like animals. That's what it took to win."[39]

In early August, the Hobacks received a package from Europe. It contained Raymond's Bible, inscribed "Raymond S. Hoback, from mother, Xmas, 1938," and a letter:

> *19 July 1944. Somewhere in France.*
>
> *Dear Mr. and Mrs. Hoback*
>
> *I really don't know how to start this letter to you folks, but will attempt to do something in words of writing. . . While walking along the beach D-DAY plus 1, I came upon this Bible and as most any person would do, I picked it up from the sands to keep it from being destroyed . . . . You have by now received a letter from your son saying he is well. I sincerely hope so. I imagine what has happened is your son dropped the book without any notice. Most everybody who landed on that beach D-Day lost something.*[40]

The letter was from Corporal H. W. Crayton of West Virginia. The Bible was the only personal belonging of Raymond the Hobacks ever received.

"There was almost nothing from Bedford," recalled Lucille Hoback. "A bill-fold, with nothing in it, and perhaps a fountain pen but that was it."[41]

The Bible had no water stains. Perhaps Raymond had gotten onto the beach before he died. "My mother always treasured the Bible so much," Lucille said. "She said that, next to her son, she would have wanted to have his Bible."[42]

A few days later, the following words appeared in the *Bedford Bulletin*:

M E M O R I A M
Do not say my sons are dead;
They only sleepest . . .
They loved each other, stayed together
And with their comrades crossed together
To that great beyond;
So weep not, mothers,
Your sons are happy and free. . . .
    MRS. J. S. HOBACK.[43]

But the Hobacks did weep. Things were never the same. That summer, Lucille was barred from going to Bedford County Lake or doing anything that might have been fun. Her mother spent hours alone and rarely left the house. Every evening felt like a wake. "My sister and I were always trying to make everybody feel better. There was [to be] no laughing and no chatting. I was very close to my mother, so anything that hurt her, hurt me. I felt helpless."[44]

Later that summer, Lucille asked if she could go to an amusement park in Roanoke. Her parents said no. She thought she understood why: "They were the only ones who lost two sons on D-Day."[45]

All across Bedford County, joy died that summer. "Life seems so useless without you darling," wrote Bettie Wilkes in a memorial notice published with dozens of others from bereaved relatives and widows in the *Bedford Bulletin*. "There is only one hope left now, to meet you up there where there is no night but eternal rest and peace."[46]

Families grieved behind closed doors, sharing their pain with relatives and God. "People didn't feel like going out and doing things for a good while," recalled Marie Powers, a junior at Bedford High School who loved nothing more than jitterbugging in her saddle shoes to Glenn Miller tunes at dinner club dances. "Most all the activities were discontinued. It was just such a sad time. It was terrible. But people loved one another, and people supported each other."[47]

By the time Powers returned to High School that fall, the War Department had confirmed that in all nineteen men from Bedford had been killed on Omaha Beach on D-Day. Three more Bedford boys had died later in the invasion. In cities close to Bedford, where blood lines also went back several generations, the slaughter had also taken a heavy toll. Eight of Bob Sales's buddies in Company B from Lynchburg had died on D-Day. Seven of Bob Slaughter's buddies in Company D would never go home to Roanoke. But no community in the state or in America or indeed in any Allied nation had lost as many sons as Bedford.

In a matter of minutes, a couple of German machine gunners had broken the town's heart.

18

Coming Home

FOR THE YOUNGEST, AT LEAST, Bedford's sad summer ended with a fresh start. In early September 1944, Bedford County's children went back to school. Ivylyn Schenk returned to Moneta grade school where she welcomed a new class. That summer, one of her thirty-five pupils, seven-year-old Booker Goggin, had written her a deeply moving letter of consolation in his small first-grade handwriting. "Those boys and girls gave me great heart to carry on," recalled Ivylyn. "They were still my children. I still claim them all as mine, and their children and their grandchildren. They're still all mine."[1]

The *Bedford Bulletin* continued to feature memorial letters and poems from relatives.

To mark Frank Draper Jr.'s twenty-sixth birthday on September 16, his mother and family sent a memorial letter to the *Bulletin* which they addressed to "Frank." His mother wrote:

I can't even see your grave except in a dream. Now my mind wanders thousands of miles across the mighty deep. To a lonely little mound in a foreign land where the body of my dear soldier boy might be lain away. This tired, homesick soldier boy who attended church in Bedford all his life. He was not buried in a nice casket, flowers and funeral procession. His dear body was laid to rest in a blood-soaked uniform. Maybe it was draped in an American flag. There will not be any more cruel wars where you have gone, dear Frank. . . . The old rugged cross has a two-fold meaning for me, for my own dear boy shed his precious blood like Jesus on the cross at Calvary. For our religious freedom, they say. A dear price to pay.[2]

Kathleen Bradshaw, the young Virginian nurse who had met John Reynolds in England and hoped to marry him, sent a poem:

How sad I was that lonely day
When I heard that you'd been called away . . .
I can't forget your smiling face,
Full of love, friendship and grace;
God called you on that other shore,
To rest with Him forever more.[3]

Elaine Coffey, the "dear sweetheart" of Bedford Hoback, wrote of how "in the stillness of midnight my tears in silence flow. . . . Will I forget you? Oh no! For memory's golden chain will always bind my heart to thee until we meet again."[4]

A Mrs. Keith Harvey, co-publisher of the *Bedford Bulletin*, "went around to see some of the families. There wasn't any weeping and wailing. It was all so quiet. There wasn't any hysteria. Everybody was just stunned. For those not involved it was hard to comprehend, but the families took it. There weren't any mothers saying, 'My son shouldn't have been over there in the first place to fight this dirty old war.'"[5]

Back in France, Company A had been decimated time and again as it had fought through St. Lô, and then taken Vire to the south. The 1st Battalion of the 116th Infantry had been awarded its second Presidential Unit Citation for the capture of Hill 203 near Vire. The first had been for actions on D-Day. The battalion had then joined Patton's Third Army during the Allied breakout of Normandy, before being sent west to take the Brittany port of Brest, a vital objective because of its many U-boat pens.

On September 16, Sergeant Allen Huddleston of Bedford rejoined Company A in the outskirts of Brest, having fully recovered from his broken ankle. "When I got back to the company," he recalled, "there wasn't a single boy I recognized from Bedford. There was Newcomb and Mitchell in headquarters but I didn't see them."[6] That afternoon, as he moved up to the frontline, Huddleston heard that Company F's Joseph Parker, Earl Parker's brother, had been killed just hours earlier in fierce fighting.

Colonel Canham, now assistant division commander of the 8th Infantry Division, accepted the German surrender at Brest two days later. When he entered the headquarters of German General Ramcke, Canham was asked for his credentials. Without hesitation he turned and pointed to the GIs accompanying him: "These are my credentials."[7]

Over 40,000 Germans were taken prisoner. "They marched past us, thousands and thousands," recalled Company B's Bob Sales, by now a platoon sergeant. "There were so many they marched past us all morning until one in the afternoon."[8]

After the fall of Brest, the 116th Infantry boarded trucks and trains headed east. It was a remarkable journey through a newly liberated and grateful France. At night, men tried to sleep in the cramped compartments but with little luck. Every few hours they would free their legs from the tangle of their buddies' limbs, and stand in the doorway, left ajar for fresh air, and watch the silhouettes of French hamlets and towns pass by.

"The days were better," recalled Joseph Ewing, a rifle platoon leader who would later write an official history of the 29th Division. "The men, sitting and crowding the open doors, waved to French civilians at the lowered gates and grade crossings, and whistled at the French girls riding bicycles along the streets. . . . French housewives came running through their backyards, down to the tracks, carrying apples and pears in their aprons or in baskets. . . . The Blue and Gray soldiers, flushed with all this fleeting attention, waved back happily until their arms were tired. It was a strange, but possibly shallow happiness that they felt as they watched the smiling people of these cities from which the war had fled . . . for the train was pursuing the war, and they knew the pursuit would end at the German border, for the war had stopped there, and had turned around and was waiting for them."[9]

Sergeant Allen Huddleston was on board one of the trains. "We went through Paris, where we stopped for a few hours," he recalled.[10] The men were not to move from their trains. They would not be getting to see "gay Pareeee" as they called it. Nevertheless, some managed to wriggle out of train windows and doors and go AWOL for a few hours in the city of lights. They just couldn't bear to roll past the fantasy city they'd heard so much about.

Before dawn, the trains groaned to life and when they stopped again, Huddleston discovered they were near Aachen on the German-Dutch border. It was September 29. "We went into Aachen on a truck some time that night and went on the line the next day. Suddenly, the artillery started and we all jumped over a bank. An 88mm hit me in the shoulder, turned me around, and killed a guy a few feet from me. It was 5 P.M., my first day in combat.

"They took me to the aid station that night, operated on me some place along the line, took out the shrapnel. I stayed in Paris for two or three days while they waited for the weather to clear and then they shipped me back to England. I wound up at the same place where I had been with my broken ankle. I had the same doctor and the same physical exercise sergeant for my rehab, a nice guy—a New Yorker."[11]

Huddleston was the last Bedford boy in Company A to fight in the frontlines. In the rest of the 116th Infantry, there were very few other men still alive who had trained in England for D-Day. Company D's Bob Slaughter had been wounded by mortar shrapnel in his back and awarded his second purple heart; he would eventually rejoin his unit in Germany. "Everybody alive today from the 116th has got two or three purple hearts," he said sixty years later. "If you don't have one, you didn't see much action."[12]

Company B's Bob Sales was, miraculously, still going strong by November 1944 as the 29th fought to defeat German forces west of the Rhine. On November 17, the 116th Infantry's B and C companies jumped off under orders to take the Rhineland town of Setterich. They had advanced to within a few hundred yards of the town by nightfall.

At 4 A.M. on November 18, Sales was called by his company commander and ordered to take up position on the other side of a field by dawn. "In those days, if you didn't like something, you had to keep your mouth shut. Well, the Germans lit that field up with flares like you could play football on it and then opened up on us with tracer fire from a machine gun. When dawn came, I crawled back and then took a tank along a road. We got the German gun. I tapped the tank and hollered, 'Okay! Let's get out of here!' The tank turned and then they hit us with an antitank rocket.

"There were balls of fire rolling out of my eyes. I couldn't find my gun, nothing. I was hit in both eyes with shrapnel, blood was pouring out of my head from a cut, where my head hit the side of the tank. That finished me. I stayed in hospital a year and a half, lost an eye. The other one is not the best in the world but a hell of a lot better than nothing. I'd been in combat six months. And in that time, you wouldn't believe how many men I saw die."[13] Sales's actions on November 18 earned him a Silver Star.

Bedford's last casualty from Company A, Sergeant Allen Huddleston, arrived in America in April 1945. "I went to the hospital, spent a night in New York, and then I got to come home." A few weeks later, on May 7, he celebrated V-E Day, marking victory in Europe. That morning, at 2:41 A.M., Central European Time, General Alfred Jodl, seated at a plain wood table in a grimy school building in Reims, had signed the official German surrender.[14]

Company A had fought all the way to the Elbe. John Barnes had spent the last months of the war as a company runner, somehow avoiding the fate of the last surviving rifleman from D-Day, Sam Rothenberg, who had died in October 1944. The 29th Division had been 14,000 strong when it arrived in England in October 1942. By war's end, it had suffered over 20,000 casualties.[15]

On V-E Day, Company A was in a small town in the Ruhr valley, preparing to move to Bremen to begin new occupation duties. Barnes and the rest of Company A celebrated long and hard. "The main claim to fame [of the town] was its gin factory. The name of the town was emblazoned on the earthen bottle that held this fabulous nectar of which we tasted the last sweet drops, our tongues licking the neck of each bottle. What was that delicious mix that we lightly added? Could it have been that awful lemon mix from our K rations?"[16]

Just a few weeks later, Company A held a profoundly moving ceremony in the town of Spaden in the American-occupied zone of Germany. Barnes stood on a parade ground as the reconstituted Company A observed the first anniversary of D-Day. "The entire company fell out for a full dress parade," Barnes recalled. "As the American flag was raised and taps was played, I tried to think back twelve months to the day of the landing, but I could not."[17]

Of the Bedford boys who had left America, Earl Newcomb and the company's supply sergeant, Jack Mitchell, were still serving with Company A. Neither had fought in the front lines. George Roach and Gil Murdock, who swam for their lives on D-Day, were still in the company but not as infantrymen. Roach was now Company A's clerk. Murdock worked in the regimental headquarters. According to Barnes: "It [was] safe to say that no rifleman now remained that had served on the front and had been in England in Ivybridge in the spring of '44."[18]

The anniversary passed quietly in Bedford. There were no special services. America was still at war with Japan and hundreds of Bedford County's sons were still fighting in the Pacific. It was widely expected that many would be involved in another huge invasion, this time in Japan.

That summer, as America girded itself to deliver to death blow to Imperial Japan, wounded Bedford boys began to return home. "Mothers who had lost sons went out and hugged the survivors who came back," recalled Elva Newcomb. "They were still family."[19]

Lieutenant Ray Nance had left Europe in October 1944 by walking along the very same wharf in Greenock in Scotland, where Company A had landed that grim October day in 1942, and then crossed the Atlantic to New York on the *Queen Elizabeth*, crammed with thousands of other wounded GIs. Nance continued his rehabilitation in a hospital in Staunton, Virginia. By late 1944, his heel had mended sufficiently for him to be able to walk unaided and the hospital gave him medical leave. He spent most of it in nearby Petersburg where a statuesque, auburn-haired Army nurse named Alpha Watson was working.

Before the war, Nance and Alpha had gone to the same high school and dated. They had corresponded throughout the war, and while in the hospital in England Nance had proposed to her.[20] They were married on November 26, 1944. Nance was mustered out of active duty on December 15 and then returned to live in Bedford.

Going home was as heart-wrenching as D-Day.

Nance often could not sleep at night and when he did the nightmare of Omaha returned with traumatizing intensity. Was there something more he could have done to save the Bedford boys under his command? Bedford seemed to be full of mothers who had lost sons. Nance stood for hours on street corners, recounting what he had seen on D-Day to widows, and to Taylor Fellers's father. "I can still see my father now," says daughter Bertie Woodford, "standing on the street corner, just hoping to see one of the survivors, talking and talking to Nance, trying to find out exactly what happened."[21]

Explaining over and over to the bereaved what had happened was soul-destroying. "You wondered what they were thinking," Nance said. "Why is he here and not my son or brother who will never be here?"[22]

Fresh-faced Roy Stevens was discharged on July 30, 1945, at Fort Meade, Maryland. From there, he hurried to Washington where he planned to catch a bus to Bedford. While waiting for his connection, he went into a bar. "They wouldn't sell me a beer! They said I was too young."[23]

The bus dropped Stevens off on Main Street, not far from Green's drugstore. Barracks bag slung over his shoulder, Stevens marched down a sun-bleached road to the farm which he and Ray had bought before the war, and where his parents were now living. On the way, he stopped at a farmhouse. "A guy lived there—Charlie Zimmerman—who had been a bootlegger before the war."[24] Roy bought some moonshine and took a good long swig. He needed something to help him face his parents alone.

Stevens's parents were waiting. His mother ran from the front door and hugged him.

"Well, at least one of you got back," she said.

"We just grabbed one another," recalled Stevens. "My Daddy was a big fella but boy he cried that day. He and Ray were very close. They'd worked on the farm together before the war. Ray's death shook him a whole lot."[25]

Stevens found it impossible to settle back into his old life. He drank hard to calm his nerves but the whiskey also fueled his rage at the deaths of his friends. "I tried to forget, wash the memories away," he said. "But you can't. As soon as that whiskey dries out it all comes right back."[26] Stevens cursed so often it was as if he was still living in a foxhole. Then one day his mother scolded him and he dropped the foul language. But he didn't stop the bad living until he met twenty-year-old Helen Cundiff at the Bedford County fairground. She was pitching pennies. He kept tossing coins until she agreed to a date. They were married on Groundhog's Day, February 2, 1946. About the same time, Roy joined a local church and vowed to dedicate himself to "God's works."

Foxhole buddy Clyde Powers returned a few days after Stevens. On his way from Washington to Bedford, he stopped in Richmond, Virginia, where his younger sister, Eloise, now a beautiful, dark-haired twenty-year-old, was a cadet nurse at the Grace Hospital. It was mid-morning when Clyde walked along its spotless corridors in his crisp uniform. "There's a good looking paratrooper asking for you," said one of Eloise's fellow nurses. Eloise was amazed to see Clyde. She had thought he was still in England. In the thirty-one months he had been overseas, he had become lean and rugged. But he was still as nonchalant, as unflappable, as she remembered.

Thirty-year-old Clyde grabbed his little sister and hugged her. He was not the kind of man to cry. For the rest of his life he would keep his emotions bottled up. Eloise couldn't hold back the tears. "I can't go home alone," Clyde said calmly. He had left Bedford with his brother. He couldn't face returning without a sibling by his side. Eloise asked the nursing director if she could have the day off to go home with her brother. Of course she could.

Eloise changed out of her nurse's uniform and called her mother, Alice, to tell her that they were on their way. They caught the 2 P.M. bus to Bedford. Later that afternoon, they arrived home. Clyde's mother hugged her son: "I'm so glad you're home." She cried but did not ask about Jack that day.

"It was very hard for Clyde coming home," recalled Eloise. "He felt enormous survivor's guilt. How could you not?"[27]

Clyde would not talk with Eloise or anybody else in his family about what had happened in France. It was too much to bear. "People say the men who died on the beach were heroes," recalled Eloise. "I think the heroes are the ones who came back and had to live with it for the rest of their lives."[28]

Elva Newcomb had waited for three years to feel her husband's arms around her. Finally, she received a telegram from Earl, who had just landed on American soil: "I'm over here from over there."[29] A few days later, Earl called her around 11 P.M., and told her to meet him in Lynchburg the next day. They drove into Bedford on June 13, 1945, in Earl's 1935 Ford coupe and fourteen days later celebrated their third wedding anniversary: "I had told him when he left: 'Just you make it back for our wedding anniversary.' He didn't make it for the first, or the second, but the third was just as good."

"Earl was different when he came back," added Elva with a smile. "I had a time getting him back to like he was. He'd been telling boys what to do for fifty-five months and I had to teach him all over that I knew better."[30]

Earl felt compelled to visit some of the grieving families of Bedford boys. He had known the Schenks well before the war but when he visited their home, John's mother, Rosa, told Earl that her husband, George, would not talk to him. "Mr. Schenk felt that if his son hadn't come home," recalled Earl, "he didn't want to speak to anyone who did."[31]

Like the rest of the 29th Division, Earl was not yet demobilized. War still raged in the Pacific. He had sixty days' leave but then he would have to return to a camp in North Carolina and then ship out to the Far East. Earl had seen enough of war so he tried to extend his leave, sending a telegram that claimed he had responsibilities he couldn't evade at home. The army promptly replied: "Regret you have not reason. Desire you to come back."[32]

On August 10, 1945, the B-29 bomber *Enola Gay*, named after its commander's mother, dropped an atomic bomb on Hiroshima. On September 2, the Japanese formal surrender was signed. Earl didn't have to ship out after all. V-J Day was celebrated in Bedford with enormous joy. It was as if the small town had won the World Series. "The wailing of the blackout siren was followed by the spontaneous blowing of car horns and the ringing of bells as people drove through the streets," reported the *Bedford Bulletin*. At Rubatex, Hampton Looms, and Belding Hemingway, the shift whistles blew late into the night. The Bedford Fireman's Band bashed out "The Star-Spangled Banner" on the courthouse steps, and hundreds of revelers sang "God Bless America," many with tears in their eyes, and then whooped and cheered and sang into the early hours. When most revelers had gone home a "lone victory serenador was heard wandering about the streets singing lustily: "Happy Days Are Here Again." He repeated the song over and over, pausing now and again like a town crier to yell with a ringing cheer: 'The war is over!'"[33]

Now all the town's sons could come home.

Sixteen million Americans had been in uniform during the war. Four hundred thousand would never come home. Half a million more had been wounded. But for many on the home front, it had mostly been a good war. Personal incomes had doubled at least since Pearl Harbor. Unemployment had virtually disappeared. Indeed, no country in the world now enjoyed such prosperity and such a high standard of living as America.

By 1947, most veterans across America were enjoying the good times too. In Bedford, several lost sons finally made it home. The first to arrive, in a casket draped with the Stars and Stripes, was Sergeant Dickie Abbott, just twenty-two when he died storming Dog Green beach. On the sixth anniversary of Pearl Harbor, December 7, 1947, the Bedford Fireman's Band again gathered at the courthouse and this time played "Nearer My God to Thee." Abbott's casket was placed on the courthouse steps before two thousand people who had to come to pay their respects to Abbott and 116 other Bedford County boys who had died in the war.[34]

The next Bedford boy to arrive back on the slow night train, the Pocahontas, was Frank Draper Jr. His sister Verona and the rest of his family walked to the station along the Norfolk and Western tracks from their home in Mud Alley, right beside the railroad. "It was around 9:30 P.M. when they took his casket off the train," she recalled. "It was draped with a flag and there was an honor guard. My brother left from that station and he came back from it in a box."[35]

Mrs. Mary Draper had her son's casket brought back to the house. "She wanted him home with her before he was buried," recalled Verona. The local undertaker, Harry Carder, who had delivered telegrams that terrible July day in 1944, was forced to squeeze the casket through a window because the Drapers' front door was too narrow.[36] A few days later, Verona and her family gathered in a private room at the Carder Funeral Home. "Mr. Carder sprayed something in the air and then they opened the casket because my Mom wanted to be sure it was Frank. I knew it was him as soon as I saw. I could tell by the form of his head—he had the prettiest little old head. He was still in his uniform. His face looked like if you blew on it the skin would just float away."[37]

The U.S. Government had given relatives the option of leaving their loved ones in war graves in Europe or reburying them in America. In all, seven Bedford boys were exhumed and shipped to America. Most of the boys who came home in coffins now rest in Bedford's Greenwood Cemetery.

On a late fall evening in 2000, Roy Stevens walked from grave to grave, smiling as he recalled each man. As the years passed, he said, Bedford struggled to come to terms with its loss. There was no uplifting fable of grief ending in redemptive healing. Therapy did not exist. The Bible sufficed. The pain faded at times but never went away.

Most of the survivors remained tormented by what they had experienced. Dickie Overstreet could not erase images from his mind of young GIs being mangled on Dog Green by the tracks of tanks. "When I first got back," recalled Stevens, "I was jumpy for a while. The wind would blow the shades at night in the summer sometimes and I'd come out of bed in a hurry."[38]

In 1948, Stevens quit drinking and the bad dreams started to fade. For other Bedford veterans, they did not: "They were hurt, not so much physically but in the brain. They'd start talking and you'd get to crying. Friends like Clyde Powers . . . they got torn up inside. The drinking—it got a lot of them in the end."[39]

Tony Marsico fared better than most. The 116 Yankees catcher returned to his job with the Piedmont Label company, where he would work until his retirement, aged sixty-two. He found solace in a deeply loving relationship with his wife, Hazel, whom he had married in Washington, D.C., in 1942, and eventually in a baby girl, Laura, who was "the apple of his eye."[40] By 1948, he had recovered sufficiently from his D-Day wounds to play golf with his 116 Yankees teammate, Pride Wingfield. Before the war, they had both belonged to the same Piedmont Label side as had Frank Draper Jr. and Elmere Wright. Although their teammates had been killed, their love of baseball had survived. Come what may, they were determined to once again stand on a diamond in the same colors and play ball.

"They did play again—for Bedford in the Skyline League," insisted Rebecca Wingfield. "I went and watched them with my sister. We would visit all the beautiful little hamlets in the hills around here. They were very good. One year, they won the league." Marsico could still catch but a wound sustained on Omaha to his upper right arm severely limited his game. Wingfield still fielded as reliably as ever at second base.[41]

"My Daddy lost a little something inside him when he couldn't play ball any more," recalled Marsico's daughter, Laura, who was born in 1958 when her father was forty-nine and her mother forty-one. "Just before he died in 1986, he was in [a] Veterans' Home and an orderly tried to lift him and touched him on his leg. The wound still really hurt. Right until he died, he loved golf and above all baseball.

"I have his Purple Heart and a signed baseball from the 1943 [European Theater] World Series," she continued. "It was probably his most valuable possession. He kept it in a cedar chest and would only occasionally bring it out. He would talk about playing baseball with Draper and Wright in the war but not about what happened to him on D-Day. It was such a horrible experience, and talking about it would have meant reliving it. That was too hard."[42]

As America boomed in the late-forties and fifties, so too did the factories in Bedford, which were quickly converted to civilian use in 1945. Roy Stevens got a job at the production line at Rubatex. In 1953, he lost his left hand in an accident. A year later, his foxhole buddy Clyde Powers lost his right hand—burnt off when Powers was electrocuted working on a power line.[43]

"I went to see Clyde in hospital," said Stevens. "He was worried to death because he smoked and he didn't know how he was going to light a cigarette. I got out a book of matches, showed him how to do it with one hand. Boy, he liked that."[44]

Like other survivors, Lieutenant Ray Nance couldn't get rid of horrific scenes from D-Day that would invade his sleep and leave him traumatized. Not long after returning to Bedford, he decided the town needed to find appropriate ways to commemorate and honor its dead before the bereaved could move on with their lives. As Nance saw it, the best way to begin that process was to start a new National Guard company in Bedford so that the town's tradition of service would live again.

Bring back Company A? Throughout Virginia, people said Nance's dream of a volunteer corps in Bedford once again would never happen. No one would support it. But Nance was determined to prove them wrong. With the help of other Bedford veterans, he got to work, writing letters, and giving interviews to as many reporters who would listen.

The plan struck a chord with teenagers in Bedford. Everyone had known someone who had not come home. Many had escaped service by just a year or in some cases months, and they were keen to do their part. When Nance held his first meeting for volunteers, he was amazed at how many turned up: "It spread like wildfire among young high school students. They flocked in. They were proud of it."[45]

By 1948, re-formed Company A had 124 men, nearly double its pre-war strength. There was no chance of this generation's meeting its predecessor's fate. National Guard units would in future be spread among different divisions to prevent a similar catastrophe.

Putting the war behind them was as hard for Bedford's widows. But some were fortunate enough to find love again. At a Christmas celebration in 1945, Ivylyn Schenk met a local farmer, Ralph H. Hardy, who had almost joined Company A before the war. Taylor Fellers had tried to recruit Hardy, but he had "been unable to commit"[46] because he had to look after his sick mother and feed and educate nine of his siblings after his father's death.

"After a wonderful Christmas meal," recalled Ivylyn, "Ralph came upstairs to meet my mother. We had a good game of carom—a board game derived from pool. It was not long until we started dating." A few months later, Hardy proposed to Ivylyn. She warned him that she would never stop loving John. "I know that," he replied promptly. "But I want to make a place for myself."[47] In July 1946, Ivylyn and Hardy were married. She still cherishes her memories of John and has kept all their correspondence, many photographs, and several of his personal belongings which she received a few months after he died. She chose to leave his body in the American graveyard above Omaha Beach with his friends.

After the war, Bettie Wilkes and Viola Parker attended a night class together in Lynchburg, home of Company B, hoping to qualify as beauticians. In early 1946, Bettie met Master Sergeant Lewis Hooper on a train from Washington to Bedford. Hooper was returning from fighting the Japanese in the Pacific. "I knew of him because his aunt was a friend of mine," recalled Bettie. "We got to talking. He was just glad to be coming home. The next week, he called me. After the war, no one had any cars, and he said he was going to Roanoke to try to find one. If he found one, could he take me out to dinner?"[48]

They were married in 1948. By then, Bettie had found work as a beautician. When people brought up the war, Bettie would sometimes criticize Eisenhower for his decision to proceed with the invasion on June 6. The bad weather and cloud cover that day meant Omaha Beach was not bombed. If it had been, perhaps John would have found cover in a crater, perhaps he would have survived, perhaps so many other Bedford boys would have come home.

Frank Draper Jr.'s father was much more outspoken, telling co-workers at Hampton Looms one day that he wanted to "blow Franklin D. Roosevelt's brains out."[49] Grant Yopp's sister, Anna Mae Stewart, was also "mad at the world." "Where were those bombers?" she asked herself. "Why didn't they get those Germans?" Today, she still questions why the invasion went ahead in such atrocious weather: "I say to this day that [Eisenhower] made a bad decision. Why he did I don't know . . . I still dream about my brother. I still dream about him coming home."[50]

Viola Parker, betrothed at nineteen, a mother at twenty, a widow at just twenty-one, also remarried in 1948. She had met and fallen in love with McHenry Nance, a local banker, fifteen years her senior. Perhaps she felt more comfortable with an older man given that D-Day had, as she put it, "taken away [her] youth."[51] As with other widows, Viola struggled to find out how her first husband had actually died, if in fact he had. At first, none of the Bedford boys would tell her much. All she had to go on was the missing-in-action telegram. Eventually, she visited Ray Nance. "I told Ray that he'd better tell me something," Viola recalled. "I told him I didn't believe Earl was dead, and he said I'd better believe it."[52]

Apparently, Earl had been hit by a mortar shell. His body had then been washed out into the English Channel, never to be found. He had died instantly without pain. That was a comfort. A far greater one was the love of her daughter: Earl had left her with the greatest of parting gifts. "I was so lucky to have my little girl," said Viola. "She was an inspiration to go out and do something instead of sitting around crying all day."[53]

19

Memorial

AFTER A STINT AT FARMING, Ray Nance became a mail carrier. His route each morning took him past several of the Bedford boys' homes. One belonged to Martha Jane Stevens, mother of the Stevens twins. Many mornings, she would be there waiting at the front gate, ready to ask Nance for news about Ray, hoping he had brought a letter or telegram to finally end her questions. "Mrs. Stevens came out each morning. She'd ask me what happened over there, where was her Ray?"[1]

Nance would often see Earl Parker's parents when he delivered mail to their box. They had aged considerably since D-Day, having lost another son, Joseph, in Normandy. A third son, Billy, survived almost a year in a brutal German prisoner of war camp and had arrived home on July 11, 1945, unaware of his brothers' deaths.[2] Mr. Parker had to break the news.[3]

Not content with bringing back Company A, Nance decided that such parents should have a focus for their grief, a permanent monument to their sons. Nance mentioned the idea to a local newspaper publisher, Kenneth Crouch of the *Bedford Democrat*. Crouch began to lobby state and town officials.[4] Members of the town's Parker-Hoback post of the 29th Division also pushed hard to get a monument built. The post was named after the two pairs of brothers who died in Normandy. Clyde Powers coordinated fundraising. Pride Wingfield was responsible for getting a memorial stone to Bedford. Allen Huddleston prepared a suitable inscription.[5]

Ten years after D-Day, Bedford got a monument to its lost sons. Over 4,000 people—the largest crowd ever to assemble in Bedford—

squeezed into roped-off streets facing the west lawn of the Bedford courthouse. The *Bedford Bulletin* reported that "older residents of Bedford said they could recall no gathering in Bedford that was larger or more deeply moved by what they heard and saw."[6]

On June 6, 1954, before a tearful crowd, Taylor Fellers's mother unveiled the memorial of polished granite, carved from the very cave near Vierville sur Mer that served as the first command post of Major General Charles H. Gerhardt. It seemed to glimmer in the sunshine.

Among the onlookers was thirty-year-old Captain Edward Gearing of Silver Spring, Maryland, who had kept his men together in the water on D-Day. "Company A was different from other organizations," he would later write. "It was made up of 'home town' folks—fathers, cousins etc. Under these circumstances it is more difficult to see these men die and as difficult to return to the same community and resume the same way of life."[7]

Bedford survivors from Company A—Ray Nance, Earl Newcomb, Tony Marsico, Anthony Thurman, Roy Stevens, Clyde Powers, Allen Huddleston, and Dickie Overstreet—were also present. Among the families were Lucille Hoback and her parents and Earl Parker's mother, Mrs. Joe E. Parker.

Earl Parker's daughter, eleven-year-old Danny, stood beside her mother, Viola, and her new husband. "I was already aware of what had happened in France because I had unveiled another monument to the boys at Bedford High School," recalled Danny. "I still have a picture of me standing near my grandmother that day [in 1954]. I was wearing my Girl Scout uniform."[8] The only other fatherless child was Earl Parker's nephew, Peter Royce. He was two when his father—Joseph Parker, Danny's uncle—had left for Europe.

The Bedford Fireman's Band played the French and American national anthems, "La Marseillaise" and finally "The Star-Spangled Banner." Admiral André Jubelin, naval attaché at the French Embassy in Washington, then spoke in appreciation of Bedford's sacrifice. "This rock, upon which are inscribed all the names of these young heroes, will stand out for generations to come as a memorial of their sacrifice, and as a token of gratitude from France to the people of Bedford."9

Then General Charles Gerhardt walked to a rostrum set up on the courthouse steps. It was his birthday. That morning, he had driven down from Baltimore, through the heart of Virginia, and had thought about the generations of men from America's first colony who had fought and died for what they believed was right. "Remember," Gerhardt told the bereaved mothers of Bedford, "your sons were with friends and that means a great deal . . . no finer tribute to a commander can be made than to be asked to come to such a ceremony as this."10

The Bedford boys had been engaged in a great crusade, an ultimately glorious battle to preserve the very foundations of Western civilization, of Christendom itself. D-Day had been the "Day of Pentecost" in the lives of Bedford's sons.

"The rushing mighty wind, the tongues of fire, the coming of the Spirit," said Gerhardt, "that great and mighty wind . . . those tongues of flame . . . those of us who were there certainly remember that phase of it. The Spirit was there, too, the spirit of the men of the 29th as typified by A Company. The spirit of those boys was an inspiration for those who went in later. It is the spirit that counts, ten to one, over material in such a contest."11

Gerhardt went on to explain why a bunch of farm boys from Bedford, who had joined the National Guard to put food on the table, had been selected for the most crucial assault of World War II:

> Why was the 116th picked for that particular job? Because they showed the characteristics necessary to assure success on that particular day. Who were these boys? The record of the 29th Division goes back to 1620, through the regimental history of Virginia troops, and their record has been unequalled. Those boys were the descendants of the men who fought with Jackson and Lee and Stuart.12

Gerhardt also spoke about the taking of the Vierville sur Mer D-1 draw: "The best exit of Omaha Beach [that had] a gun position which had to be taken only by individuals. The quarry from which this stone came was about 200 yards from that gun. It was our first command post on the night of D-Day." Gerhardt ended with a prayer that "A Company, as it now stands, will not be asked to face what A Company of ten years ago faced and conquered."[13]

Three days before the dedication, Clyde Powers had placed an urn beneath the memorial. It contained a SHAEF shoulder patch with a drawing of the patch autographed by President Dwight D. Eisenhower. Dr. Editha von Rundstedt, daughter-in-law of the late Field Marshal Gerd von Rundstedt, German commander-in-chief in France during the 1944 invasion, had sent her father's field marshal sticks.[14]

That week, many locals had expected to open *Life* magazine and read a special commemorative story about Bedford. But sadly the piece was spiked. Space was needed to honor Robert Capa, who had died in Vietnam. On D-Day, Capa had been the only photographer to cover the first wave assault on Omaha Beach.

Many Bedford veterans had hoped that one officer above all others would be at the ceremony: Brigadier General Norman Cota, who had done so much to achieve Company A's initial objective on D-Day. But "Dutch" was too ill to make it. On July 10, he wrote Kenneth Crouch to express his regret at not being able to attend. "My health is coming along just fine," he added, "am myself once again, and think I might possibly be able to cross Omaha Beach again if I had to, but certainly would not choose to do so. . . . Roll On." [15]

Cota's fellow officer Colonel Canham was also unable to attend. Since D-Day, he had been promoted to major general and he was now one of the most decorated officers fighting in the Korean War. Canham did, however, send a message to the Parker-Hoback Post in time for the dedication: "The 116th Infantry was composed of the finest group of men that I have encountered and a unit that had no peers as fighters. I deeply regret that I cannot be present to pay homage to our departed comrades."[16]

The crowds dispersed, the uniforms were mothballed, and the walls of silence went up again. The survivors from D-Day never spoke about their experiences publicly, and very rarely with each other. It was too painful. Some mothers would return each Memorial Day to the courthouse and quietly weep but there were no more public commemorations. It was as if the unveiling of the stone had closed the curtain on a tragic drama. D-Day, it seemed, was finally over, assigned to history, buried like the urn beneath the memorial.

In private, of course, Bedford continued to grieve and commemorate. As relatives and widows got older, many tried to rationalize their loss— it was part of a heroic sacrifice that had marked the beginning of the end for Hitler, and America's finest hour. But mostly those left behind still tried to overcome grief that seemed for some to get greater as their time left grew shorter.

Viola Parker told Danny as much as she could about Earl as she grew up, hoping she would always be able to cherish an image of the father she had never even touched: "[Earl] had a great sense of humor. That's what I tried to tell her, the funny things, anything pleasant instead of dwelling on the sadness. You don't get over it. You learn to live with the memories and thank goodness there are some good ones."[17] Today, Danny remembers her mother describing Earl as "the great love of her life. . . . She also told me he didn't set out to be a hero. None of those boys did. They had joined the National Guard to make extra money."[18]

Time did not assuage Viola's heartbreak. As the years passed, often when she had drunk a little too much, the old ghosts would return. She found Earl's letters too upsetting to read. They took her back to that day when her most precious dreams had been destroyed. So she put a match to the old V-grams and sepia-toned envelopes. "One night, I burned all his letters in the fireplace," she explained. "My brother said if I didn't stop reading those letters, I'd go plum crazy."[19]

In 1975, Frank Draper Sr. shot himself to death. "It wasn't over Frank's death like some say," insists Verona Lipford, Frank's sister. "My Daddy was sick, real sick for twenty years with emphysema. My Momma cared for him day and night—he wouldn't let anybody else do it. Finally, he told the doctor he couldn't take it no more. He was going to take his life. And he did. Three weeks later, my husband died."[20]

In 1988, Company A survivors decided to return to Normandy to pay their respects before they became too infirm to walk the sands they had once stormed. They also wanted to witness the unveiling of a National Guard Memorial at the base of the Vierville draw.

Bettie Wilkes Hooper was one of several widows who were to visit Normandy for the first time. Since John's body had been brought back from Normandy in 1947, she had wondered about his last moments. It still tormented her to think that he had died alone and in great pain. Bettie joined a party of 29th Division veterans and their families for the trip to Normandy. At Dulles airport in Washington, as Bettie was about to board her plane to France, two gentlemen noticed she was wearing a badge with the 29th Division insignia. Bettie was laden down with luggage. One of the men, a man of medium height and build with a friendly face, asked if he could take some of her bags.

Where was she from?

Bedford.

The old man said he had known many men from Bedford during the war.

"Did you happen to know Master Sergeant Wilkes?" asked Bettie.

"Did we know Sergeant Wilkes!" replied Cecil Breeden.

"Were you in his company?"

"I sure was. He drilled the hell out of us, but he also made us men."

A few days later, Bettie stepped off a tour bus parked near Omaha Beach. Breeden was waiting for her.

"I'll take you down, if you want to go, to where I found John."

Breeden walked with Bettie across the promenade road above the beach. There was no longer a sea wall. The skies were overcast and out in the channel a gale was blowing, just like on D-Day. Pebbles crunched under foot and then they were on the sand, a few yards from the water.

"When I got to your husband," said Breeden, "there wasn't a damn thing I could do. He had gotten it right between the eyes. You don't have to worry. He never knew what hit him. He never suffered."[21]

Bettie stood and stared at the beach, the bluffs, and the other veterans and their families milling around. At last she knew. John had died fighting. He'd almost made it across the beach. There had been no pain. Before Cecil Breeden died of heart failure in 1993, he wrote to Bettie explaining that he had told her that day about John because he hoped she would be able to sleep better at night. She did.

It was not until 1994 that Bedford's lost sons came to massive public attention, during the national celebration of the fiftieth anniversary of the Normandy landings.[22] In Bedford, television cameras invaded homes and reporters from around the world kept phones ringing late into the night. Ray Nance gave several interviews, camera lights shining in his pale blue eyes, but then the survivor's guilt and repressed trauma became too much. He stopped talking to the press and stayed at home, his memories suddenly as vivid as when he'd come home from Omaha Beach fifty years before.

Roy Stevens was one of many who returned to Omaha Beach for the official fiftieth anniversary commemoration. He still had dreams about his lost twin—good dreams, set in a sunny Bedford before the war when they'd boxed each other for a few nickels.[23] Finally, he got to the crossroads in Vierville sur Mer, the promised rendezvous with Ray. Stevens stuck his good hand in the air as if Ray was actually there to finally shake it.

Other veterans around the world began to share their experiences. Here was a generation that had fought and won a "good" war and then possessed the dignity to keep quiet about their sacrifice. America had suddenly discovered its "greatest" heroes—hundreds of thousands of them.

In 1994, by contrast, Viola Parker had had enough of digging up the past. "People still expect to see [me] crying with a long face," she said before she died in 1996. "We've cried long enough. Let's do something that lets us love, respect and honor them without being morbid all the time."[24] Viola's second husband had passed away in 1968. Since then, she had become more somber, less witty, increasingly withdrawn. Many friends felt she had never recovered from Earl's death, and the loss of the second great love of her life was just too much for even the most resilient of the Bedford widows to endure in one lifetime.

What of the Bedford boys' parents? How did they feel about the "good" war? Sadly, by 1994 there was only one parent of a Bedford boy still alive: ninety-four-year-old Gordon Henry White Sr. According to a relative, George Sumpter, D-Day had meant only tragedy to him: "Mr. White always said the war took his son and his wife."

Mr. White's wife, Rose, had suffered a terrible stroke on February 20, 1948, the day after her son returned to Bedford in a casket. His burial had to be postponed when she fell into a coma but finally went ahead, her family slipping away unnoticed from Rose's bedside to pay their final respects to Gordon Henry White Jr. He was interred in the family's corner of the graveyard at Forest Baptist Church. In 1958, Rose was buried beside him, leaving her husband to care for their six children. "It just broke [the] home completely," said Sumpter.[25]

To the day he died in 1995, Mr. White couldn't let go of the past, his grief, nor belongings that had been so precious to his son. He had once refused to put down his son's beloved shire horse, Major, even though the horse was old and infirm. Incredibly, the horse had lived until 1959.[26]

Raymond and Bedford Hoback's mother, Macie, died, like most of the bereaved parents, of old age and a broken heart in the 1970s. For many years, Macie had a deep loathing for Germans, once even refusing to attend her church when a German missionary visited. "She never allowed us to take the pictures of my brothers off the top of her TV," recalls daughter Lucille Hoback Boggess. "She would never let go of them. As she got more and more feeble, it seemed that she felt they were going to come back. She'd wake up in the night asking over and over: 'Where are my boys? Where are my boys?'"

The fiftieth anniversary of D-Day was not the end of the saga of Bedford's lost sons. Given the nation's new fascination with D-Day, it was hoped that perhaps the first national memorial to commemorate D-Day might be built in the town. For several years, Company D's Bob Slaughter had been pushing for such a memorial. "After the war, I went to

work, finished school, and then I married, had children," he said. "I
didn't have any time to think about the war or any other thing. At first, I
didn't like to talk to people who had not seen combat. They didn't know
what you were talking about. They didn't understand.

"Some people would say to me 'all you think about is war.' At reunions,
we survivors would talk, but it wasn't done otherwise. Then, around the
time I retired, I found out that many people had forgotten D-Day around
[Roanoke]. People, especially younger generations, didn't know that June
6, 1944, was the largest air, ground and sea battle ever fought."27

Slaughter had formed a committee in 1988 to explore ways to erect a
memorial, envisioning a modest statue somewhere in Roanoke, but the
project was too ambitious, he was told, for the town to afford. Slaughter's
dream languished until 1994. "Then, with all the publicity about the fiftieth anniversary, people saw that D-Day was worth remembering."28

Town officials in Bedford were told about Slaughter's plan and provided eleven acres of land. Slaughter's committee bought more. When
Virginia's Republican Senator John W. Warner heard of Slaughter's plan,
he introduced legislation in Congress and Bedford was officially made
the site for a national D-Day memorial.

Plans and designs were debated. Finally, it was agreed that America's
first national World War II memorial would comprise three core features
denoting the key stages of Overlord: the years of preparation, the actual
invasion, and, finally, victory in Normandy. There would be an English
formal garden, an education center, over eighty acres of landscaping,
many life-size bronzes of soldiers. A landing craft would sit in a reflecting pool leading to a wall representing the bluffs and cliffs along Omaha
Beach.

A local historian and businessman, Richard Burrow, was brought in to
make the monument a reality. Hired in January 1996 as the executive director of the National D-Day Foundation, Burrow set out to raise the
many millions needed to build such an ambitious memorial. In October
1997, he was delighted to hear that one of America's most famous World
War II veterans, *Peanuts* cartoonist Charles M. Schulz, wanted to pledge

$1 million. Schulz was then asked to head a fund-raising campaign. He and his wife had long known about Bedford's sacrifice and were eager to give the campaign a jump start. Soon other high-profile figures such as Steven Spielberg, director of *Saving Private Ryan*, also donated significant sums. Spielberg's Oscar-winning film had included powerful scenes of the first minutes on Omaha Beach.

Burrow's next challenge was staying on schedule for a planned opening of the memorial on June 6, 2001. In press interviews, Lucille Hoback Boggess said she hoped the memorial would act as a place of solace for veterans from all over the world. "We actually considered Washington to be the wrong place for this memorial,"[29] Burrow added just before the memorial was opened by President George W. Bush on June 6, 2001.

Company A veterans too infirm to join 15,000 people at the actual memorial saw President Bush honor them and the Bedford boys on national television: "Here were the images these soldiers carried with them, and they thought of when they were afraid. This is the place they left behind. And here was the life they dreamed of returning to. They did not yearn to be heroes. They yearned for those long summer nights again, and harvest time, and paydays. They wanted to see Mom and Dad again, and hold their sweethearts or wives. . . ."[30]

The National D-Day Memorial now sprawls across an eighty-eight-acre site and has become a major tourist attraction in Bedford County, bringing much needed revenue to the area. "It seems like a lot of [men] who survived the war almost have a guilty feeling that they survived and these men died," said Lucille Hoback on the memorial's completion. "It'll give them a place to go and have some quiet moments with their thoughts and memories of those who died."[31]

On September 11, 2001, just three months after President Bush opened the memorial, over three thousand Americans died in a single day, victims of the worst terrorist attacks in history. That morning, a shaken Lucille Hoback Boggess visited the D-Day memorial. Dozens of people stood in silence.

"I hadn't had that kind of pain in my chest since I lost my brothers in the D-Day invasion," she later told the *New York Times*. "So devastating to watch the suffering in New York. And the numbers—5,000 dead— why, that's the same losses as D-Day." New York would need a memorial, she added, because the city would stay in pain just as Bedford had.

"This little town was a vale of tears with all those telegrams coming in," said Roy Stevens. "Not a day I don't remember [Ray], just like those poor people in New York and Washington have to remember their dead now."[32]

Bedford had become a place for the nation to mourn, its memorial a touchstone for generational loss. But some veterans wondered whether the latest generation would be prepared to endure what they had. "I'm not sure if people are up to it right now," said Bob Slaughter. "The enemy doesn't come in a uniform. The front lines are going to be cities and water supplies and the air we breathe."[33]

A couple of months later, Bedford again hit the *New York Times* headlines. This time, the story was not so poignant. The FBI had been called in to investigate allegations of fraud at the National D-Day Foundation. The prime suspect was Richard Burrow, the man who had the memorial built in time for President Bush's much-publicized visit in June 2001. Bush had thanked Burrow personally for his hard work.

Burrow was eventually charged with four counts of fraud. It was claimed that instead of waiting to amass enough money to build the $25 million memorial, foundation officials had borrowed it in the hope that donations would come in before creditors demanded their money back. Burrow's indictment accused him of falsely telling a Lynchburg bank he had collected pledges in excess of $2 million in an effort to gain a $1.2 million loan in June 2001. In October 2002, the National D-Day Foundation filed for bankruptcy, hoping to be able to renegotiate payments to creditors.

Before Burrow was indicted, the foundation's board members resigned, including a deeply saddened Bob Slaughter and Lucille Hoback Boggess. Slaughter began writing his memoirs and was still tireless in his efforts to ensure that his comrades on D-Day would continue to be remembered. So was Company B's Bob Sales, a close friend of Slaughter. For many years, he held Company B reunions at his home in Lynchburg. In his enchanting garden, Sales also erected a memorial stone listing the names of his lost buddies. "I'm glad of one thing," he said. "I never killed a prisoner and I never sent one back when I thought a man would kill him."[34]

As with so many whose lives were changed forever by D-Day, Lucille Hoback Boggess continued to dedicate herself to church and community. The first woman elected to office in Bedford County, Lucille became a member of the county's Board of Supervisors. Whenever possible, she spoke to local school children about Company A and D-Day. "Think what it would be like to take nineteen kids out of a class," Lucille told them. "That's what it was like."

Hoback Boggess also helped organize annual reunions for Company A for over twenty years. Until 2002, candles were lit for veterans who had died the previous year. Sadly, in 2002 there was no reunion for Company A. Too few were alive and well enough to watch yet more candles flicker. Of the 5,000 men who landed on D-Day with the 116th Regiment, less than two hundred were still breathing. It is estimated that 500,000 of their generation die each year. Soon no one will be left to tell what it was like to be on Omaha Beach.

Company A veterans Hal Baumgarten, an ebullient doctor living in Florida, and John Barnes, a retired school teacher in upstate New York, kept going strong. Both wrote books about their experiences. Baumgarten attended the premiere of *Saving Private Ryan* in New Orleans in 1998. His book includes photographs of him with the actor Tom Hanks and director Steven Spielberg.

Seventy-eight-year-old Verona Lipford could still picture her brother, Frank Draper Jr., with a smile on his face that February day in 1941 when he packed his foot locker and left for war. "I have a nineteen-year-old grandson in the marines," she said. "I wish to goodness he had never gone in. But the recruiter got him. I just hope history does not repeat itself with what's going on now. They're nothing but kids over there, don't know what they're getting into. My dad always said war makes rich people richer but a lot of poor young boys have to die. He knew that all right. You lose a son, you never get over it. That's what war's really about."[35]

Eighty-six-year-old Elaine Coffey still wondered how Bedford Hoback was buried and wished his parents had brought his body back home. If they had, she would have been able to put fresh flowers on his grave, as other widows had for so many years. "I wasn't married to him," she said wistfully. "So I couldn't tell them what to do."[36] The Hobacks had decided to leave the brothers together in France, thinking that was what they would have wanted. Raymond's body was never found. Today, he is listed on a wall of remembrance, a hundred yards from where Bedford Hoback rests beneath an immaculate white cross.

Elaine used to treasure all of Bedford's letters but then she tore them to shreds one day in a fit of anger. Now all she has is a picture of his old station wagon, which she drove after he died. "War is a terrible thing," she said, tears in her eyes as she clutched the small photograph. "You wonder why they have it."[37]

Roy Stevens came to look back on D-Day with immense pride. "Freedom is not free," he said when asked to reflect on the loss of his brother and so many friends. He recently battled cancer and was still madly in love with the woman he met in 1946 at Bedford County Fair. He and Helen now have three great-grandchildren.

Eighty-five-year-old Earl Newcomb was, in 2003, still married to the woman he fell in love with before D-Day. And he still cried at the memory of Earl Parker's saying he wouldn't mind dying if first he could just see his daughter, Danny.

Today, Danny prizes her father's letter to her before Christmas 1943, a set of his dog tags, and his Purple Heart. "His body was never found," she said, "but just a couple of years ago one of the Bedford boys' relatives sent me his dog tags. I don't know how they were found. It's a mystery. But I do know they have my mother's name on them."[38] Danny also has a colorized photograph of a good-looking young man smiling happily and

sporting a red and green plaid tie. A black and white photograph shows
Earl wearing a kilt in Scotland in 1943, the year Danny was born.

"I went to Omaha Beach in 1997," said Danny. "I was amazed that
any of them got off alive. It was just because of sheer numbers that they
did. Those boys—they were all just unbelievable." Danny also went to
the graveyard above the beach where her father is listed on a wall in a
Garden of the Missing commemorating 1,557 men whose bodies were
never found.

Sixty years after he crawled across Omaha Beach, the last living officer from Company A on D-Day was still plagued by survivor's guilt and
the occasional episode of post-traumatic stress disorder. Not a day went
by when Ray Nance didn't think about the men he once commanded
and the lives they might have led had they been as lucky as he was.
Nance was also the last survivor from Bedford who landed on D-Day.

At eighty-eight years of age, Nance was tempted to go back to Omaha
Beach but, having recently survived a quintuple heart bypass, he said he
didn't want to die there. Returning to those cold sands might be too
much for his heart to bear. This is a shame because it is not so much in
Bedford that the spirits of its lost sons are most palpable, but rather a
few hundred yards from the beach where they died, in the American
cemetery at Colleville sur Mer.

Eleven of Bedford's sons still lie there in graves overlooking the
beach, beside 9,386 other American dead from the battle for Normandy.
In a chapel at the heart of the rows of dead, each with a cross pointing
west—towards home—the following words are inscribed for all to see:
"Think not only upon their passing. Remember the glory of their spirit."

THE BEDFORD BOYS
AND D-DAY

Twenty-two Bedford Boys were killed in the Normandy campaign:

Leslie Abbott
Wallace Carter
John Clifton
John Dean
Frank Draper Jr.
Taylor Fellers
Charles Fizer
Nicholas Gillaspie
Bedford Hoback
Raymond Hoback
Clifton Lee
Earl Parker
Joseph Parker
Jack Powers
Weldon Rosazza
John Reynolds
John Schenk
Ray Stevens
Gordon White
John Wilkes
Elmere Wright
Grant Yopp

Six Bedford Boys landed on D-Day and survived:

Robert Goode

James Lancaster
Robert (Tony) Marsico
Elisha (Ray) Nance
Glenwood (Dickie) Overstreet
Anthony Thurman

**Five Bedford Boys missed landing on D-Day when
their landing craft sank, but landed days later:**

Robert Edwards
Charles Fizer
Clyde Powers
Roy Stevens
Harold Wilkes

**Four Bedford Boys served in support capacity
and did not land on D-Day:**

Earl Newcomb
Jack Mitchell
George Crouch
Cedric Broughman

The entire 116th Infantry Regiment suffered 797 casualties, including 375 killed or missing in action. The 116th received a Distinguished Unit Citation for "extraordinary heroism and outstanding performance of duty in action in the initial assault on the northern coast of Normandy, France."

BIBLIOGRAPHY

Ambrose, Stephen. *Citizen Soldiers*. New York: Touchstone, 1997.

Ambrose, Stephen. *D-Day*. New York: Touchstone, 1994.

Astor, Gerald. *"June 6 1944."* New York: St Martin's Press, 1994.

Balkoski, Joseph. *Beyond the Beachhead*. Mechanicsburg: Stackpole Books, 1989.

Barnes, John. *Fragments of My Life*. self-published, 2000.

Baumgarten, Harold. *Eyewitness on Omaha Beach*. self-published, 2000.

Bradley, Omar. *A General's Life*. New York: Simon and Schuster, 1993.

Butler, Daniel A. *Warrior Queens*. Mechanicsburg: Stackpole Books, 2002.

Capa, Robert. *Slightly Out of Focus*. New York: The Modern Library, 1999.

Carell, Paul. *"Invasion, They're Coming."* New York: Bantam, 1960.

Chronicle of America. New York: Dorling Kindersley, 1995.

D'Este, Carlo. *Eisenhower, A Soldier's Life*. New York: Henry Holt, 2002.

Drez, Ronald. *Voices of D-Day*. Louisiana State University Press, 1994.

Eisenhower, Dwight. *Crusade in Europe*. New York: Doubleday, 1948.

Ewing, Joseph. *29 Let's Go*. Washington: Infantry Journal Press, 1948.

Frank, Anne. *The Diary of a Young Girl*. New York: Doubleday, 1967.

Hall, Tony, editor. *D-Day*. New York: Salamander Books, 2001.

Harrison, Gordon A. *Cross-Channel Attack*. Washington: Office of the Chief of Military History, 1951.

Ingersoll, Ralph. *Top Secret*. New York: Harcourt Brace, 1946.

Isby, David C. *Fighting in Normandy*. London: Greenhill Books, 2001.

Kennett, Lee. *GI: The American Soldier in World War 2*. New York: Scribner's, 1987.

Keegan, John. *Six Armies of Normandy*. New York: Viking, 1982.

Kershaw, Alex. *Blood and Champagne*. London: Macmillan, 2002.

King, Ernest. *"Fleet Admiral."* New York: Lipincott, 1947.

Lewis, Adrian R. *Omaha Beach—A Flawed Victory*. University of North Carolina Press, 2001.

Lewis, Nigel. *Exercise Tiger*. New York: Prentice Hall Press, 1990.

Masters, Anthony. *Nancy Astor*. New York: McGraw-Hill, 1981.

Matchett, J. H. "Let's Teach Battlefield Training." *Infantry Journal*, January 1946.

Miller, Russell. *Nothing Less Than Victory*. New York: William Morrow, 1993.

Morison, S. E. *The Invasion of France and Germany*. New York: Castle Books, 1957.

Pyle, Ernie. *Brave Men*. New York: Grosset & Dunlap, 1944.

Reynolds, David. *Rich Relations*. London: Phoenix Press, 2000.

Ryan, Cornelius. *The Longest Day*. New York: Touchstone, 1994.

Sulzberger, C. L. *World War II*. New York: Houghton Mifflin, 1987.

Tobin, James. *Ernie Pyle's War*. New York: The Free Press, 1997.

War Department. *Omaha Beachhead*. Historical Department, War Department, 1984.

Wilson, George. *If You Survive*. New York: Ivy Books, 1987.

Wilson, Theodore A. *Eisenhower At War*. Lawrence, KS: University Press of Kansas, 1994.

NOTES

Chapter 1

1. Lynchburg (Va.) *News & Advance*, June 3, 2001.
2. Roy Stevens, interview with author.
3. Bill Geroux, "The Suicide Wave," *Richmond Times-Dispatch*, June 3, 2001.
4. This proved correct. Of eighteen landing craft, six were lost. The casualties were similar—around a third of his men.
5. Roy Stevens, interview with author.
6. *Richmond Times-Dispatch*, ibid.
7. "Virginians at Normandy," WDBJ7 public television station, Virginia.
8. Ibid.
9. Joseph Balkoski, *Beyond the Beachhead* (Mechanicsburg, Pennsylvania: Stackpole Books, 1989), p. 7.
10. Bill Geroux, "The Suicide Wave," *Richmond Times-Dispatch*, June 3, 2001.
11. Ray Nance, interview with author.
12. John Barnes, *Fragments of My Life* (self-published, 2000), p. 61.
13. Cornelius Ryan, *The Longest Day* (New York: Touchstone, 1994), p. 178.

Chapter 2

1. Roy Stevens, interview with author.
2. Ibid.
3. Ibid.
4. Ibid.
5. Ibid.
6. Lynchburg (Va.) *News & Advance*, June 3, 2001.
7. Roy Stevens, interview with author.
8. Brookings also found that over 70 million people, 60 percent of American families, got by on less than $2,000 a year, an amount "sufficient to supply only basic necessities."
9. In 1937, the U.S. Government purchased 657.4 acres of land, including Sharp Top and Flat Top, for $60,000 in order to protect them from logging and other development.
10. *Chronicle of America* (New York: Dorling Kindersley, 1995), p. 686.

11. C. L. Sulzberger, *World War II* (New York: Houghton Mifflin, 1987), p.57

12. Lynchburg *News & Advance*, June 3, 2001.

13. Ibid.

14. Roy Stevens, interview with author.

15. Elaine Coffey, interview with author.

16. Roy Stevens, interview with author.

17. *Bedford Bulletin*, February 4, 1941.

18. Lynchburg *News and Advance*, June 3, 2001.

19. Roy Stevens, interview with author.

20. Lynchburg *News & Advance*, June 3, 2001.

21. Roy Stevens, interview with author.

22. Lee Kennett, *GI: The American Soldier in World War II* (New York: Scribner's, 1987), p. 17.

23. Roy Stevens, interview with author.

24. Ibid.

25. Eloise Rogers, interview with author.

26. Eloise Rogers, letter to author, November 24, 2002.

27. Lynchburg *News & Advance*, June 3, 2001.

28. Ibid.

29. Eloise Rogers, interview with author.

30. *Bedford Bulletin*, February 20, 1941.

31. Joseph Ewing, *29, Let's Go* (Washington: Infantry Journal Press, 1948), p. 1.

32. Lucille Hoback Boggess, interview with author.

33. "Morale in the U.S. Army: An Appreciation," *New York Times*, September 29, 1941.

34. Roy Stevens, interview with author.

35. Lucille Hoback Boggess, interview with author.

36. Roy Stevens, interview with author.

37. Franklin D. Roosevelt, Pearl Harbor speech, National Archives Web site.

38. Ray Nance, interview with author.

Chapter 3

1. Bob Sales, interview with author.

2. Bertie Woodford, interview with author.

3. Lynchburg *News & Advance*, June 3, 2001.

4. Ibid.

5. Dorothy Wilkes Goode, interview with author.

6. Ibid.

7. Roy Stevens, interview with author.

8. Bettie Wilkes Hooper, interview with author.

9. Bettie Wilkes Hooper speech, May 2000.

10. *Bedford Bulletin*, December 11, 1941.

11. Lynchburg *News & Advance*, June 3, 2001.

12. Billy Parker, interview with author.

13. Bob Slaughter memoirs, The Eisenhower Center for American Studies, University of New Orleans.

14. Elva Newcomb, interview with author.

15. "Remembering D-Day," *Baltimore Sun*, June 6, 1998.

16. Ivylyn Hardy, interview with author.

17. Ibid.

18. Ibid.

19. Ibid.

20. Verona Lipford, interview with author.

21. Bettie Wilkes Hooper, interview with author.

22. Elaine Coffey, interview with author.

23. Bettie Wilkes Hooper, interview with author.

24. Earl Newcomb, interview with author.

25. Roy Stevens, interview with author.

26. Joseph Balkoski, *Beyond the Beachhead* (Mechanicsburg, Pennsylvania: Stackpole Books, 1989), p. 34.

27. Bob Slaughter memoirs, Eisenhower Center.

28. Bob Slaughter, interview with author.

29. Bettie Wilkes Hooper, interview with author.

30. Ibid.

31. Like other wives, Viola vowed to write to her husband every day. She did, and to the day she died, in 1994, she remembered his dog-tag number by heart—20363625.

32. *Bedford Democrat*, June 6, 1994.

33. Anna Mae Stewart, interview with author.

34. Daniel Allen Butler, *Warrior Queens* (Mechanicsburg, Pennsylvania: Stackpole Books, 2002), p. 46.

35. Lee Kennett, *GI: The American Soldier in World War II* (Scribner's, New York, 1987), p. 115.

Chapter 4

1. The *Queen Mary* was designed to carry 2,119 passengers with a crew of 1,035.

2. Daniel Allen Butler, *Warrior Queens* (Mechanicsburg, Pennsylvania: Stackpole Books, 2002), p. 129. Infantrymen had to carry their M-1 rifles wherever they went.

3. Roy Stevens, interview with author.

4. Ibid.

5. Butler, *Warrior Queens*, p. 132.

6. That July's issue of the popular *Yank* magazine had cautioned: "Don't brag. Don't tell an Englishman we came over and won the last war for them. We didn't. England lost a million men; we lost only 60,000."

7. Butler, *Warrior Queens*, p. 131.

8. Lynchburg *News & Advance*, June 3, 2001.

9. Men often lost their pay within hours of it being issued. In 1942, lieutenants made $125 a month, sergeants around $70, and privates just $30.

10. Earl Newcomb, interview with author.

11. Clipping from Elva Newcomb's scrapbook. The incident would later receive prominent space in the *Bedford Bulletin*.

12. Roy Stevens, interview with author.

13. Ibid.

14. Lee Kennett, *GI: The American Soldier in World War II* (New York, Scribner's, 1987), p. 116.

15. Docks further south were in range of the Luftwaffe.

16. Butler, *Warrior Queens*, p. 99.

17. Ibid., p. 107.

18. Ibid., p. 110.

19. Ibid., p. 113.

20. Ibid., p. 114.

21. Earl Newcomb, interview with author, January 2002.

22. Bob Slaughter, interview with author.

23. Allen Huddleston, interview with author.

24. Butler, *Warrior Queens*, p. 114.

25. Ibid., p.118.

26. Bob Sales, interview with author.

27. Butler, *Warrior Queens*, p. 116.

28. Ibid. Also see: Captain Harry Grattidge, *Captain of the Queens* (London: Oldbourne Press, 1956).

29. Roy Stevens, interview with author.

30. Ibid.

Chapter 5

1. Joseph Ewing, *29 Let's Go* (Washington: Infantry Journal Press, 1948), p. 15

2. Bob Slaughter, interview with author.

3. Ibid.

4. Ibid.

5. Ibid.

6. Bob Slaughter memoirs, The Eisenhower Center for American Studies, University of New Orleans.

7. Ibid.

8. Lee Kennett, *GI: The American Soldier in World War II* (New York: Scribners, 1987), p. 73.

9. Lynchburg *News & Advance*, June 3, 2001.

10. Ivylyn Hardy, interview with author.

11. Mrs. George P. Parker, Bedford County World War II Committee, *Reports and Correspondence Concerning Bedford County in World War II, 1943–1945*, May 1, 1943.

12. *Bedford Bulletin*, February 4, 1943.

13. John Barnes, *Fragments of My Life* (self-published, 2000), p. 50.

14. Bertie Woodford scrapbook. Fellers was proud of his family's Scottish roots and had purchased a special plaid called the "Royal Stewart" in Scotland; Sergeant John Laird's parents had located the plaid.

15. Taylor Fellers to his parents, private correspondence, March 27, 1943.

16. Not every 29th Division soldier hated the moors. Brigadier General Norman Cota, who would be the most senior 29th Division officer to join the Bedford boys in combat, was so taken by their bleak beauty that he often spent his free weekends camping in a small pup tent.

17. Allen Huddleston, interview with author.

18. Roy Stevens, interview with author.

19. Ibid.

20. Joseph Balkoski, *Beyond the Beachhead* (Mechanicsburg, Pennsylvania: Stackpole Books, 1989), p. 55.

21. Roy Stevens, interview with author.

22. Earl Newcomb, interview with author.

23. In the nearest town to Tidworth Barracks—Ivybridge—the landlady was still alive in 2003 and remembered many of the Bedford boys with great fondness.

24. Ewing, *29 Let's Go!*, p. 17.

25. Ellen Quarles, interview with author.

26. Beulah Witt, interview with author.

27. One hundred twenty thousand U.S. servicemen were in the United Kingdom as of January 31, 1943. [Morison, *The Invasion of France and Germany*, p. 51.]

28. Parker report, July 15, 1943.

29. Ray Nance, interview with author.

30. Roy Stevens, interview with author.

31. Ibid.

32. Letter from Bedford Hoback to Mabel Phelps. Quoted by Lucille Hoback Boggess.

33. Lynchburg *News & Advance*, June 3, 2001.

34. Roy Stevens, interview with author.

35. Ibid.

36. Bertie Woodford, interview with author.

37. Stevens would name his first daughter after her and stay in touch for over sixty years.

38. *Bedford Bulletin*, May 20, 1943.

39. Roy Stevens, interview with author.

40. Ibid.

41. Bob Sales, interview with author.

Chapter 6

1. Joseph Balkoski, *Beyond the Beachhead* (Mechanicsburg, Pennsylvania: Stackpole Books, 1989), p. 44.

2. Ibid., p. 45.

3. Roy Stevens, interview with author.

4. David Draper, interview with author.

5. Information provided by Laura Burnette.

6. Verona Lipford, interview with author.

7. *Stars and Stripes*, October 1, 1944.

8. Quoted from Elva Newcomb's scrapbook, private collection.

9. Roy Stevens, interview with author.

10. Grant Yopp, letter to Anna Mae Stewart. Private correspondence, Anna Mae Stewart.

11. Allen Huddleston, interview with author.

12. David Reynolds, *Rich Relations* (London: Phoenix Press, 2000), p. 113.

13. Ray Nance, interview with author.

14. See Ewing, *29, Let's Go!*, and Balkoski, *Beyond the Beachhead*, for excellent character portraits of Cota and Gerhardt.

15. Bertie Woodford scrapbook. Letter from J. H. Wyse to Captain Fellers, December 3, 1943.

16. "Stories of Heroes: Virginians At Normandy," WDBJ7 television station. Broadcast June 1, 1994.

17. John Barnes, *Fragments of My Life* (self-published, 2000), p. 48.

18. Hal Baumgarten, interview with author.

19. Barnes, *Fragments of My Life*, p. 49.

20. Ibid., p. 49.

21. Ibid., p. 49.

22. Hal Baumgarten, interview with author.

23. Ibid.

24. Earl Newcomb, interview with author.

25. Taylor Fellers, letter to his parents, March 17, 1943.

26. Private correspondence, Bertie Woodford. Also see biographical sketch, provided by Woodford for unpublished book by Ray Nance.

27. John Barnes, interview with author.

28. Felix Branham, oral history, The Peter S. Kalikow World War II Archive, The Eisenhower Center for American Studies, University of New Orleans.

29. Roy Stevens, interview with author.

30. Felix Branham, oral history, The Peter S. Kalikow World War II Archive.

31. Ibid.

32. Gerald Astor, *June 6, 1944* (New York: St Martin's Press, 1994), p. 89.

33. Roy Stevens, interview with author.

34. Rebecca Wingfield, interview with author.

35. Roy Stevens, interview with author.

36. Bedford Hoback to Mabel Phelps, January 1944. Letter quoted courtesy of Lucille Hoback Boggess.

37. Ray Nance, interview with author.

38. Ibid.

39. Reynolds, *Rich Relations*, p. 324.
40. Balkoski, *Beyond the Beachhead*, p. 1.

Chapter 7

1. John Barnes, *Fragments of My Life* (self-published, 2000), p. 51.
2. Hal Baumgarten, oral history, The Peter S. Kalikow World War II History Archive, The Eisenhower Center for American Studies, University of New Orleans.
3. Bob Slaughter, interview with author.
4. Barnes, *Fragments*, p. 53.
5. Stephen Ambrose, *D-Day* (New York: Touchstone, 1994), p. 45.
6. Harold Baumgarten, *Eyewitness on Omaha Beach* (self-published, 2000), p. 10.
7. George Roach, oral history, The Peter S. Kalikow World War II History Archive.
8. Roy Stevens, interview with author.
9. Sibyle Kieth Coleman, interview with author.
10. Earl Newcomb, interview with author.
11. Sibyle Kieth Coleman, interview with author.
12. Roy Stevens, interview with author.
13. *Richmond Times-Dispatch*, June 2, 2002.
14. Ivylyn Hardy, interview with author.
15. *Liberty Magazine*, April 1944.
16. Raymond Hoback, letter to his parents, April 13, 1944.
17. Ray Nance, interview with author.
18. Ernest King, *Fleet Admiral* (New York: Lippincott, 1947), p. 621.
19. Arthur Victor, personal log. Quoted in Nigel Lewis, *Exercise Tiger* (New York: Prentice Hall, 1990), p.65.
20. Lewis, *Exercise Tiger*, p. 108.
21. Ibid., p. 109.
22. Ibid., p. 111.
23. Ibid., p. 121.
24. Ibid.
25. Eisenhower to Marshall, April 29, 1944, Eisenhower Library.
26. David Reynolds, *Rich Relations* (London: Phoenix Press, 2000), p. 365.
27. Ibid.
28. Roy Stevens, interview with author.
29. Ralph Ingersoll, *Top Secret* (New York: Harcourt Brace, 1946), p. 105.
30. Ibid.

Chapter 8

1. John Barnes, *Fragments of My Life* (self-published, 2000), p. 57.
2. Ray Nance, interview with author.

3. Quoted, Bedford Museum newspaper piece, undated, World War II File.

4. June 23, 1944, V-mail, Mrs. B. Abbott to Dickie Abbott. Quoted, Lynchburg *News & Advance*, June 3, 2001.

5. Lucille Hoback Boggess, interview with author.

6. "Remembering D-Day," *Baltimore Sun*, June 6, 1998. Also private correspondence, Ivylyn Hardy.

7. Ivylyn Hardy, interview with author.

8. Ibid.

9. Bertie Woodford, interview with author.

10. Bill Geroux, "Sacrifice," *Richmond Times-Dispatch*, May 28, 2000.

11. Mrs. George P. Parker, Bedford County World War II Committee, *Reports and Correspondence Concerning Bedford County in World War II, 1943–1945*, April 15, 1944.

12. Lloyd Ayers and Jesse H. Jones, letter to editor of the *Bedford Bulletin*, March 15, 1944.

13. Rebecca Wingfield, interview with author.

14. Geroux, "Sacrifice."

15. Parker report, January 15, 1944.

16. Bertie Woodford scrapbook, private collection.

17. Elouise Rogers, interview with author.

18. Bettie Wilkes Hooper speech, Bedford County Museum World War II File.

19. Parker report, April 15, 1944.

20. Ibid., February 1, 1944.

21. Geroux, "Sacrifice."

22. Parker report, November 1, 1943.

23. *Richmond Times-Dispatch*, May 28, 2000.

24. Hal Baumgarten, interview with author.

25. Barnes, *Fragments of My Life*, p. 58.

26. Allen Huddleston, interview with author.

27. Robert Capa, *Slightly Out of Focus* (New York: Modern Library, 1999), p.134.

28. Hal Baumgarten, oral history, The Peter S. Kalikow World War II History Archive.

29. Barnes, *Fragments*, pp. 57–58.

30. Ronald Drez, *Voices of D-Day* (New Orleans: Louisiana State University Press, 1994), pp. 40–41.

31. Cornelius Ryan, *The Longest Day* (New York: Touchstone, 1994), pp. 27–28.

32. Barnes, *Fragments*, p. 55.

33. Drez, *Voices of D-Day*, pp. 40–41.

34. Leroy Jennings, oral history, The Peter S. Kalikow World War II History Archive.

35. William Dillon, oral history, The Peter S. Kalikow World War II History Archive.

36. Joseph Balkoski, *Beyond the Beachhead* (Mechanicsburg, Pennsylvania: Stackpole Books, 1989), p. 124.

37. Roy Stevens, interview with author.

38. Drez, *Voices of D-Day*, pp. 40–41.

39. Ibid.

40. Ibid.
41. Omar Bradley, *A General's Life* (New York: Simon and Schuster, 1993), p. 238.
42. Carlo D'Este, *Eisenhower, A Soldier's Life* (New York: Henry Holt, 2002), p. 527.
43. David Reynolds, *Rich Relations* (London: Phoenix Press, 2000), p. 360.
44. Ibid.
45. Brooke diary entry for June 5, 1944, Liddell Hart Centre for Military Archives, King's College, London.
46. Bradley, *A General's Life*, p. 242.
47. Balkoski, *Beyond the Beachhead*, p. 62.
48. Hal Baumgarten, interview with author.
49. Thomas Valance, oral history, The Peter S. Kalikow World War II History Archive.
50. Balkoski, *Beyond the Beachhead*, p. 64. See archives, HQ Company, 116th Infantry Regiment.
51. Ibid.
52. Bertie Woodford, quoted, "Stories of Heroes," WDBJ7 television station broadcast June 1, 1994.
53. Anna Mae Stewart, interview with author.
54. Earl Newcomb, interview with author.
55. Ibid.
56. Roy Stevens, interview with author.
57. Ibid.
58. Balkoski, *Beyond the Beachhead*, p. 60.
59. Carlo D'Este, *Eisenhower, A Soldier's Life* (New York: Henry Holt, 2002), p. 510.
60. Barnes, *Fragments of My Life,* p. 60.

Chapter 9

1. Jimmy Green, interview with author.
2. Ibid.
3. Ibid.
4. Ibid.
5. Dwight Eisenhower, *Crusade in Europe* (New York: Doubleday, 1948), p. 249.
6. Ibid., p. 250.
7. Robert Walker, oral history, The Peter S. Kalikow World War II History Archive, The Eisenhower Center for American Studies, University of New Orleans.
8. *Roanoke Times*, June 4, 1994.
9. Group Captain James Stagg, Imperial War Museum, Sound Archives, 002910/02.
10. Carlo D'Este, *Eisenhower, A Soldier's Life* (New York: Henry Holt, 2002), p. 525.
11. Dwight D. Eisenhower, *Crusade in Europe* (New York: Doubleday, 1948), p. 249.
12. Joseph Balkoski, *Beyond the Beachhead* (Mechanicsburg, Pennsylvania: Stackpole Books, 1989), p. 6.
13. Baumgarten, *Eyewitness on Omaha Beach* (self-published, 2000), p. 34.
14. "Nobody Slept That Night," *Roanoke Times*, June 4, 1994.

15. Roy Stevens, interview with author.

16. Theodore Wilson, *Eisenhower at War* (New York: Random House, 1986), p. 253.

17. John Barnes, oral history, The Peter S. Kalikow World War II History Archive.

18. Hal Baumgarten, interview with author.

19. Betty Wilkes Hooper, interview with author.

20. Eisenhower Papers, No 1735, Dwight D. Eisenhower Library, Abilene, Kansas.

21. Roy Stevens, interview with author.

22. Ibid.

23. Ibid.

24. Ibid.

25. John Barnes, interview with author.

26. Roy Stevens, interview with author.

27. John Barnes, interview with author.

28. Jimmy Green, interview with author.

29. Ibid.

30. Ibid.

31. Balkoski, *Beyond the Beachhead*, p. 9.

32. John Barnes, interview with author.

33. Roy Stevens, interview with author.

Chapter 10

1. Jimmy Green, interview with author.

2. Ibid.

3. Ibid.

4. 29th Division D-Day action report, headquarters report, composed by Jack Shea, November 1, 1944, p29d—9.

5. Ray Nance, interview with author, and "The Suicide Wave," *Richmond Times-Disptach*, June 3, 2001.

6. John Barnes, *Fragments of My Life* (self-published, 2000), p. 63.

7. Jimmy Green, interview with author.

8. Roy Stevens, interview with author.

9. John Barnes, interview with author.

10. Jimmy Green, interview with author.

11. Monitor Radio report commemorating D-Day, June 1984.

12. Roy Stevens, interview with author.

13. Jimmy Green, interview with author.

14. Verona Lipford, interview with author.

15. Jimmy Green, interview with author.

16. Ibid.

17. Barnes, *Fragments of My Life*, p. 65.

18. *Omaha Beachhead*, Historical Department, War Department, 1984, p. 29.
19. Jimmy Green, interview with author.
20. Ibid.

Chapter 11

1. George Roach, oral history, The Peter S. Kalikow World War II Oral History Archive, The Eisenhower Center for American Studies, University of New Orleans.
2. *Bedford Bulletin*, June 6, 1989.
3. Monitor Radio report commemorating D-Day, June 1984.
4. Beulah Witt, interview with author.
5. George Roach, oral history, The Peter S. Kalikow World War II History Archive.
6. Ibid.
7. *Omaha Beachhead*, Historical Department, War Department, 1984, p. 29.
8. Thomas Valance, oral history, The Peter S. Kalikow World War II Oral History Archive.
9. Ray Nance, quoted in Donald Drez, *Voices of D-Day* (Louisiana State University Press, 1994), p. 213.
10. Ibid.
11. Monitor Radio report commemorating D-Day, June 1984.
12. Ray Nance, interview with author.
13. Ibid.
14. Ibid.
15. Ibid.
16. Ibid.

Chapter 12

1. Account of Breeden's first actions, see S.L.A Marshall's "First Wave on Omaha Beach," *Atlantic Monthly*, November 1960.
2. Ibid.
3. Russell Pickett, interview with author.
4. Ibid.
5. Bob Sales, interview with author
6. Ibid.
7. Ibid.
8. Joseph Balkoski, *Beyond the Beachhead* (Mechanicsburg, Pennsylvania: Stackpole Books, 1989), p. 152.
9. Bob Sales, interview with author.
10. Ibid.
11. Ibid.
12. Ibid.

13. Ibid.

14. One of the few photographs of 116th Infantry wounded on Omaha shows Sales a few feet from a bandaged Smith.

15. Bob Sales, interview with author.

16. Ibid.

17. Hal Baumgarten, oral history, The Peter S. Kalikow World War II History Archive, The Eisenhower Center for American Studies, University of New Orleans.

18. Harold Baumgarten, *Eyewitness on Omaha Beach*, (self-published, 2000), p. 21.

19. Ibid.

20. Ibid.

21. Baumgarten, oral history, The Peter S. Kalikow World War II History Archive.

22. Baumgarten, interview with author.

23. John Barnes, interview with the author.

24. John Barnes, *Fragments of My Life* (self-published, 2000), p. 66.

25. Ibid.

26. Roy Stevens, interview with author.

27. Jimmy Green, interview with author.

28. Ibid.

29. Russell Pickett, interview with author.

30. Verona Lipford, interview with author.

31. John Barnes, *Fragments of My Life*, p. 66.

32. Bob Slaughter, interview with author.

33. The Battle of Omaha Beach is thought to be the only time in history when American wounded were not evacuated to the rear but instead dragged forward into the front line.

34. Along the four miles of Omaha, there were three thousand other dead or seriously wounded men.

35. Paul Carell, *Invasion, They're Coming* (New York: Bantam, 1960), p. 86.

36. Ibid., p. 85.

Chapter 13

1. Joseph Balkoski, *Beyond the Beachhead* (Mechanicsburg, Pennsylvania: Stackpole Books, 1989), p. 134.

2. Lieutenant Shea, after-action report, D-Day, 29d, p. 12.

3. Ibid.

4. His body was later recovered from the shallows where it had lain floating. Shea report, p. 12.

5. "21 of the 743rd's 51 medium tanks were finally knocked-out on the beach. Only 30 successfully passed through the exits. They left at about 1930 hours on D-Day, all of them through the Vierville exit." Shea report, p. 13.

6. Ibid.

7. Ibid., p. 17.

8. Monitor Radio report commemorating D-Day, June 1984.

9. Untitled memoir, Bedford County Museum, World War II File.

10. Ray Nance, interview with author. See also the *Bedford Bulletin*, June 6, 1994.

11. *Richmond Times-Dispatch*, June 3, 2001.

12. Harold Baumgarten, *Eyewitness on Omaha Beach* (self-published, 2000), p. 31.

13. Bob Slaughter, oral history, The Peter S. Kalikow World War II History Archive, The Eisenhower Center for American Studies, University of New Orleans. Quoted in Russell Miller, *Nothing Less Than Victory* (New York: William Morrow, 1993), pp. 328–329.

14. Baumgarten, *Eyewitness on Omaha Beach*, p. 32.

15. Quoted, Web-site report, United States Army Medical Department & School Information Service.

16. Bob Slaughter, oral history, The Peter S. Kalikow World War II History Archive.

17. Presley would later be awarded the Distinguished Service Cross, as would Canham and Cota.

18. Bob Slaughter, oral history, The Peter S. Kalikow World War II History Archive.

19. *Omaha Beachhead* (Washington: Historical Department, War Department, 1984), p. 56.

20. Ronald Drez, *Voices of D-Day* (Louisiana State University Press, 1994), pp. 219–220.

21. Cornelius Ryan, *The Longest Day* (New York: Touchstone, 1994), p. 265.

22. Russell Pickett, interview with author.

23. Hal Baumgarten, interview with author. Mitchum would later play Cota in the film, *The Longest Day*, based on Cornelius Ryan's eponymous classic.

24. Shea report, p. 17. Account of Cota's actions on D-Day taken mainly from Shea's excellent report.

25. Ibid., pp. 18–19.

26. Ibid., p. 19.

27. Ibid., p. 20.

28. Ibid.

29. Ibid.

30. Baumgarten, *Eyewitness on Omaha Beach*, p. 38.

31. Robert Walker, oral history, The Peter S. Kalikow World War II History Archive.

32. Barnes, *Fragments of My Life*, pp. 65–67.

33. Shea report, p. 23.

34. Roy Stevens, interview with author.

35. Monitor Radio report commemorating D-Day, June 1984.

36. *Omaha Beachhead*, p. 95.

37. Warner Hamlett, oral history, The Peter S. Kalikow World War II History Archive.

38. Ray Nance, interview with author.

39. Baumgarten, *Eyewitness on Omaha Beach*, p. 40.

40. Ibid., pp. 42–43.

41. Thomas Valance, oral history, The Peter S. Kalikow World War II History Archive.

42. Gerald Astor, *June 6, 1994* (New York: St. Martin's Press, 1994), p. 297.

43. Harry Parley, oral history, The Peter S. Kalikow World War II History Archive.

44. Bob Slaughter, oral history, The Peter S. Kalikow World War II History Archive. "I realized it didn't make any difference whether one was a superior soldier, was more religious, or better character. People were being killed randomly and they could not help themselves."

45. Bob Sales, interview with author.

46. Baumgarten, *Eyewitness on Omaha Beach*, p. 43.

47. Hal Baumgarten, interview with author.

Chapter 14

1. Stephen Ambrose, *D-Day* (New York: Touchstone, 1994), p. 489.

2. Elva Newcomb, interview with author.

3. *Richmond Times-Dispatch*, May 28, 2000.

4. Ivylyn Hardy, interview with author.

5. Bettie Wilkes Hooper, interview with author.

6. Bertie Woodford, interview with author.

7. *Bedford Bulletin*, June 1, 1944.

8. Advertisement, *Bedford Bulletin*, June 8, 1944.

9. Eleanor Yowell, letter to "Pinky," June 6, 1944.

10. Rebecca Wingfield, interview with author.

11. Allen Huddleston, interview with author.

12. *The Times* (London), June 7, 1944.

13. Typescript, D-Day Museum, New Orleans.

14. Eloise Rogers, interview with author.

15. Anne Frank, *The Diary of a Young Girl* (New York: Doubleday, 1967), p. 268.

16. *Bedford Bulletin*, June 7, 1944.

17. Mrs. George P. Parker, Bedford County World War II Committee, *Reports and Correspondence Concerning Bedford County in World War II, 1943–1945*, June 6, 1944.

18. *Bedford Bulletin*, June 8, 1944.

19. *Richmond Times-Dispatch*, May 28, 2000.

20. Parker report, June 7, 1944.

21. *Richmond Times-Dispatch*, May 28, 2000.

22. *Bedford Bulletin*, June 1, 1944.

23. *New York Times*, June 7, 1944.

Chapter 15

1. John Barnes, *Fragments of My Life* (self-published, 2000), p. 67.

2. Ibid., p. 68.

3. Ronald Drez, *Voices of D-Day* (Louisiana State University Press, 1994), p. 221.

4. Roy Stevens, interview with author.

5. Ibid.

6. Ibid.

7. Ibid.

8. Barnes, *Fragments of My Life*, p. 68.

9. Roy Stevens, interview with author.

10. Barnes, *Fragments of My Life*, p. 68.

11. Ibid., p.70. Gearing would fight on with Company A until October when he would be evacuated after his legs were crushed by a wall blown away by the Germans during fierce street fighting. He was later awarded the Distinguished Service Cross.

12. Ibid.

13. Earl Newcomb, interview with author.

14. Barnes, *Fragments of My Life*, p. 68.

15. Ibid., p. 78.

16. Joseph Ewing, *29 Let's Go!* (Washington: Infantry Journal Press, 1948), p. 83.

17. Roy Stevens, interview with author.

18. Ibid.

19. Clyde Powers to Mrs. H. B. Powers, August 17, 1944. Private collection, Eloise Rogers. Quoted with permission.

20. Roy Stevens, interview with author.

21. Ibid.

22. Ibid.

23. Ibid.

24. Bob Sales, interview with author.

25. Roy Stevens, interview with author.

26. Ibid.

27. Bob Slaughter, interview with author.

28. Bob Sales, interview with author.

29. Ibid.

30. Bob Slaughter, interview with author.

31. Roy Stevens, interview with author.

32. Bob Sales, interview with author.

33. Roy Stevens, interview with author.

34. Balkoski, *Beyond the Beachhead*, p. 200.

35. Bob Slaughter, interview with author.

36. Roy Stevens, interview with author.

37. Earl Newcomb, interview with author.

38. Roy Stevens, interview with author.

39. Ibid.

40. Ibid.

41. Brockman survived the war only to die in an industrial accident—he was electrocuted while working on a power line.

42. Roy Stevens, interview with author.

43. Ibid.

44. Ibid.

45. Ibid.

46. James Tobin, *Ernie Pyle's War* (New York: The Free Press, 1997), p. 185.

47. See Ambrose, *Citizen Soldiers*, pp. 52–53 for further statistics on extent of losses and relative strengths of Germans and Allies.

48. David C. Isby, editor, *Fighting in Normandy, The German Army from D-Day to Villers-Bocage* (London: Greenhill Books, 2001), p. 236.

49. Roy Stevens, interview with author.

50. Poem composed by Roy Stevens, July 1944.

Chapter 16

1. *Richmond Times-Dispatch*, May 28, 2000.

2. Ivylyn Hardy, interview with author.

3. *Bedford Democrat*, June 6, 1994.

4. Ernie Pyle, *Brave Men* (New York: Grosset & Dunlap, 1944), p. 251.

5. *Bedford Bulletin*, July 27, 1944.

6. *Bedford Bulletin*, June 6, 1994.

7. Lucille Hoback Boggess, interview with author.

8. Lynchburg *News & Advance*, June 3, 2001.

9. Sibyle Kieth Coleman, interview with author.

10. *Bedford Bulletin*, July 6, 1944.

11. Verona Lipford, interview with author.

12. Elva Newcomb, scrapbook.

13. Ibid.

14. Betty Wilkes Hooper, interview with author.

15. Ibid.

16. Ibid.

17. Ibid.

18. Bertie Woodford, interview with author.

19. Ibid.

20. Ibid.

21. *Bedford Bulletin*, July 8, 1944.

22. Ibid., July 15, 2002.

23. *Richmond Times-Dispatch*, May 28, 2000.

Chapter 17

1. *Washington Times*, Weekend Section, June 5–11, 2000.

2. Lucille Hoback Boggess, interview with author.

3. Elaine Coffey, interview with author.

4. Elizabeth Teass, interview with author.

5. By now some were saying that the 29th Division commander, General Gerhardt, had "a division in the field, a division in the hospital, and a division in the cemetery." Balkoski, *Beyond the Beachhead*, pp. 253–254.

6. Earl Newcomb, interview with author.

7. John Barnes, *Fragments of My Life* (self-published, 2000), pp. 80–83.

8. Elizabeth Teass, interview with author.

9. "Uncommon Valor," Lynchburg *News & Advance*, June 3, 2001.

10. Ibid.

11. Elizabeth Teass, interview with author.

12. Ibid.

13. Ibid.

14. Rebecca Wingfield, interview with author.

15. Elizabeth Teass, interview with author.

16. Ibid.

17. Ibid.

18. *Richmond Times-Dispatch*, May 28, 2000.

19. *Bedford Democrat*, June 6, 1994.

20. *Richmond Times-Dispatch*, May 28, 2000.

21. *Bedford Democrat*, June 6, 1994.

22. Elizabeth Teass, interview with author.

23. Elva Newcomb, interview with author.

24. Bettie Wilkes Hooper, interview with author.

25. *Richmond Times-Dispatch*, May 28, 2000.

26. Helen Stevens, interview with author.

27. "D-Day Widow Recalls Husband's Sacrifice," *Bedford Bulletin*, June 6, 2000. Original speech given on May 8, 2000.

28. *Richmond Times-Dispatch*, May 28, 2000.

29. Verona Lipford, interview with author.

30. Elizabeth Teass, interview with author.

31. Ivylyn Hardy, interview with author.

32. Elva Newcomb, interview with author.

33. "Memorial to Honor a Town's Sacrifice," *Baltimore Sun*, June 6, 1998.

34. Lucille Hoback Boggess, interview with author.

35. Sibyle Kieth Coleman, interview with author.

36. Anna Mae Stewart, interview with author.

37. *Bedford Bulletin*, July 19, 1944.

38. Eleanor Yowell, letter to "Pinky," July 25, 1944.

39. David Draper, interview with author.

40. Letter, private correspondence, Lucille Hoback Boggess.

41. Lucille Hoback Boggess, interview with author.

42. Lynchburg *News & Advance*, June 3, 2001.

43. Elva Newcomb, private scrapbook.

44. Lynchburg *News & Advance*, June 3, 2001.

45. *Washington Times*, June 5–11, 2000.

46. "In Memoriam," *Bedford Bulletin*, undated, contained in World War II File, Bedford County Museum.

47. Lynchburg *News & Advance,* June 3, 2001.

Chapter 18

1. Ivylyn Hardy, interview with author.

2. Letter from Mr. and Mrs. Frank Draper, and children Verona, David, and Gamiel; from Elva Newcomb's scrapbook.

3. Elva Newcomb's scrapbook. Poem by Kathleen Bradshaw, Quinby, Virginia.

4. Ibid., poem by Elaine Coffey.

5. *Richmond Times-Dispatch*, May 28, 2000.

6. Allen Huddleston, interview with author.

7. Quoted, Canham biographical information, Staunton Armory Records of 116th Infantry.

8. Bob Sales, interview with author.

9. Joseph Ewing, *29 Let's Go!* (Washington: Infantry Journal Press, 1948), p. 149.

10. Allen Huddleston, interview with author.

11. Ibid.

12. Bob Slaughter, interview with author.

13. Bob Sales, interview with author.

14. Huddleston ran his own photography business until retiring in the eighties. The wife he had married in 1942 before going overseas with the Bedford boys died in 1988. He has three sons and in 2003 lived in Bedford's Elks home with several other relatives of Company A men and played Rook almost as often as he did in the army. His shoulder wound, he said, had recently given him "a lot of trouble."

15. Information on casualties provided by Bob Slaughter.

16. John Barnes, *Fragments of My Life* (self-published, 2000), p. 131.

17. Ibid.

18. Ibid.

19. Elva Newcomb, interview with author.

20. *Richmond Times-Dispatch*, June 2, 2002.

21. Bertie Woodford, interview with author.

22. Ray Nance, interview with author.

23. Roy Stevens, interview with author.

24. Ibid.

25. Ibid.

26. Ibid.

27. Eloise Rogers, interview with author.

28. *Richmond Times-Dispatch*, June 2, 2002.
29. Elva Newcomb, private scrapbook.
30. Elva Newcomb, interview with author.
31. *Richmond Times-Dispatch*, June 2, 2002.
32. Elva Newcomb, private scrapbook.
33. *Bedford Bulletin*, August 16, 1945.
34. *Bedford Bulletin*, December 8, 1947.
35. Verona Lipford, interview with author.
36. Ibid.
37. Ibid.
38. Roy Stevens, interview with author.
39. Ibid.
40. Rebecca Wingfield, interview with author.
41. Ibid.
42. Laura Burnette, interview with author.
43. *Bedford Democrat*, April 29, 1954.
44. Roy Stevens, interview with author.
45. *Bedford Bulletin*, June 7, 2000.
46. Ivylyn Hardy, interview with author.
47. Ibid.
48. Bettie Wilkes Hooper, interview with author.
49. *Richmond Times-Dispatch*, June 2, 2002.
50. Anna Mae Stewart, interview with author.
51. *Bedford Bulletin*, June 6, 1994.
52. *Virginia Pilot*, June 2, 1968.
53. Ibid.

Chapter 19

1. John Lang, "A town's gift: The valor of its sons," *Washington Times*, June 5, 2000.
2. Billy Parker memoir, Bedford County Museum, World War II File.
3. Billy Parker, interview with author.
4. Bedford Museum World War II File. Untitled clipping.
5. *Bedford Bulletin*, March 25, 1954.
6. Ibid., June 7, 1954.
7. Edward Gearing, letter to Kenneth Crouch, September 20, 1954, Bedford County Museum, World War II File.
8. Mary Daniel Heilig, interview with author.
9. *Bedford Bulletin*, June 7, 1954.
10. Ibid.
11. Ibid.
12. Ibid.

13. Ibid.

14. *Bedford Bulletin-Democrat*, June 23, 1982, "Liberty Bicentennial Edition."

15. Norman D. Cota, Maj. Gen., US Army, Ret., letter to Kenneth E. Crouch, July 10, 1954.

16. Major General D. W. Canham, letter to Parker-Hoback Post, April 30, 1954.

17. *Bedford Democrat*, June 6, 1994.

18. Mary Daniel Heilig, interview with author.

19. *Potomac News*, June 5, 1994.

20. Verona Lipford, interview with author.

21. Bettie Wilkes Hooper, interview with author.

22. In the meantime, most D-Day veterans had died.

23. *Baltimore Sun*, June 6, 1998.

24. *Bedford Democrat*, June 6, 1994.

25. Lynchburg *News & Advance*, June 3, 2001.

26. Ibid.

27. Bob Slaughter, interview with author.

28. Ibid.

29. "D-Day Memorial to Salve Town's Terrible Loss," *Washington Post,* January 8, 1998.

30. Various broadcasts as well as the *New York Times,* June 7, 2001.

31. "Talk of War Where One From Past Still Haunts," *New York Times,* September 15, 2001.

32. Ibid.

33. Ibid.

34. Bob Sales, interview with author.

35. Verona Lipford, interview with author.

36. Elaine Coffey, interview with author.

37. Ibid.

38. Mary Daniel Heilig, interview with author.

INDEX

CO. A